Education Together for a Change

Integrated Education and Community Relations in Northern Ireland

Acknowledgements

Fortnight Educational Trust has been established with the aim of promoting understanding of social, political, economic and cultural issues relevant to Northern Ireland through education, discussion and debate. It is funded by the Joseph Rowntree Charitable Trust and the Northern Ireland Voluntary Trust.

This book has received support from the Cultural Traditions Programme of the Community Relations Council which aims to encourage acceptance and understanding of cultural diversity.

Education Together for a Change

Integrated Education and Community Relations in Northern Ireland

Edited by Chris Moffat

Fortnight Educational Trust

Published by Fortnight Educational Trust
7 Lower Crescent, Belfast BT7 1NR

First published 1993
© Fortnight Educational Trust and the authors 1993

ISBN 09509081 4 2

British Library Cataloguing-in-Publication Data
A catalogue record for this book is available from the British Library

Cover illustration: Emma Hutchinson, Bridge Primary School, Banbridge
Cover design: Lynne Hastings
Typesetting: December Publications
Printed in Northern Ireland by

Contents

Contributors

Sister Anna, Anglican Sister of the Love of God, was brought to Belfast in February 1972 by Mother Teresa to work with her nuns for reconciliation. She was co-founder of *Children's Community Holidays* and member of *All Children Together* since 1974 and chairman of the movement when Lagan College started in 1981. She has worked full-time for it fund-raising world-wide ever since as Co-Treasurer, Director and Governor. *All Ireland People of the Year Award* 1984. Awarded MBE 1993.

Colm Murray Cavanagh is a founder member and co-chairperson of Foyle Trust for Integrated Education which opened Oakgrove Primary School in 1991 and Oakgrove College in 1992. A solicitor, Colm volunteered with the UN Development programme in Tanzania 1969-72. He has since worked with economic and social self-help projects, primarily in L'Derry. Currently chief executive of the Waterside Project he is married with two daughters and a son.

Priscilla Chadwick read theology at Girton College, Cambridge before becoming head of religious education in three different schools, the last of which was a joint Anglican/Roman Catholic comprehensive school in Surrey. She was appointed by the Archbishop of Canterbury to the English Anglican/Roman Catholic Committee and published a discussion document, *Joint Schools*. She is now Dean of Educational Development at South Bank University, London.

Terence Flanagan was educated at Magee University College, L/Derry and Trinity College, Dublin. He taught in Kenya for two years, was Head of Religious Studies at Ballymena Academy until 1984 when he became Principal of Lagan College.

Grace Fraser is Research Officer in the Centre for the Study for Conflict, University of Ulster, Coleraine. She graduated in History and Education, and has taught at primary and secondary level in Scotland and Northern Ireland, including both controlled and maintained schools. She has researched and published on integrated education.

Charles Graham was appointed Principal of Bridge Integrated Primary School in 1987. He was educated in England and Northern Ireland, holding degrees in Education from the London University and the University of Ulster. His wife, Pauline, is from Belfast and their three children, all born in England, have been educated at Bridge.

Anne Hovey joined NICIE in September 1992 after many years in curriculum and management development posts and in educational consultancy throughout England and Wales. Immediately before joining NICIE she was Regional Officer in Wales for the National Association of Head Teachers.

Áine Hyland is Chairperson of Educate Together in the Republic of Ireland and lecturer in Educational Policy and the History of Education at University College, Dublin.

Colin Irwin is Honorary Research Fellow in the Department of Social Anthropology, The Queen's University, Belfast. His research on social theory and conflict resolution has included work for native organisations in Canada as well as studies in Northern Ireland and Israel.

Mrs Margaret Kennedy is a retired biology teacher from Orangefield Girls' School. In the 1960s she taught in a Convent School in Trinidad and later lectured in a teacher training college in Maseno, Kenya. She has represented ACT on CRIS (Community Relations in School) and currently represents ACT on the Focus Group (Forum on Community Understanding and Support). She is a member of the Church of Ireland and co-author with Bill Brown and Thelma Sheil of ACT's submissions to the Churches Core Curriculum Drafting Group on Shared RE.

Brian Lambkin was educated at Queens' College, Cambridge. He began teaching in 1977 at Rathmore Grammar School, Belfast. He joined Lagan College in 1981 at its foundation where he is now Vice-Principal.

Errol Lemon is Head of History and member of the senior management team of Brownlow College.

Cecil Linehan MBE, orthodontist, was a member of South Eastern Education and Library Board 1973-77 and Secretary to Lagan College Board of Governors 1982-85; Development Officer with Co-operation North, with special responsibility for the School-links Programme 1986-88, and now a Council member. A Roman Catholic and founder member of All Children Together, she is now a director of Forge Integrated Primary School.

Terence McMackin was Head of History at St Malachy's College, Belfast, and Head of RE at St Louise's Comprehensive School, Belfast, before becoming joint Head, with a Protestant colleague, of RE at Lagan College. He is currently on secondment to Brownlow College.

Chris Moffat is education materials editor of Fortnight Educational Trust, co-founder and secretary of NAGIE (North Armagh Group for Integrated Education), a governor of Portadown Integrated Primary school and a co-opted governor of Brownlow College, both of which schools one or other of her children attend.

Anne Murray is Principal of Oakgrove Integrated Primary School and was a founder member of Foyle Trust for Integrated Education. She has taught in Sudan and England as well as in L'derry.

Trevor Parkhill and his family have been associated with Hazelwood Primary School and Hazelwood College since their establishment in 1985. His three children attend one or other. His wife, Sheila, is a foundation governor of the Primary School. He is a parent governor of the College, having previously been

8

Contributors

secretary to the Hazelwood Primary School board and chairperson of Hazelwood College Parents' Council. In real life he is an archivist who has published extensively on historical topics.

Tom Rowley graduated from, and trained as a teacher at Queens University Belfast. He taught at Holywood High School and Gransha Boys High before moving to Hazelwood College in 1985 as its first Principal.

Alan Smith is a research fellow at the Centre for the Study of Conflict, University of Ulster, Coleraine. As a parent he helped establish Mill Strand Integrated Primary School in 1987 and is a founder trustee of the North Coast Charitable Trust for Integrated Education. He has been a director of All Children Together (1988-89) and was chairperson of the Northern Ireland Council for Integrated Education during its formative years. He is currently a governor of the Integrated Education Fund.

Fiona Stephen taught for nineteen years and wrote and worked for the Open University before taking up her appointment as Director of the Northern Ireland Council for Integrated Education in 1989.

The late **Frank Wright** lectured in Politics at Queen's University, Belfast, before being appointed to the chair of Peace Studies at Limerick University in 1992. A member of the Corrymeela Community and dedicated to working for better inter-communal understanding, he died in 1993 before being able to complete his contribution to this book.

Introduction

The emergence of a small but steadily growing sector of integrated schools in Northern Ireland inevitably raises questions about the shape of its future development. Will it continue to grow or will it remain marginal in comparison with mainstream segregated education? Will it contribute to better cross-communal understanding or will it add new pressures for exclusivity and fragmentation? Will it help to bring about a fairer and more equal society?

The purpose of this book is to contribute to the continuing discussion and debate within integrated schools about these issues and about the best ways of achieving in practice the aims of the integrated education movement. It is also intended to explain how the efforts to create integrated schools are contributing to better community relations in Northern Ireland. A great deal of research has been carried out on integrated schools but its results have not always been readily available to those most involved and have not necessarily contributed to a wider understanding of what integrated schools are trying to achieve.

Integrated Schools Now
The first section of the book looks at how integrated schools are operating now: how and why they have been set up; how this affects the way they function both in terms of the kind of education they offer and in terms of their principles of shared participation and management. The contributors are parents and teachers and others who have been deeply involved in the day-to-day practice of the schools. In Chapter 1 the Director of the Northern Ireland Council for Integrated education, Fiona Stephen, gives an overview of the current state of development of integrated schools and describes the work of the Council in promoting and supporting new developments under the provisions of the Education Reform (Northern Ireland) Order 1989. In Chapter 2 Colm Cavanagh describes the impact of the creation of two new integrated schools on his local community in L'Derry. He identifies some of the reasons why support for integrated education has grown over the past twenty years: an increasing awareness amongst parents

that the inexorable slide into communal polarisation and educational apartheid is cutting them off from others with whom they have much in common; and a growing realisation that this is something which neither politicians nor the churches are willing or able to tackle.

The next three chapters give some idea of what integrated schools in their different ways are trying to achieve educationally. Anne Murray, Anne Hovey and Tom Rowley examine in turn the ethos, processes and context of teaching and learning in integrated schools. There is now a vast literature on the social, pedagogic and curricular implications of segregated schooling, both in the explicit and the 'hidden' sense. Teachers in integrated schools, with the positive support of parents, have been able to move beyond this by building on the opportunities offered by a multi-cultural and multi-faith context. The social and educational advantages of a child-centred approach are now fairly widely accepted as particularly appropriate to pupils from diverse cultural and religious backgrounds. So too, increasingly, is the anti-bias approach to curriculum which seeks to prepare pupils for what goes on outside the school by equipping them with positive strategies for countering prejudice and stereotyping. The emphasis in integrated schools at nursery, primary and secondary levels is on both socialisation and nurture, while at the same time providing opportunities for pupils to explore, appreciate and also question their own and others' cultures. This makes special demands on the communal values of the school and requires, as Tom Rowley points out, continuing attention to staff development.

The ethos of integrated schools includes a Christian dimension which also has important practical implications. In Chapter 6 Terence McMackin offers a personal perspective on the nurture of religious faith, particularly for Catholics, and outlines an integrated schools model for partnership in faith provision.

In Chapter 7 Colin Irwin shows from his research in Lagan College that integrated education works for pupils as much through informal social relations and the organisation of school-based social life as through the formal curriculum. He also draws attention to the often neglected issue of the rights of pupils in education, under such international conventions as the UNESCO Convention on the Prevention of Discrimination in Education and the UN Convention on the Rights of the Child.

In Chapter 8 Grace Fraser describes her research on teachers in the first generation of integrated schools. The commitment of founders, both teachers and parents, which she discusses remains central to the ethos of the movement as a whole. In Chapter 9 Trevor Parkhill discusses the role of parents in integrated schools and the effectiveness of the structures that have been deliberately created to foster partnership between them and teachers, both in management and in day-to-day activities and decisions. Parental involvement is increasingly important in all schools. But in integrated schools it is vital that new parents are able to play a full part in developing the shared communal context and values which are transmitted to their children. In Chapter 10 Charles Graham focuses on the issue of management of an integrated school in the crucial early period of growth and change and argues that a degree of conflict in such situations is perfectly normal and usually a sign of healthy commitment.

In Chapter 11 the alternative strategy for the development of integrated education by transformation of an existing school, rather than the creation of a entirely new one, is discussed from two perspectives. It tells the story of the transformation of a secondary school first from the point of view of a parent group which wanted to create the option of integrated education for their children, and secondly from the point of view of a member of staff at the school. The practicability and the merits of this strategy have significant implications for the longer term development of integrated education.

Equally important for integrated education, as Alan Smith argues in Chapter 12, is the need to underpin the community development processes of integrated schools by providing safeguards which ensure that balance is maintained between the two main religious and cultural traditions without undermining the rights of staff, parents and children. His contribution also raises more general questions about the role of parents and pupils with regard to the organisation and administration of education in a plural and democratic society.

Issues and Ideals
The second part of the book looks at some of the issues and ideals that are likely to be important for the future development of integrated education. All the contributors are again people who have been closely involved in integrated education here or in neighbouring societies.

The focus in the first two chapters is on the experience of educational innovations in the Republic of Ireland and in Britain. In Chapter 13 Áine Hyland describes how in the Republic pressure for multi-denominational education began to emerge at the same time as pressures for integrated education in the North, and showed a similar consciousness among parents of the lack of opportunity for them to play a part in determining policy and institutional arrangements for education. The parent-led movement for multi-denominational schools in the

Republic also reflected a growing consciousness of the need for a more pluralistic sense of Irish identity. In Britain, as Priscilla Chadwick argues in Chapter 14, joint Christian schools have developed partly as a response to economic pressures and partly from ecumenical ideals. The British experience shows that Christian churches can play a significant role in inter-church cooperation in educational developments.

In Chapter 15 the late Frank Wright argues from a historical perspective that separate school systems in Irish education have provided a means of managing mistrust between communal traditions with differing national aspirations. Neither integrated education nor curriculum developments can remove or socialise away in children the underlying differences of their parents. But if integrated schools are founded on voluntary commitment and shared parental involvement, they can create small scale opportunities for genuine reconciliation and, in the healing of old wounds, the possibility of the creation of new shared values.

In Chapter 16 Brian Lambkin and Terence Flanagan argue that Christians who take the transmission of Christian values and commitment seriously must also take integrated education seriously. Since all schools are now required to teach mutual understanding and respect for the two cultural traditions, including religious traditions, the difference between segregated and integrated schools is one of degree rather than kind. In Chapter 17 three leading members of All Children Together, Sister Anna, Cecil Linehan and Margaret Kennedy, take up this theme with a challenge to the Churches in Northern Ireland to grasp the opportunity to make good their disappointing lack of engagement with reconciliation in education thus far.

The Future Development of Integrated Schools
The reluctance of government to face up to many of the problems regarding the organisation of integrated education is understandable. As many have pointed out, segregated schools in Northern Ireland are as much the *consequence* of segregative tendencies in other spheres as they are a *cause*. It is not necessary, however, to argue that the emergence of integrated schools is a 'response' to conflicts 'caused' by segregated schooling, or to assume that there is a single cause or explanation for the growing support for integrated education. It is also possible that new economic, social and demographic changes and international pressures on Northern Ireland are creating new kinds of segregative tendencies which make new forms of integrative processes both desirable and, to many people, necessary.

The failure of the government to develop a coherent policy on these wider aspects of integrated education is nonetheless regrettable. The right of all parents to have the opportunity of integrated education for their children has not been clearly acknowledged. It is true that the Education Reform (Northern Ireland) Order has provided the opportunity for the establishment of new grant maintained integrated schools with 'day one' public funding of recurrent costs if 'adequate' parental demand can be demonstrated. It is also true that it has simplified the procedures for the conversion of established segregated schools to integrated status by parental ballot. But this adaptation of the Conservative Government's policy on 'opting out' does not in practice amount to a policy of securing parity of provision, in comparison with the established segregated sectors, for those parents who want integrated education. Establishing a new integrated school still involves substantial burdens on those involved in raising the initial capital and organising the development of the new school which are not – or are no longer – faced in the established segregated sectors.

These difficulties do not end when an integrated school has been established. There is no clear statutory protection in the 1989 Order or otherwise for their planned cross-communal character and ethos. The statutory definition of an integrated school as one likely to attract reasonable numbers of both Roman Catholic and Protestant pupils is very much less demanding than the integrated school movement's current objective of a minimum of 40 per cent from each of the two main communal traditions amongst the pupils and staff and on the board of governors of the school. Anti-discrimination legislation and open enrolment provisions pose a threat to the maintenance of the essential character of integrated schools, particularly in those areas of Northern Ireland where demographic and other pressures towards segregation are most acute. The fact that all schools are exempt from the Fair Employment Acts gives some flexibility to the integrated sector in securing balance among teaching staff. But this may not be sufficient to counteract the limitations on the mobility of teachers posed by the strength of the traditional segregated sectors and the natural concerns of individual teachers over career development. The absence of a clear definition of the essential features of integrated schools may eventually undermine their credibility for both parents and teachers.

A further difficulty is that while the 1989 Order imposes a duty on the Department of Education to encourage and facilitate integrated education, it imposes no corresponding duty on area boards. Nor does it impose any specific requirement that the Department or area boards should ensure adequate provision of integrated schools, both primary and secondary, throughout Northern Ireland for those who want it, or even that they should take any steps to ascertain the wishes of parents. This is in stark contrast to the response of the Department to the criticism by the Standing Advisory Commission on Human Rights over differences in access to grammar school places in the two segregated sectors. The Department has undertaken to provide additional grammar school places in Belfast and L'Derry for the Catholic maintained sector but has not even acknowledged the issue of equitable provision for qualified pupils in the integrated sector. The prohibition of the inclusion of academic ability in any form as an admissions criterion for non-grammar schools makes it particularly difficult for newly founded integrated secondary schools to develop appropriate sixth form provision within an all-ability ethos which will meet the legitimate needs of their pupils or the aspirations of their parents.

These considerations indicate that the continuation of the Government's current policies towards integrated education could lead to increasing problems. In practice most of the integrated schools which have been created to date have been established by parents, teachers and other supporters in spite of, rather than because of, the law. The danger is that the integrated schools will be seen, as time passes, to be divorced from or irrelevant to the more general problems of the educational system in helping to create a fairer and more pluralistic society in Northern Ireland, just as the policy of encouraging schools to 'opt out' in Britain is beginning to reveal its divisive and exclusivist tendencies.

A Comprehensive Policy for Integrated Education

If it is accepted that current Government policy on integrated education is flawed in many respects, it is important to consider what else should be done and why it has not been more seriously considered.

One of the justifications for the government's apparent determination to rely on voluntary action by others in the development of an integrated sector is the continued reluctance of the churches to participate in joint educational provision, even when, in the case of integrated schools, this meant denying any pastoral responsibility for members of their own communion. A second has been the widely held assumption in government circles that the very high level of support for integrated education repeatedly shown in surveys over the past twenty years cannot be a true measure of real demand. The government has continued to take the position that these surveys were based on a misunderstanding of the 'real' nature of integrated education or that they were more significant as an indication of dissatisfaction with other aspects of education. The idea that they were roughly accurate may have been too threatening to be acceptable. A final explanation may be the absence of any very clear external pressure on the UK Government under international human rights conventions to take seriously the rights of parents and pupils to challenge the legitimacy of the established segregated structures and interests groups.

Whatever the reason, the Department has clearly shown itself to be unwilling to take an interventionist role on any aspect of educational organisation, as opposed to its content, despite its now prodigious array of powers to do so. This may be due to its unease about its capacity to marry what it thought of as an impartial system of educational administration with an education policy designed to improve both community relations and social inequalities. There is now increasing evidence that structural inequality in Northern Ireland society, both in class and communal terms, is a significant factor in sectarian antagonism and mistrust. This has been recognised in the considerable range of interventionist legislation designed to curb discrimination in housing and employment, to promote equality of opportunity and shared participation and to ensure equality of representation in a wide range of public appointments.

The problem is that these measures have not been matched by equivalent provisions designed to reduce inequality and encourage shared participation in education. Instead the government has adopted a limited policy of securing equity of provision between the two segregated systems, one of which is explicitly confessional and the other so in practice. Issues of equality in education have thus been avoided by focusing almost exclusively on those of individual communal identity which is assumed without question to be ascribed to all children at birth and to be willingly accepted thereafter.

There are strong arguments for saying that the provision of both segregated and integrated schools should be seen as a basic right for parents. But there are also strong arguments for saying that children's educational rights should be addressed irrespective of their communal background. The provision of integrated schools is only a small part of a general policy of integration in education. Such a policy should also address inequalities in the education system which undermine children's rights irrespective of their communal identity. The development of such a policy would contribute greatly to the general effectiveness of measures to improve communal integration in other spheres such as employment and housing.

One objective which might be included in such a policy would be to lessen the influence that the school attended by any pupil has on his or her chances of obtaining a job or further education. A way of doing this would be to encourage joint provision or sharing of sixth form facilities and to give incentives for pupil 'cross-overs' for specific courses – a fairly common practice in other 'dual' education systems. Another might be to widen educational choice, not just for those who pass the selection test at eleven, but for all pupils by delaying selection. The integrated school movement is committed to all-ability education for precisely these reasons. A policy for building an integrative system of education will have to face up to segregation based on imputed ability as well as segregation based on imputed communal or religious affiliation.

Reorganising education with such objectives in mind would provide an opportunity for establishing clear rules for joint or cross-communal management and control and for inviting people to participate on the basis of an explicit commitment to power-sharing. The principles of shared participation developed by the integrated schools provide a valuable model of how others might progress in stages towards a more embracing concept of structural equality in all spheres. Similarly, a more positive approach could be adopted to encouraging existing educational institutions, such as colleges of further education which serve both communities and claim to be 'mixed', to adopt NICIE principles of shared management and control. Likewise, it should be a statutory responsibility of local education and library boards and other formal bodies to be involved in the planning, provision or promotion of explicitly integrated educational institutions, so that it is clear that shared participation is here to stay and not merely a short-term expedient.

Such a policy would not be easy nor could it be implemented overnight. However, what the integrated education movement has demonstrated is that how changes are achieved is as important as the end result. Thus a genuine integrated education policy would begin by giving real choice to parents and pupils by carrying out surveys of demand which included questions about a range of options which might be considered in deciding the extent and nature of integrated options in any one area. If past surveys of the demand for integrated education can be faulted, it is that they failed to get beyond a relatively simplistic single question. A more realistic survey of demand would include questions such as whether parents and pupils favoured the pooling or sharing of particular educational facilities like nursery schools or the provision of joint sixth forms or possible transformations or amalgamations of existing local schools. The churches might also consider how they could give more say to their lay members – parents and students. Teachers might be given an opportunity to consider whether continued exemption from fair employment legislation in all schools is compatible with their professional aims and the model they are providing for their students.

Such objectives would point towards a much more interventionist educational policy than anything which the government has yet attempted. But interventionist and integrative policies have been typical of the approach adopted in nearly every other modernising western society. They were employed in the introduction of comprehensive reorganisation in the 1970s in Britain and in the Irish Republic in the introduction of comprehensive and community colleges. The fact that the Northern Ireland government made no attempt to maintain parity with British, Irish or European developments in this sphere was assumed to be in accord with parental wishes. But in practice no real attempt was made to find out whether that was true. There are problems in reconciling different ideas of freedom and equality and no easy solutions. But in a democratic society seeking such solutions is the first duty a government owes its citizens.

PART 1

Issues in Organising Integrated Schools

1
Integrated Education in Northern Ireland
Current Provision and Legislation

Fiona Stephen

The development of the current model for planned integrated schools in Northern Ireland began with the establishment in September 1981 of Lagan College with 28 pupils in the now almost legendary scout hut. All Children Together (ACT), the first pressure group for integrated education, intended Lagan College as an exemplar, to prove to government that the concept of an integrated school could and would work in reality. The growth of subsequent schools was initially rather hesitant and the process of development very much one of learning by doing. Despite the tremendous obstacles, particularly financial, the creation of new integrated schools continued. Each new school project learned from the previous parent group, and with each successive project there was an increasing body of knowledge and confidence to bolster everyone's sense of purpose.

The Education Reform (NI) Order 1989 brought recognition and financial support for integrated education where sufficient numbers of Catholic and Protestant parents showed there was the demand. This recognition, although welcome, has had the effect of both raising the public expectation that integrated schooling should be a readily available option for those who wish it, and, perhaps less helpfully, identifying integrated education with government political strategy.

The new legislative provision for integrated education was, however, a major milestone. For everyone involved in the development of the early schools, and those individuals whose calls for integration had created a climate for change, it was the long awaited response from government. The legislation places a statutory duty on the Department of Education to 'encourage and facilitate' the development of integrated education.[1] Under its terms there are two categories of integrated status: controlled integrated (CI) and grant maintained integrated (GMI). In 1990 when the legislation was enacted, the existing integrated schools were able to opt for either model of integrated status. Only two of the then eight integrated schools opted for controlled integrated rather than grant maintained integrated status. For new integrated school projects seeking day-one funding, GMI status is the only option.

Both grant maintained integrated and controlled integrated status are open to any existing school (apart from a nursery or special school) which wants to build on a mixed enrolment, plan to develop a more integrated structure to enhance its integrating ethos and 'transform' into a recognised integrated school. So far, from the controlled sector, two schools, Brownlow College, Craigavon, and Carhill Integrated Primary School, Garvagh, have opted to 'transform', both to controlled integrated status. From the voluntary or maintained sectors, no school has yet elected to seek a change, whether to controlled or grant maintained integrated status, although the option remains a realistic possibility for the future.

The legal process of transformation is launched by a parent ballot which recent experience has shown has the potential to be divisive. If successful, it entails specific changes in the scheme of management and composition of the board of governors as well as other changes in the organisation of the school. The atmosphere in which this takes place will reflect the circumstances within the surrounding community and how politically sensitive the proposed change is perceived to be.

Recent Developments

There are now eighteen integrated schools, fourteen at primary level, including seven with nursery classes. A further three integrated primary schools plan to open in September 1993 and other new school projects are in the process of development at both levels. Two new schools have opened each year since 1988 and the pattern of steady, incremental growth seems firmly established. The total number of pupils represents just over one per cent of the Northern Ireland school population. This number is increasing each year and not simply in relation to the opening of new integrated schools. (See table and map.)

Integrated sixth form provision is now available at both Lagan College and Hazelwood College. Lagan College has successfully introduced the International Baccalaureate to Northern Ireland while Hazelwood College offers a range of courses at A level and hopes to introduce General National Vocational Qualifications (GNVQs) for those students who wish to continue at school post-sixteen but do not find the A level programme appropriate. For both schools the introduction of sixth form provision was a new phase in their development initiated in response to demand and without Department of Education financial support until firmly established. This pattern of parent initiative, unsupported by

The Growth of Integrated Schools in Northern Ireland

Date of foundation and current (1993 provisional) enrolment of integrated schools

Second level (all ability and co-educational)

1981	Lagan College	Belfast E	860	
1985	Hazelwood College	Belfast N	600	
1991	Brownlow College *	Craigavon	209	
1992	Oakgrove College	L'Derry	180	

Primary/nursery schools

1985	Forge Primary	Belfast S	180	
1985	Hazelwood Primary	Belfast N	303	+ 25 nursery
1986	All Children's Primary	Newcastle	156	
1987	Mill Strand Primary	Portrush	171	+ 25 nursery
1987	Bridge Primary	Banbridge	232	
1988	Windmill Primary	Dungannon	115	+ 24 nursery
1989	Braidside Primary	Ballymena	118	+ 24 nursery
1989	Enniskillen Primary	Enniskillen	160	
1990	Omagh Primary	Omagh	110	+ 18 nursery
1990	Portadown Primary	Portadown	112	+ 23 nursery
1991	Corran Primary	Larne	96	+ 25 nursery
1991	Carhill Primary *	Garvagh	51	
1991	Oakgrove Primary	L'Derry	215	
1992	Acorn Primary	Carrickfergus	60	+ 24 in playgroup

* transformed

New schools opened September 1993: Saints and Scholars Primary, Armagh; Loughview Primary, Belfast SE; Cranmore Primary, Belfast S. New projects planned for 1994: (Second level) Fermanagh; South Down; (Primary) Ormeau, Belfast.

government and requiring independent funding to start with, is not new to integrated education but it is one which many had expected would change as a result of the Education Reform Order. It is certainly at odds with the generally held – but unfounded – perception that integrated education is not only fully government funded, but generously so in comparison with the traditional controlled and maintained sectors.

Structure

Perhaps the most significant ingredient in the success of the integrated schools to date is attributable to the carefully planned structure which governs the membership and management of each school community. The premise on which it is based is that in any culturally mixed group where there is a minority smaller than 40 per cent of the total, the minority feels, behaves and is perceived as a minority; and conversely, where a group amounts to more than 60 per cent of the total, they feel, behave and are perceived as the dominant group. Therefore, to guard against inequality or bias (conscious or unconscious), it is essential to ensure the representation of either cultural group never falls below 40 per cent of the total. Public confidence in the 'integrated' quality of integrated schools has been clearly established around this balance factor.

The 40 per cent minimum representation is a key element in the composition of the enrolment, staffing and management of the integrated schools. A further key structural element is the involvement and representation of parents. The structure of the board of governors of a grant maintained integrated school fully reflects both these cultural and parental elements in its composition. According to size, it may have 16 or 24 voting members, plus the principal as a non-voting member. Voting members consist of:

Board of Governors: GMI Schools

Members	16	24
Foundation Governors	6	9
(one third must be parents of pupils at the school)		
Department of Education appointees	4	6
Elected Parents	4	6
Elected Teachers	2	3

case of a new school, the foundation governors will be appointed the body or persons submitting the proposal. Subsequent foundation governor appointments are made by the foundation governors themselves, as the 'guarantors' of the school's integrated ethos. All governor appointments are made according to the Northern Ireland Council for Integrated Education (NICIE) model scheme of management, approved by DENI, which ensures that balance of representation between the two major religious/cultural traditions is maintained.

Finance

It would be difficult to underestimate the importance of the contribution from the charitable trusts and foundations which supported the early development and consolidation of integrated education. This contribution amounted to over £2.5m in the eight years between 1982 and 1990. By January 1990 however, the financial need experienced by the integrated schools was so acute that government assurances of good intent under the terms of the new legislation had to be accepted. There was a desperate question as to how sufficient funds were to be found to provide for teachers' salaries and running costs in three schools during the months before they become eligible for government funding under the terms of the new GMI status. These costs, combined with the ever-mounting interest on bank loans for five schools premises, far exceeded the funds promised by the group of charitable trusts led by the Nuffield Foundation, generous as these were. Although there was tremendous financial relief at the prospect of the legislation, it was marred by considerable anxiety surrounding the issues of enrolment and the non-definition of an integrated school in the legislation – issues which continue to be contentious.

By September 1990 the scale of need and ever increasing level of demand had moved far beyond that which was reasonable for charitable fund-raising to support. It was already recognised in the plans for two new schools for that year that their opening would have been seriously in question without the promise of day-one funding under the legislation. However, much more than simply money was involved. In addition to ensuring that salaries would be secure, the 1989 Education Order also meant that teachers' superannuation and career prospects would no longer be automatically jeopardised. Teachers making the tremendous professional commitment involved in taking up an appointment with a new integrated school, would not be taking quite such a gamble with their long-term financial security. Equally, the integrated school governors could discharge their duties in a proper manner without necessarily incurring an ever-increasing bank overdraft and coping with all the associated anxieties. Most important of all, though, was the formal acceptance of integrated education as a legitimate option.

Recurrent funding for the integrated schools, as for other schools, is allocated by Local Management of Schools (LMS) formulae based on the age weighted pupil unit (AWPU) and pupil numbers. In the case of the controlled integrated schools, the formula is the same as that set by the local education and library board (ELB) for all the schools within their area. For the GMI schools, the formula is set by the Department of Education, but according to the same principles as the other LMS formulae to ensure that there is no preferential treatment for integrated schools. The GMI schools do not receive any special supplementary allowances for being opted out (as is the case with the opted out schools in England and Wales) and they look to their local ELB for all the services which are provided free of charge to the controlled and maintained schools. Statutory services such as school meals and educational psychology have to be provided for the GMI schools on the same basis. However, services such as transport, peripatetic teaching support (eg. for music and remedial subjects) and governor and teacher training are available on a more variable basis depending on which ELB is involved and how its particular policy and resource considerations present themselves.

Commitment
The provision of limited government funding from the day the first pupils cross the threshold, has not changed the fact that any new integrated school project still depends utterly on the determination and hard work of the parents and staff if it is to come to fruition. This heavy drain on energy and commitment continues to make integrated schooling a tough option for parents if they live in an area without an already established integrated school. The possibility of transforming existing schools is a very sensitive issue and a daunting prospect for individual parents who seek integrated schooling for their children. If parents are prepared to work very hard, there is a good chance that they will succeed in building up a sufficiently substantial parent body to start a new integrated school project. Furthermore, they can do this without being a direct threat to any particular existing school or section of parents. Until there is a more general acceptance of integrated education in the educational political and religious status quo, doubts are likely to remain about the logic of transforming existing schools. New school projects are likely to continue to be the preferred option of most parents, despite the problems of finance.

The financial burden involved with new school development is, however, substantial. In the case of rented premises, there is usually the need for some building adaptation, the costs of which are non-recoverable from government. Where a school has to open on a green field site in temporary buildings or purchase an existing building, the capital outlay may be recoverable eventually. In such cases, grant may be paid by the Department of Education, but only if the expenditure received prior approval. Payment is usually after a period of three to four years, during which the school in question must have become firmly established and proved its viability. A loan in the region of £500, 000 may be involved. This represents a considerable tying-up of resources in just one project, effectively restricting the number of projects and the rate of expansion for integrated education – resources being the ultimate enabling factor.

The Role of NICIE

Whether a project is an emerging new school, or a transformation school, it needs advice and support. The Northern Ireland Council for Integrated Education (NICIE) was formally launched in 1989 'to assist the development of integrated education and schools in Northern Ireland for the public benefit'. The creation of the council as a central body and umbrella organisation for the integrated education movement was a reflection of both the movement's energetic growth and increasing maturity. Following the enactment of the Education Reform Order, there was an urgent need for the development of processes to support the implementation of integrated education provisions. With the acquired wisdom of its membership and the support of professional staff, NICIE was in a position to coordinate the broader integrated movement, drawing together the knowledge and experience of individuals and groups and making it accessible to all. One of the council's most significant achievements to date has been the drawing up of a *Statement of Principles and Practical Guidelines* which is endorsed by the membership and defines clearly what an integrated school strives to achieve and by what means. (See Appendix) Although NICIE is a voluntary organisation and still dependent on charitable funding, it has received an annual grant from government since June 1991. This financial recognition for NICIE helps it to provide the development, support and advice services it gives to integrated schools and projects.

One inevitable result of the legislation has been the development of a close working relationship between NICIE and the Northern Ireland Department of Education. The linking of integrated education with the government's 'opting out' policy meant that DENI assumed a direct executive role in relation to the grant maintained sector. With no real precedent for this role apart from the voluntary grammar schools, and with five distinctively different education and library boards to look to for guidance on school administration, DENI found the development of processes and formulae for the GMI schools challenging. In the context of Northern Ireland, where the government's primary focus is on issues related to parity of treatment between sections of the community, it was an overwhelming priority for DENI (as well as NICIE) to ensure that integrated schools did not receive preferential treatment. However, it was also essential to ensure that there was not only parity of treatment between integrated, controlled and maintained schools, but also consistency of treatment between one integrated school and another. The result has been an attempt to establish a 'golden mean' for the integrated schools, with a balance being struck, so far as is possible, between the lowest common denominator and the highest common factor as established from information gleaned from the five area boards. In a different, but not completely unrelated context, research into educational discrimination[2] by the Standing Advisory Commission on Human Rights has also revealed some of the complexities involved in trying to establish a clear cross-board picture of provision under any one heading.

The public expectation that integrated schooling should be a readily available option has been further reinforced by the *Parents' Charter*. This has encouraged parents to set up integrated schools in the expectation of full government support. While the emergence of integrated schools can only reflect the readiness for change within specific local communities (if it is to be firmly rooted), it is also dependent on the availability of resources. Integrated education remains the only area of educational provision where the initial money to provide for premises has to be found by the parent body.

The Integrated Education Fund

To ensure that the long-term provision for such financial needs was available while it was not being met by statutory sources, an endowment fund was established by the Nuffield Foundation and the Joseph Rowntree Charitable Trust in 1992. The Integrated Education Fund is independent but receives administrative support through NICIE. The fund's capital base is used by its governors to secure loans on school premises, while the income is used to make grants for other integrated school developments. As the capital base of the fund can only support a limited number of capital projects, so the size of the fund effectively defines the potential rate of growth for integrated education.

Integrated Nursery Education

The integrated education movement has encouraged nursery provision in the belief that nursery education and the pre-school stage is the bedrock for the whole educational process, and perhaps the most underrated natural channel for creating an atmosphere of mutual respect and tolerance. There are seven integrated nursery classes, each one part of an integrated primary school, created through the efforts and determination of parents. But although nursery classes have an established role within a planned integrated school, they have not been accepted as integral by the Department of Education and there is no statutory provision for integrated nursery education. This has resulted in the anomalous position where seven integrated primary schools have a nursery class which is legally separate from the main body of the school under the terms of the scheme of management, is funded completely separately and is not permitted to derive any financial or material benefit from sharing the same site as the rest of the school. As the nursery classes are all staffed by qualified nursery teachers and childcare assistants the operating costs involved are considerable.

The nurseries coordinate their funding and policy through NICIE by way of the nursery committee. In the early spring of 1992 all the nursery classes were forced to contemplate closure as their financial situation had reached a crisis point. Five of the seven were in such a financially desperate position that it seemed unlikely they would be able to continue paying salaries until the end of the school year. Faced with the possibility of these classes being forced to close mid-year as they ran out of money, it was decided to make one last bid to put a collective funding strategy together and to seek some government input; and failing this, to close all nurseries at the end of the summer term.

It was therefore a significant breakthrough when the Department of Education agreed to make a grant through NICIE for integrated nursery education. The grant, while only representing 19% of the running costs (excluding capital) of each of the existing nursery classes, is an important recognition that integrated education has as much right to educational provision at nursery level as any other sector. The development of an anti-bias approach to the curriculum which the integrated nursery classes have been working on will, it is hoped, provide the basis for the future development of community-based nursery education provision. This is an area the government should not ignore. Education for Mutual Understanding as reflected in the Northern Ireland Curriculum shows that the government recognises the importance of tackling these issues. Attitude formation begins very early in a child's life and research has shown the value of early years education. Government policy, as yet, has not absorbed the many compelling arguments for nursery education as cost-effective, pre-emptive action on both the educational and personal/social development fronts, although the benefits have been clearly established by research in the USA and Scandinavia.[3] In Northern Ireland, where the percentage of under-five children per head of population is the highest in the UK and the provision of nursery education the lowest, the clearly defined need provides an exciting opportunity for fresh vision in planning and implementing provision.

Conclusion

The often expressed concern as to whether integrated schools could survive and deliver quality education has proved ill-founded. Integrated education as a social force is working well. There are results which clearly demonstrate that this is not to the detriment of the quality of education. The goal for the integrated education movement in the short to medium term continues to be the creation of new integrated schools. At least one integrated school at primary level plus one at second level in each of the 26 district council areas is the minimum necessary to make the choice of integrated schooling a realistic option for parents. Integrated education is not an instant panacea but it can play an important part in the process of creating a reconciled community.

Notes

1   Education Reform (Northern Ireland) Order 1989, Article 64 (1).

2   Standing Advisory Commission on Human Rights, Education Project 1989-1992, Consultants' papers.

3   Berrueta-Clement, J., et al. (1984) *Changed lives: the effects of the Perry pre-school programme on youths through age 19*, Monographs of the High/Scope Educational Research Foundation No 8; Kathy Sylva, Peter Moss, (1992) *Learning before School*, National Commission on Education, Briefing No 8.

2
Integrated Schools and their Impact on the Local Community

Colm Murray Cavanagh

...in twenty years of working in various ways at cross-community relations and reconciliation within this City, the setting up of Oakgrove Integrated Primary School and the work towards an integrated college here, have proved, in terms of inter-community relationships and coming together, the most positive, the most fruitful, the most hopeful, the most constructive, the most forward-looking, the most heart-warming and at times the most moving work of reconciliation we have been involved in.

Co-Chairpersons' Report, first AGM of Foyle Trust for Integrated Education, December 1991.

'If you get involved in opening an integrated school', said Fiona Stelfox, founder member of Mill Strand Primary School in Portrush and at that time Chairperson of the Northern Ireland Council for Integrated Education, 'it will change your life. It is tremendous. And it *will* change your life!'

Fiona Stelfox said this to us in 1990. At that time there were no formally integrated schools anywhere in the city or county of L'Derry. Now in April 1993 we have Oakgrove Integrated Primary School with 183 pupils; and Oakgrove Integrated College with 80 first form students and heavily oversubscribed for the next 100 first year places in September 1993. Fiona Stelfox was right. It *is* tremendous. And it *did* change our lives. When you create your own school you educate yourself twice!

Parent Power
The founding of new integrated schools in Northern Ireland from 1981 to 1993 has been a superb example of parent power. Some of the form 1 students at

Oakgrove Integrated College are younger than Lagan College which was founded by the trail-blazing Belfast visionaries of All Children Together in September 1981. Those ACT people demonstrated that it *is* possible; that change *can* be achieved. In L'Derry we continually pay tribute to their courage and determination.

The great demonstration of the last ten years has been that *structural* change can be accomplished by ordinary individuals. Ordinary people can come together and actually make permanent changes to the structure of our battered Northern Ireland society.

In 1993 Oakgrove Primary School not only had 183 pupils, it also had 16 members of the board of governors and 17 staff members. And all of these pupils and adults had families who were affected by the new institution. I know, because I am one of them. Oakgrove Integrated College not only has 80 form 1 students, it also has 15 staff members and is in the process of finalising its 16-person board of governors. And all of these students and adults have families who have been affected by the new institution.

For both primary school and college, enrolment more than doubled in the first year and Oakgrove College itself played host to 900-1000 visitors at its first Open Day. September 1993 will see 100 new form 1 students and 6 new teachers.

One began the whole process by thinking primarily of the effect that integrated schools would have on the students in the desks. It became very clear very quickly that in addition to this transformation of the pupil experience, the whole community was affected.

Effect on the Community

What has the effect been in L'Derry? (That 'L'Derry' is one effect: it reminds us all the time that we live in a society with two different vocabularies, as well as two different aspirations.)

So, who is affected?

1. The pupils;
2. The adults immediately involved (parents, teachers, other staff, governors);
3. The relations of those pupils and adults;
4. The other schools, to some extent; and
5. The whole community, to some extent.

1. The people most affected by our new integrated schools are clearly the pupils themselves – an additional 130 per year in L'Derry rising to at least 150 per year

from September 1994 into the indefinite future. Those pupils get the straightforward, intended benefit of having the kind of cross-community, pluralist experience sought by their parents.

2. Then those parents have the highly stimulating and rewarding experience of shaping the kind of life they want for themselves and for their children. And I am now profoundly aware of the vital importance of the actual *process* of cross-community work. Familiarity and trust are certainly anticipated at the outset. But they eventually become real in fact – copperfastened by months and then years of shared discussion, shared planning, shared committee work, shared fund-raising, shared problems and shared success. This depth of understanding and trust cannot come quickly; it requires actual time.

Staff members, especially the principal and teachers, have to face what is largely a new experience – both for the pupils and themselves – in terms of ordinary life in Northern Ireland, in terms of individuals' experience and in terms of creating a new approach to teaching a plural class with its previously one-sided experiences.

This new learning is also encountered by the board of governors and parents' council of each school. Although goodwill and good intentions can be assumed as a starting point, it is only in the joint working out of daily decisions and practicalities that the pluralist way forward emerges. ('How would it be if...?' 'Would it be an acceptable venue if we were to go to...?' 'How would Catholics approach...?' 'How would Protestants find...?' 'Do Jehovah's Witnesses...?' 'Would Bahá'ís understand if...?') In these ongoing – usually quite mundane, but significant – decisions, do we create the actual shape and learn the actual sensitivities of a new society.

3. The effects of this then automatically extend to the relations of all these people: the cousins of pupils, the parents of the parents, the brothers of the staff, the sisters of the governors, etc. The intentions are chatted about. The problems are aired. The relationships are teased out as part of the locality's new reality.

4. The existing local schools will be conscious of the new arrival in their midst. 'Is it necessary?' 'Are existing schools not integrated enough?' 'Why do all grant maintained integrated schools have a parents' council?' 'Will it take some of our pupils?' 'How is Religious Education taught at an integrated school?'

5. In addition to all these growing ripples throughout the community, the community has seen a long-term structural change and a very clear public declaration by local people in favour of reconciliation and co-operation. The

community as a whole now has access to that third, shared option which did not exist before.

For generations – ever since the national schools were established 160 years ago – there were always parents who had wanted their children to have the benefit of attending school with pupils from the other community. Until 1981, with the opening of Lagan College, few opportunities existed in Northern Ireland, or indeed Ireland as a whole, other than in the dozen factory schools and in rural areas. Now the third option is being made available in a steadily increasing number of areas throughout Northern Ireland. At last those parents are giving their children the kind of education which had largely been unavailable before.

A Clear Public Statement

The creation of a new integrated school must be seen in its own locality as an unambiguous public statement by a group of local adults that:

(1) they are actively committed to working for reconciliation, co-operation and dialogue between the two communities. The very structures designed by the integrated school movement to share representation and responsibility ensure that this is done on a basis of acceptance, equality and consensus.

(2) that our present education structures (like most other structures) can be made even better.

The highly successful progress of Oakgrove College and Oakgrove Primary has been part of the steady growth of the integrated education sector. Oakgrove pupils represent 263 of the 3,300 pupils in Northern Ireland's grant maintained integrated schools. The two Oakgrove schools have strengthened and reinforced the ripple effect of the new integrated schools founded in the 1980s.

More importantly, the demonstration effect of a group of individual parents setting up these schools has spread further. Just as we in turn brought speakers to our public meetings from Enniskillen Integrated Primary School, Omagh Integrated Primary School, NICIE, Lagan College and Hazelwood College, so we also have responded to invitations to send speakers to groups interested in establishing new primary schools in Carrickfergus and in Ormeau, Belfast, and new integrated colleges in North Derry, South Down and Fermanagh.

We have followed the example of others and have thus, in turn, provided the demonstration effect to those who are seeking integrated education facilities in their own locality. Our particular experience has been extremely useful in that the Foyle Trust for Integrated Education is currently the only local trust with the actual experience of establishing both a primary school and a college under the provisions of the 1989 Education Reform Order. In the light of this experience, what have we found in the North West?

No Arguments!

From the very beginnings of our work in 1990 we were advised by the knowledge and expertise of Geoff Starrett, retired Principal of Greenhaw Controlled Primary School, the first MA graduate in Peace Studies at the University of Ulster. On his advice it was agreed by the whole group from the very start that we would not engage in public controversy while we were in the process of creating the new primary school. This was simply to avoid public rancour and public arguments which would probably not change anyone's mind, but would tend only to attract negative comments to the project.

On the other hand, we continually produced press releases and publicity regarding our positive progress in creating the new school and college. As one would expect, given the catastrophic community divisions in Northern Ireland over the last two decades, and the well established results of several public opinion surveys regarding integrated education, there was a widespread public sympathy for our work. Much of this was articulated on a quiet individual basis and in a non-public manner. It was often quite impossible to judge in advance which local person would be strongly supportive of, indifferent to, or opposed to integrated schools.

The only overt opposition to our work to open an integrated primary school and college in L'Derry came from some staff and governors of some existing schools. This opposition seemed to be largely based on the totally pragmatic functioning of the school market. New schools simply increase the competition for students. As the Department of Education says: 'The money follows the child', although, from some education officials there was also a distinct coolness regarding our wish to set up the integrated college.

In terms of actual effect I have witnessed a wonderfully strong benefit both to the community and to my own life from my contact and co-operation with like-minded adults from the different historical and religious traditions in this City.

Likewise as a parent my own life has been enriched by the new range of friends which the schools have brought to me personally and the cross-community contacts and friendships which my children now have both at the primary school and college.

Laissez-Faire and Politicians

In the 1970s and 1980s, individuals in L'Derry interested in integrated education declined to take action. There was increasing mixing of children from the two traditions at existing local primary and second-level schools. A form of integration seemed to be taking place naturally. However the passage of time and the very major movement of population across the Foyle seemed by 1990 to indicate that rather than moving towards a mixed population, the apparent mixing was actually a 'snapshot' of a transition process which showed many indications of ending up by the year 2000 with schools as mono-cultural as they had been in 1960.

But the situation was actually worsening. This greatly increased geographical polarisation in the city was clearly removing from current children and teenagers much, perhaps *most*, of the previous cross-community contact which had been experienced by the current adult population.

In 1975, 21 councillors of the then Londonderry City Council in a public meeting of the Council, responded to a presentation which encouraged integration of schools. Councillor after councillor spoke in favour of integrated schools. Only one was opposed. Three had major reservations. Seventeen actually rose to speak in favour. By a nice coincidence, the council's temporary address in 1975 at Rectory Field now forms part of the site of Oakgrove Integrated Primary School.

One councillor in particular said in 1975 that he had changed his mind about integrated education. Previously he would have opposed it. Now he was in favour. It emerged later that the reason for this change was because he had become stunningly aware that whereas he himself had grown up in a mixed community, widening community polarisation meant that his son had now been raised almost totally without contact across the community divide. The father now felt that active steps must be taken to increase cross-community contact. By 1990 when the matter of integrated education was raised informally with local politicians, one senior politician said: 'Keep away from integrated education. The schools are already mixed'.

One city councillor when asked for his views on integrated education, clasped his hands to his head in mock horror: 'Oh Jesus! Don't ask us to support integrated education. If you want our support ask us for money. But don't ask us to support integrated education!' The point was clearly made: there are no votes in integrated education. A dismaying example of how our local politics are pulled apart by our community division rather than knitted together by efforts to cooperate.

On the other hand, in the establishment of Oakgrove Primary School, the acceptance and encouragement of some councillors has been very positive. While some councillors actively opposed our intentions, many councillors approved. At worst they felt that we were a responsible group and would do no harm, at best they wished to support our wish to work for reconciliation.

This was a clear indication that in the larger political parties – other than the Alliance Party – there will be little initiative towards integrated education. If it is to come from anywhere then it will come from individuals. The same seems to be true as regards the churches. All the evidence indicates that this form of practical reconciliation will come not from the pulpit but from the individuals in the pew.

And so by the end of the 1980s in L'Derry, those people who felt the increasing polarisation and who were frustrated at our community's lack of progress towards reconciliation and cooperation, knew that they themselves would have to take action. Leadership was not going to come from the existing structures. A classic case of the maxim:

If not now, then when?

If not me, then who?

Local parents decided it was time for action.

One chance conversation among several people on a sunny spring day in May 1990 seemed to indicate that the time was ripe. It was near the time of the 11+ results – Northern Ireland's selection process. Others were contacted: would they be interested? Further informal discussions took place. Then several meetings were held in the deliberately neutral venue of a local hotel. The Community Relations Council was approached for cash to help cover the local expenses (stamps, advertising, room hire). A public meeting was held in November attended by 115 people. They were interested in integrated education at nursery, primary and secondary level. The way seemed clear.

The task was simple but daunting. Find a minimum of 25 pupils for the first year. Demonstrate continuing viable enrolment. Hire staff. Find premises. Set the whole structure up. Let people be sure that it would happen. Demonstrate to people that the ideal was attainable. Show the Department of Education that it would be viable.

Critically important was the advice and assistance from NICIE – especially from Fiona Stephen, Director, and Kevin Lambe, Development Officer. Without NICIE we would have opened not in September 1991 but in September 1992. Without NICIE we would not have found £90,000 worth of loan guarantees to refurbish the building premises from the Nuffield Foundation and the Joseph

Rowntree Charitable Trust. Those foundations unlocked the door.

Effect

So, what did we provide? By far the largest group of adults who supported the integrated school movement and enrolled their children were those people who knew that cross-community relationships simply had to be improved and who felt a commitment to do something personally about it. They saw this as a way to create one new, cooperative and cross-community bond. One parent with children at Oakgrove IPS in an interview for Canadian television described the new school as: 'an antidote to the poison that is affecting this community'.

Oakgrove IPS also provided an outlet for inter-church families ('mixed marriages') who felt that it accommodated both traditions in a welcoming and fruitful way. This approach was most poignantly – and pointedly – articulated by a young child shortly after Oakgrove IPS opened its doors. Her family represented both traditions – a 'mixed marriage'. The child was then aged eight, one of the first intake of pupils at Oakgrove Primary. Out of the blue one day she said to her mother 'At my last school I just talked about Daddy. I didn't say anything about you, Mammy. At Oakgrove I can say I'm proud of both of you.' Out of the mouths of babes...

This child had experience of one of the existing schools from the segregated system. Obviously, of course, no teacher in that previous school had ever made any distinction between Catholic and Protestant children. It does not even matter which side of the divide that school was. But the child knew from our lacerated society that some relationships are usually better left unspoken. The whole beauty of the integrated schools is that they welcome and celebrate children from both of Northern Ireland's two main traditions. And children of other traditions. And children of no political or religious tradition at all.

This is perhaps particularly the case with children who come here from abroad. If they feel no part of either the unionist/Protestant or nationalist/Roman Catholic traditions here, then the integrated school can provide them with a welcoming and non-partisan home. This foreign mixture has, of course, an enriching effect on the integrated school as well. Pupils from Pennsylvania. Pupils from Greece.

In terms of religion the integrated school provides a home for both ends of the spectrum i.e. those who are not members of any church; and those who feel that their faith brings them to share actively and personally with not only their own church adherents, but those of other faiths.

Leadership

The experience of Northern Ireland in the last twenty years indicates that leadership in this field will not come from any source other than local individuals and groups. The two main political and religious communities show no likelihood of coming together in the field of education to set up shared structures. Clearly the government has no intention of placing itself in the middle ground or of seeming to dictate to the politicians and the churches in this hyper-sensitive field. However, Dr Brian Mawhinney's 1989 Education Reform Order drew up permissive legislation which allows parents and individuals to create local structures and satisfy Government regulations in order to provide themselves with this cross-community facility. Parents are on all sides accepted as having the unassailable right to decide the education of their own children.

The Northern Ireland Department of Education has been entirely professional in all its dealings with our projects: explaining our rights and responsibilities; clarifying DENI's role; and providing non-partisan opinion and advice – even when we did not take it!

The work is very long term. After ten years only one per cent of the population of Northern Ireland schools are at these integrated schools (i.e. approximately 3,300 pupils out of the total 330,000). At the same time the evangelical Christian schools have opened in some twelve locations and are paid for not out of public funds but entirely at the expense of the fundamentalist parents – a striking evidence of the commitment of those parents. Irish language schools have gone through a similar process.

A Future for the 95 per cent?

So, what is the way forward? In the year 2000 at the present rate of development, will there be a further sixteen integrated schools throughout Northern Ireland – a total by then of 30 schools and seven nurseries? Will we continue indefinitely to open entirely new schools? What will parents do in the controlled and maintained schools as they see the increasing demand of parents for integrated education?

Will the demand for integrated schools continue to grow? Will it reach a plateau? Will existing schools transfer to integrated status? So far only two have done so – Carhill Primary and Brownlow College, both from the controlled sector.

At present one per cent of Northern Ireland school pupils are at integrated schools. An estimated further 4 per cent are at schools in which there is a significant degree of mixing of students from both sides of the community divide.

What then of the 95 per cent? Will the demand for integrated education and reconciliation encourage these schools to seek ever more cross-community contact? Will EMU be enough? Does the movement towards integrated schools leave the students in the other schools in an even more mono-cultural situation than before? In an even more polarised situation?

Parents involved in our grant maintained integrated schools have no doubt as to the effectiveness and thus the desirability of integrated education. It enriches the lives and experience of all involved. Its steady spread is profoundly encouraging. But it is a small start on a very long road. What we have achieved is so very small. And the work of reconciliation in our society remains so enormous.

That is the challenge.

3
The Educational Ethos of an Integrated Primary School

Anne Murray

In the NICIE *Statement of Principles* the core aim of an integrated school 'is to provide the child with a caring, fulfilling, educational experience which will enable him/her to become a fulfilled and caring adult'. This educational ethos or character of integrated schools has strong links with the concept of child-centred education. The term became unpopular, even derogatory, some years ago in educational circles; but it best describes the educational philosophy that parents who send their children to integrated schools want for them.

The links between child-centred and integrated education were explored at a series of seminars organised by NICIE in 1992. It was found that both approaches allow children and adults from diverse backgrounds to feel comfortable together. Both promote equal respect for self and others, and for each others' traditions and cultures and both celebrate diversity in identity. They encourage openness to issues; and welcome and can accommodate differences.

Child-Centred Learning

In a recent survey, parents of children at an integrated primary school were asked whether the ethos of the school made any difference to the education their children were receiving. The parents had no doubt that it *was* very different from other schools. They felt the schools brought children into a plural society. Integrated schools were all ability and therefore not elitist, as in grammar schools. They were not sectionalist, as in the Protestant and Catholic sectors. The participation of the parents made the schools very different. The 'banking' system where teachers have all the knowledge was not prevalent. Parents owned the school and the teachers worked for them, so relationships were different.

Many parents felt that happiness was the essence of the difference. Happy children are more open to learning. The well-being of the child was paramount. The emphasis on developing self-esteem was crucial. Parents said that while children felt liberated, they were also taught that with freedom comes responsibility. As well as children being better motivated, parents thought a broader pluralist picture of the world was being painted for them. In specific curricular areas such as history, geography, RE, literature, art and music, the resources of the two communities within the classroom were an invaluable asset which fostered openness in both staff and pupils.

But when teachers were asked what was special or distinctive about their schools in terms of the organisation of teaching and learning relationships and in terms of pupils' needs, the response was surprising. Most teachers felt that there should not be any difference; but that in reality there was. If all are charged with teaching a common curriculum why then should there be any difference?

Parental Influence
Many teachers feel that the reason why teaching and learning relationships are different in integrated schools is because the level of parental involvement and expectations are higher than in other schools. Parents set the schools up and 'own' them in a way that they do not own other schools. They do not expect teachers to have a traditional view of education, but rather presume a more child-centred approach, where their children will be treated as individuals, their self-esteem developed and their voices heard. Teachers feel that parents expect a broader education for their children and they are prepared to give more when parental expectations are high; they feel that because the children are so happy in school they are more eager to learn! Children too, accept that there is a close home–school link and this knowledge encourages them to do their best.

In integrated schools teachers give greater consideration to the differences in the children they come into contact with. They note and use what people say to them. Because parents think their children are special then the teacher treats them that way – as individuals, and with care. At the NICIE seminars, the teachers acknowledged that the educational ethos is more child-centred and that this is important from a motivational point of view.

The majority of teachers thought that in an integrated school children receive a more rounded education, with an emphasis on the creative and emotional as well as the academic development of the child. Again there is no reason why this should be especially distinctive of integrated schools, since on examination it appears to be simply 'good practice'. However, having children from different cultural backgrounds within the classroom is a ready-made and valuable resource in curricular terms.

Children from the two communities bring different experiences and perceptions from each of their different backgrounds. The sharing of these is a bonus resource in class. Teachers are also more conscious of teaching children from different traditions; they feel this helps them to think in a more pluralist way.

Whole School Policies

Most teachers at the NICIE seminars felt the educational ethos of their school was working well. The schools set out to be very democratic and place a high value on consultation among the whole school community. For example in one school the board of governors had considered an outline for a *Positive School Discipline Policy* and passed it on to staff and parents for consideration. Staff had worked through it themselves and with pupils in class. Parents were working at it through evening workshops organised by the school. Staff in another school were very proud of the work done in the *Pastoral Care Programme* in which the development of the self-esteem of staff, pupils and parents had all been considered. They felt they had embraced the philosophy of child-centred education in the right sense of the word.

Teachers at the seminars felt it important for integrated schools to ensure that they considered the NICIE *Statement of Principles* regularly. If school policies are reviewed regularly bearing these principles in mind, then the ethos will remain healthy. Induction was also recognised to be an important area. New people join the school community all the time – pupils, parents, governors and staff. Each year a programme of induction is needed to ensure these people are not left behind or left out.

In their booklet *Integrated Schools – Information for Parents* (1989), Wilson and Dunn argue that the style and character of each school is obviously different in many ways, but each shares the general philosophy which includes child-centred education and good interpersonal relationships within the school community. They suggest that the integrated curriculum should attempt to understand and define what a local Ulster culture might involve. In the meantime, they hoped that integrated schools would 'reflect the variety of cultural expressions in Northern Ireland, with special emphasis on the two major cultures summarised as British and Irish. The curriculum will therefore include, where appropriate, an appreciation of historical and religious differences as well as the obvious cultural forms such as language, art, music, literature and folklore'.

In practice, Wilson and Dunn suggest that this will be difficult. I believe it is becoming easier. The Education Reform Order (NI) 1989 brought in cross-curricular educational themes as well as a common curriculum. One of the education themes, Cultural Heritage, has a special relevance for integrated schools. As result many people are now working on Cultural Heritage materials. The integrated schools sector may have much to offer and share in this area.

The debate, discussion and shared views and experiences at the NICIE seminars produced many ideas of ways in which child-centred education could be promoted in our schools. This is what people found practical and effective:

- personal development workshops for children, and all those who work in the school, as well as parents and governors;
- weekly class meetings addressing issues important to the child and teacher;
- skills register for parents, to enable the skills of parents to be used to enhance the curriculum;
- balanced approach to sport in terms of gender, competitive/cooperative games, ability and cultural tradition;
- good classroom organisation and on-going monitoring and development of classroom management;
- letters of praise sent home/certificates of praise/certificates of merit;
- social gatherings, including formal staff, pupil and parent contact;
- governor involvement in in-service training;
- positive and egalitarian approaches and attitudes in the classroom;
- regular parent involvement;
- personal records of the whole child and her/his achievements, activities, progress and developments, to which the child contributes and which is shared with the parents;
- ensuring policy is put into practice in the day to day activity and organisation at the school;
- pupils' council;
- involvement of and in the local community;
- having a comprehensive range of policies prepared with the involvement of teachers, governors, parents and all those who work in the school.

What We Teach

There are implications in what we teach. Participants in the seminars agreed that we need to go beyond the Northern Ireland Curriculum and reflect the all-ability, child-centred character and integrative purpose of the school itself. An active and progressive programme for the development of self-esteem needs to be set in place, with staff training built in to complement it. The recognition and acknowledgement of difference should include religion, gender, class, sexuality and race. Equal opportunities and anti-bias issues should be explored.

We should teach a curriculum content that is accessible to all children so that all may experience success. Special needs should be catered for at both ends of the spectrum. As well as specialist programmes for the less, and more able, we should ensure that ordinary classroom teaching is differentiated.

Regular in-service training which focuses on and promotes a child-centred approach should be provided for teachers. Whole school and subject policies must include strategies which promote child-centredness. A positive school discipline policy should be implemented.

How We Teach

There are also implications in how we teach. Teachers must have high expectations for every child; be positive about each child as well as realistic. In getting to know each child, teachers can help them develop their skills and potential. Account should be taken of children's maturity, age and stage of cognitive development; the difference in their physical, social, emotional and intellectual stages of development; their strengths and weakness; and also very important, their rights.

Planning: Schemes of work should be prepared which reflect these differences as well as statutory requirements. A variety of teaching strategies (cross curricular, thematic, subject led) should be used. Plans should be made on a whole school and developmental basis. Reviews and evaluation of work should be undertaken regularly, sometimes with children and sometimes with parents. Team teaching might be considered in order to use all available expertise and strengths.

Resources: These should be managed effectively. Criteria should be established for the choice of resources e.g. countering cultural bias, gender, race. Where possible, reasonable class sizes should be maintained.

Classroom organisation: Teachers should have in-service training which develops positive classroom organisation and management styles. Parents should be encouraged to assist and participate in class. Teaching styles should be adaptable to different situations. The use of different types of groups could be considered, for example, interest, ability, friendship, subject. Children should be praised and encouraged and their parents told when they do something right, rather than just when they do something wrong. Child-centred education and integrated education should enable children and adults from diverse backgrounds to feel comfortable together. They should encourage openness to issues and welcome differences. They require a commitment which is consciously shared. Together they promote equal respect for self and others, for others' traditions and cultures, while at the same time celebrating diversity in identity and culture.

Conclusion

The integrated education sector in Northern Ireland has much to offer parents pupils and teachers. The educational ethos is underpinned by a common child-centred educational philosophy which both influences and is influenced by school policies. If these are measured and reviewed regularly against the NICIE *Statement of Principles* we can demonstrate that integrated education is a very positive model of education in Northern Ireland terms, reflecting the richness of our diversity. Integrated schools could do much to promote this richness, through the development and sharing of curriculum materials. We could blast a breath of fresh air through the cobwebs of teaching morale and illustrate that a very positive approach to teaching and learning, benefits all participants. We might show that democracy in education can work. As one parent said, we might even begin to counteract the effects of the divided society in which we live.

4
As Easy as Abc... The Anti-Bias Curriculum

Anne Hovey

Abc is the culmination of a project to pool ideas and expertise on combating bias and prejudice through early intervention in education. The nature of integrated schools, with their predisposition to nurturing child-centred learning, provides an ideal environment in which to foster an effective anti-bias curriculum. The development of abc in integrated nursery classes in Northern Ireland is an outstandingly successful example of teacher and parent partnership, reflecting unity and harmony of both purpose and curriculum content. The written results of the project are collected in an advisory and support handbook[1] which is aimed at awareness-raising for both adults and children. This handbook is essentially a practical guide to help schools analyse and plan an individual abc for themselves. Its application and relevance extends far beyond the integrated movement.

Some of the key principles of abc in integrated schools are:

- consider the nursery class in the context of the whole school and involve colleagues from the outset; anti-bias is a whole school matter and continuity, consistency and progression should underpin anti-bias learning in the same way as in other areas of the curriculum;

- children may be as susceptible to what isn't said or shown, as to the explicit — don't forget that omissions convey messages which influence attitudes;

- every member of staff needs to acknowledge and challenge her/his own prejudices and bias in order to implement an anti-bias curriculum;

- agreeing a common anti-bias language is essential.

Because abc is basically about attitudes, judgements, and the processes through which we acquire our own particular views, awareness-raising among both adults and children is an essential part of abc work. Abc in integrated schools is based on the firm belief that very young children do know about prejudice and stereotypes, and that this knowledge shapes attitudes and behaviour from as young as two years. Young children know which behaviours attract reward and approval! They understand adult and social expectations and how to meet them. This is a conditioned response and it is likely to reflect gender, disability, cultural and racial bias if left unchallenged.

Integrated schools have deliberately targeted the nursery class to begin the process of whole-school abc development, because this class represents the first formal experience of education for many children, and good practice can be established through a spiral approach to learning which builds on the nursery experience. Starting in the nursery also addresses the fact that children turn experience into opinion from the age of 3 to 5 years.

Positive Identity

The construction of a positive identity is crucial to effective abc, and this necessitates challenging the notion, both theoretically and practically, that gender, culture, disability or race are legitimate limits to the achievement of any individual's true potential. Preparation for adult life is one of the statutory requirements of the education provided for all children in Northern Ireland. The holistic and positive nature of abc, as constructed in integrated schools, is certainly a major contribution to preparation for a positive adult life. It is because of the unique position of the school, and the part it can play as a major structure of a prejudiced and biased society, that it is essential to negotiate and establish clear methods to address bias through the school system. Abc is interventionist; it recognises and tackles the pivotal role that education can play in the reinforcement, production and reproduction of environmental and social conditioning. It is both a damage limitation process and a positive building process.

In the integrated movement, abc influences and shapes the entire ethos and practice of each school. It achieves change by questioning the purpose and thinking behind the process and procedures of education as well as by questioning the nature and presentation of curriculum content. It defines the curriculum in the broadest terms, as the sum total of the set of formal and informal learning experiences and opportunities occurring in the school.

It acknowledges and balances the power of the hidden curriculum by analysing:

- the amount of time and status attached to different aspects of learning;
- the attention and specific help given by teachers to individual children;
- the 'value' clearly attached to various people, places, objects and situations;

(Nb. staff gender roles, especially in the nursery class: What needs to be done if it is males who have disciplinary roles, and females who have the caring role?)

• the ratio of praise given to achievement/outcome, versus that given to effort.

Abc is controversial, and unavoidably so, because it seeks to challenge beliefs held about children, learning and society, which have hitherto remained intact. It urges a response from teachers which is planned and linked to stages of child development, as well as one which is incidental or opportunistic. It insists on direct action, so that questioning the uncomfortable reality of society and its prejudiced norms cannot be avoided. Controversy also occurs because abc cannot be confined within the physical boundaries of the school and quite rightly so. Children in integrated schools take their questions and new skills of critical analysis home. It is at this point that the strength of home-school cooperation and mutual support is tested.

The efficacy of the communication systems between home and school is also vitally important at this stage. Many individuals have reservations about the radical nature of abc, but fears are usually allayed by discussion and illustration of the relevance of the work to real life, and to widening rather than restricting opportunity. Given the fundamental nature of abc, and the inevitable work it generates, it has been greeted by the integrated schools with great enthusiasm and commitment. Its enabling potential for both children and adults has been recognised quickly, and schools have been keen to introduce abc as a way of life and not as a token gesture.

All staff and parents involved have agreed that the syndrome of learned helplessness should be cured by radical intervention through training for independence and non-passivity. The concept of empowerment is a guiding principle towards which all the integrated schools are consciously aiming. Given the natural diversity of experience, approach and attitude among staff, great change has taken place quickly, in a team spirit and by negotiation.

The key areas involved in abc in integrated schools are:

• culture and race
• gender
• disability
• parent involvement
• class and health

The principles involved apply equally across each of the above issues, and so do the core themes:

- stereotyping
- reviewing books and planning to redress and balance bias in these materials
- images and messages conveyed in plays, performances and concerts e.g. choice of subject matter and characters.

In practice, each school has had to undertake a process of analysis, review and change. This has meant scrutinising and auditing all aspects of the school, including:

- policies e.g. positive discipline;
- the nature and application of rules;
- interactions between pupils, pupils and teachers, and between teachers themselves;
- the use of language, and the agreement of a common anti-bias language e.g.
    - person with disabilities
    - person who has Down's Syndrome
    - fire officer
    - police officer
    - postie/post person/post officer
- whole-curriculum   hidden/formal
- behaviour and expectations;
- sports, games and play;
- messages – formal and informal, covert and overt, e.g. letters, displays, choice and use of children's work, school plays, choice of play and its characterisation;
- partnership between home and school.

Integrated schools are encouraged to use a needs analysis checklist and process to monitor, review, assess and develop abc.

What do we need to make abc work in our school?
- We need a bi- and multi-cultural dimension;
- a positive self-identity, and a positive view of our own culture;
- to know how to act and react within and to the existing culture, so that

difference and equality of tradition are valued, and demonstrably so;

- to know that non-conformity to a dominant culture is O.K., and to know how to intervene against discrimination.

- We need a culturally relevant approach within the context of Northern Ireland, which also acknowledges that there is a racial and natural pluralism in our society.

- We need to evaluate all material and ask: Which can stay? Which needs modification? Which are acceptable?

- We need to incorporate an anti-bias approach into everything we do, and to understand how issues of gender, culture, and ability interlink and interact;

- We need to know how to intervene in *all* discriminatory activity – otherwise we are *condoning* it;

- We need a great deal of self-knowledge, particularly about behaviour and motivation;

- We need to begin an evolving practice of anti-bias teaching and environment;

- We need to work together and inclusively, and that means including the children in negotiation and change of ground rules;

- We need a negotiated and clear monitoring and evaluation procedure to tell us what is happening, what we need, and what to change;

- We need common and unbiased testing and assessment procedures throughout the school;

- We need to formulate a whole-school, unbiased marking policy and revamp all school policies to reflect abc principles.

Abc will take many years to achieve the influence and change for which it has both the potential and the support. It is an evolutionary process, yet its introduction needs to be both radical and comprehensive. It is worthwhile, and should become an essential part of education for all children in Northern Ireland.

Note
1. *As Easy as Abc,* is available from the Northern Ireland Council for Integrated Education, 16 Mount Charles, Belfast BT7.

5
Contextual Education
The Hazelwood Model

Tom Rowley

People's ideas of what integrated education is about, and how effectively it can operate, vary. It is my intention to describe the model and systems developed at Hazelwood College. Our basic premise is that education can and does make a difference, and it can change society. Its role is to lead society to a better understanding of itself and to an improved system of operation. Halsey maintains that society can only change through economic and social reforms; the role of education is to maintain such a society once change has been attained.[1] Our belief is that social, economic and political reforms can only come about when the people who make them have been transformed – thus education has a vital role in producing the future leaders, citizens and politicians.

Schools should not simply reflect the existing divisions, prejudices and injustices, for in doing so they legitimize them; instead they should take a lead in providing a working model where every structure and activity is permeated by the concepts of justice, equality, democracy and fairness.

When state education was first funded, it was out of fear of the masses and what they might do once their inevitable enfranchisement took place. It is no coincidence that every major political reform concerning the franchise was quickly followed by educational reforms. Education was seen as a way of maintaining control of a potentially volatile electorate – to maintain the political and socio-economic status quo.

It should come as no surprise then that the history of educational innovation and progress has come from schools outside the state system. Educational writers from Plato to Bruno Bethlehem,[2] have described educational systems that would promote a new society; the power of education and educators has been long recognised, abused and manipulated. In the case of integrated education the drive for reform of the state funded system came from independent, self-funding schools.

Recent research by the Education Department at Queen's University came to the conclusion: 'There can be little doubt that much of the dynamic for this controversy was provided by a minority integrationist lobby. Their very existence exerted pressure on the other schools to be seen to be doing something, thus smoothing the way for the introduction of EMU as a cross-curricular theme in all schools. It might therefore be said that the integrated schools, even though representing only a small fraction of the total education system in Northern Ireland, have exercised an influence out of all proportion to their current strength.'[3]

It remains to be seen how integrated schools can hold onto their unique approach once they have been absorbed into the state system as grant maintained integrated schools. The opinion at Hazelwood College is that education can make fundamental positive changes in society both in the short and long term. We are unashamedly reconstructionist and make no apology for it. Our own approach came from looking at existing models for integrated education and at a range of psychological research.

Models of Integration

The most obvious model of integration is the 'contact' model where we educate children together, function as any other school, and hope that contact between groups will in itself lead to changes in out-group perceptions and attitudes to other groupings. A variation on this is where we also structure the school in such a way that no external problems, political cries or crimes impinge upon the day-to-day running of the school. The weakest form of this contact model is where the contact is intermittent and infrequent in the hope that such fraternisation will lead to a better understanding and a bridging of the religious divide. As integrationists we believe that daily contact at work and play is an essential aspect of what we provide; this, however, in itself is not nearly enough to effect the fundamental changes necessary for progress to be made. Much more needs to be provided.

A second model is the 'deficiency' model which basically assumes that the source of misunderstanding is ignorance and lack of information. It presupposes that if children from different backgrounds are given information about each other's religion, history and culture, then they will not feel the need in later life to dominate, control or even kill each other. Again there is only a little truth in this approach: its chief flaw being that it is not lack of information that is the problem, but an unwillingness to be changed by it.

The third model, the 'balance' model, is an outcome of the contact model. Each school should have an appropriate balance in staffing, parents, governors and pupils in order that no one group should feel they are merely a tolerated minority. This of course is a structural prerequisite for proper integrated education to take place, but again it is not enough. All of these models have a part to play in an integrated school, but for the requisite individual attitudinal changes to take place we must look deeper than contact, information and balance.

The Hazelwood College argument is that a major source of the problem in Northern Ireland is limited perception and this perception is dependent upon the individual's self-esteem. As an integrated school we aim at improving acceptance of others through acceptance of self. We believe it is impossible to instruct individuals to be tolerant, accepting and understanding. If a new idea, situation or person is perceived by the individual as threatening, then it will be distorted, denied or rejected.

Contextual Model
Our philosophy is based on the belief that how a person perceives, understands or accepts an alternative viewpoint is dependent upon how he values or sees himself, his self-esteem. Much research has been conducted over the years to support this understanding of what true integrated education should be about. Rogers concluded that when an individual's self-esteem is low: 'There is no real understanding of the other as a separate person, since he is perceived mostly in terms of threat or non-threat to himself.'[4]

Rogers' findings have been confirmed by many studies.[5] Significant correlations have been found between favourability of self ratings and ratings of a stranger[6] and between low self-esteem and dogmatism.[7] Highly dogmatic people are those who feel insecure and threatened.[8] Rokeach talked of people as having open and closed minds. 'A closed way of thinking could be associated with any ideology regardless of content, an authoritarian outlook on life, an intolerance towards those with opposing beliefs and a sufferance of those with similar beliefs'.[9] In answer to those who believe that the dissemination of information will bring about changes in the individual, he warns: 'One can distort the world and narrow it down to whatever extent necessary, but at the same time perceive the illusion of understanding it.'[10]

With this in mind we aim to create a learning environment or context which raises the individual's self-esteem and thereby enhances his/her perception and thus acceptance of others. It is of fundamental importance to the development of self-acceptance that the appropriate learning and moral environment be created. This is often known as the ethos or hidden curriculum of the school. It implies the deliberate creation of an environment based on empathy, genuineness, acceptance of self, acceptance of others, unconditional positive regard, tolerance, cooperation and self-discipline. (See Appendix p. 59) These together constitute the context within which every other activity occurs. The formal curriculum exists within this context and is enhanced by it. The ethos or hidden curriculum delineates a model of society as it should be; not just as an intellectual exercise, but as living, breathing reality. The delivery of this model depends upon the recognition that everything and everyone is connected and it relies on congruence between the value and belief system of individuals and that of the school to make it work.

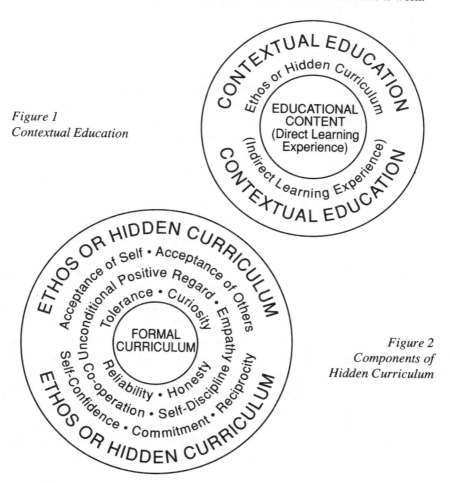

Figure 1
Contextual Education

Figure 2
Components of
Hidden Curriculum

Staff Development

There is insufficient space in this chapter to describe all the methods used in Hazelwood College so I will restrict myself to those I feel are most important. Staff induction and development are obviously of great importance to the creation of this educational environment.

Since 1985 when the college opened, we have worked on a staff development programme aimed at creating congruence in approach and a full understanding of the college's aims and objectives. All schemes of work, for instance, must make reference to how a particular teacher and particular subject department are working towards achieving the college's objectives. All new staff, including students on teaching practice, are educated in detail about our philosophy of education and approaches. This does not however mean that all staff are exact clones in a closed system. It is recognised that all of us are at different stages of personal development and that positive as well as negative incongruence can occur. (See figure 3.) As the school matures it is expected that the organisation as a whole will gradually move towards a much more advanced model of operations.

Figure 3 Teaching and Learning Objectives

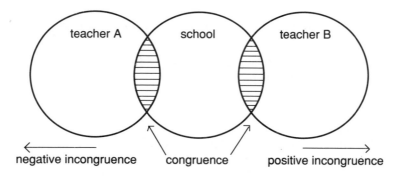

With the idea of inter-connectedness in mind it is an absolute necessity that all policy documents be in harmony with the central philosophy of the school. The policy on school discipline for example, refers to everyone, exhorting the whole community of pupils, staff, parents and governors:

- be courteous to each other
- show consideration for others
- show respect for themselves and others
- show respect for their own property as well as others

– be industrious and punctual
– be honest at all times
– contribute as fully as possible to the life of the school.

This may constitute a tall order, but if the adult role models do not attempt to make this part of their daily operations, then we cannot expect our pupils to do so.

Pastoral System

The creation of an appropriate pastoral care system is also of vital importance if the child is to see him/herself as a person of worth, regardless of religion, sex, social background or intelligence. Every teacher has pastoral responsibility for one class throughout their time at school. This creates an informal and close relationship which is beneficial to the child.

Communication with parents is frequent, thus developing a high level of trust between teachers and parents. It includes monthly progress reports, twice yearly main reports and monthly newsletters as well as letters from class tutors. In addition we have an open door policy where parents are encouraged to visit the school at any time and to participate in school activities.

The raising and maintenance of high self-esteem is a very important activity in the college. Ideally every staff member should be familiar with and use Rogerian counselling. A start has been made on this through the construction of a short course of training on this type of counselling. It is hoped that all staff will eventually become proficient in it and apply it to the teaching situation. Pressure on time with the introduction of the National Curriculum training programme has reduced the opportunities for counsellor training; however when this government sponsored programme comes to an end, such training will resume. In the area of reporting on pupils' achievements we stress the necessity for positive reporting. A foreshortened version of Bloom's Taxonomy is used whereby each subject area is subdivided into various skills and each one is reported upon, stressing the highest achievement in each skill or attainment. We feel it is very important to encourage pupils to achieve, and compliment them on what they have achieved, rather than condemning them for what they have not. The logic is simple; the momentum of success or partial success in one area will encourage better performance in other areas.

Classes are organised on a mixed ability basis for the same reasons. We feel that nothing can be more demoralising for pupils than to find themselves in a bottom stream. It is interesting to note also that in a streamed situation, the teachers who take the bottom streams (often the most difficult and least motivated youngsters) are perceived by the pupils as also being of low status and held in low esteem in their organisation. Mixed ability organisation is difficult for teachers; however it does raise the expectation level for everyone in the class, including the teachers; no pupil can feel that they are lesser people than the rest and no teacher can feel that they are being victimised.

Moral Environment

The moral education of pupils is achieved through the context of the school as well as the curriculum. As described earlier, the hidden curriculum or ethos is deliberately constructed, and part of this is the creation of a moral environment based on openness, justice, reciprocity, altruism, fairness and democracy. While difficult to operate, this does effectively raise the ceiling or expectation for moral development in the school. Kohlberg [11] maintains that institutions tend to have low ceilings of moral expectations and consequently have problems when individuals reach this ceiling and attempt to go beyond it. It is the duty of every school to help pupils develop the highest level of moral reasoning possible. However it is not sufficient simply to instruct pupils to behave in a certain way; they must see it in the everyday operation of the school.

Some aspects are possible within the formal curriculum; the principle component of moral reasoning is empathy with another person or persons. Understanding how another person feels in a situation is an essential component in deciding how you behave towards them. With this in mind we introduced drama for every pupil until third form; this is an ideal medium for developing self confidence, but primarily it is to develop the skill of empathy – understanding of another person's cognitive, affective or perceptual perspective. In addition, a moral education programme has been introduced based on the moral dilemmas developed by Lawrence Kohlberg. He believes that an individual's response to and rationalisation of any situation varies according to his/her intellectual grasp of it and level of moral reasoning, the two being linked. His programme is basically Platonic in origin, in that if an individual is presented with and understands a higher level of moral reasoning, he will naturally move towards that level. Kohlberg's programme has been adapted to include everyday school situations particularly those with a potentially difficult sectarian origin. It relies on a moral dialogue which creates a disequilibrium in the individual and then, given the correct conditions, resolution at a higher level than before.

Thus, the deliberate construction of a therapeutic and moral environment is of vital importance to the work of the school; without it, work done within the formal curriculum would be undermined and inefficient. It is fundamental to the development of self-esteem, acceptance of others, social intelligence and cognitive and moral development. It is an extremely difficult model of integrated education to work and we are a long way from achieving all we would wish; but the model does provide the map with which we will plot our future path.[12]

Appendix

Theoretical Approach

The Learning Environment
1   An individual is born with the capacity for positive and negative behaviour
2   Behaviour and attitude patterns are learned:
     (a) indirectly through imitation;
     (b) directly through specific culturally based instruction.
3   Behaviour and attitude patterns are the outcome of primary socialisation in the home and secondary socialisation in the immediate environment, peer group and schools.
4   For schools to influence attitudes and behaviour effectively they must reproduce the conditions of primary socialisation. Parents are the ideal partners in the reinforcement of this school environment.
5   The conditions of primary socialisation are empathic understanding, unconditional positive regard and genuineness.
6   These three are also the pre-conditions of a therapeutic environment which the teacher, as a role model, must seek to construct.
7   For a school to be effective in influencing behaviour and attitude patterns it must create the appropriate learning or therapeutic environment.
8   This therapeutic environment is usually called the ethos or hidden curriculum.

Ethos
9   This ethos/hidden curriculum is produced by every individual in the school community; pupils, staff, parents and governors.
10   It is essential then for every teacher to understand the ethos and apply it according to their capabilities and understanding. To operate an alternative ethos which to varying degrees is at odds with that stated, leads to incongruence and therefore considerable stress within the community.

11   The traditional purpose of schools was and is to replicate the conditions of an existing society and therefore produce it in the future. If we feel that our society is flawed then it is our duty to redefine it.

12   The components of the ethos/hidden curriculum are those which form an ideal society, which should be our aim to see exist.

13   The ethos of the school should be based around concepts like justice, openness, honesty, reciprocity and altruism – these components are essentially those of a positive moral environment.

Self-Esteem

14   The development of the self-esteem of the individual is the key to their acceptance of others and their moral development.

15   The development of self-esteem is also the key to cognitive development.

16   The development of self-esteem is a precondition to acceptance and internalisation of anything or anyone new.

17   The development of the self-esteem of the individual is central to the concept of child-centred education – such an education aims at the development of the child's own moral, cognitive social and personal awareness.

18   Self-esteem in individuals may be enhanced through a positive direct learning experience through formal curriculum and positive assessment.

Child-centred Education

19   Child-centred education takes place in the context of the ethos/ philosophy of the school.

20   Child-centred education in an integrated school also involves a specific content and methodology
     (a)   content – the child must be made aware of other cultures, religions, classes, ideas;
     (b)   methodology – a 'forms of knowledge' approach is the most appropriate, encouraging children to take an active part in the learning process – knowledge is something achieved by the pupil, not given by the teacher.

21   Child-centred education aims therefore at encouraging the development of autonomous individuals who have the capacity to think, question and research.

22   Such autonomous individuals are more capable of coping with novel or threatening situations (like a totally unknown future).

Social Development

23 Autonomy must be coupled with social awareness – this is learned from the experience of the child's environment and from direct instruction.

24 The essence of social awareness is empathy with, and the acceptance of, others.

25 The function of the school is therefore to produce a socially aware environment coupled with the encouragement of altruism through various projects.

26 Social awareness or social intelligence can be developed through the experience of, and teaching of, empathic understanding – this can be done most obviously in drama, moral education, history and English.

Notes

1. Hasley, A. H., 'Sociology and the Equality Debate', *Oxford Review of Education*, Vol 1, 1975, pp. 9-23. See also Dunn, S., (1986) 'The Role of Education in the Northern Ireland Conflict', *Oxford Review of Education*, Vol 12 No 3.

2. Bethlehem, B., (1971) *The Children of the Dream: Communal child-rearing and its implications for Society*, Paladin, London.

3. McEwan, A., and Salters, J., (1992) *Integrated Education: The View of Parents*, School of Education, Queens University, Belfast, pp. 40-41.

4. Rogers, C. R., (1951) *Client-Centred Therapy*, Houghton Mifflin, Boston, p 520. See also Rogers, C. R., (1961), *On Becoming a Person*, Houghton Mifflin.

5. Zuckerman, M., Baer, M. and Monashkin, I., (1956) 'Acceptance of self, parents and people in patients and normals', *J. Clin. Psychology*, 12, pp. 327-32; Wylie, R. C., (1961), *The Self Concept*, U.N.P. London; Bosson, J., and Maslow, A. H., (1957), 'Security of judges as a factor in impressions of warmth in others', *J. Abn. Soc. Psych.*, 55, pp.147-8.

6. Crandall, V J., and Bellugi, U., (1954) 'Some relationships of interpersonal and intrapersonal conceptualizations to personal-social adjustment', *J. Personality*, 23, pp. 224-32.

7. Larsen, K. S. and Schirendiman, G., (1969) 'Authoritarianism, Self-Esteem and Insecurity', *Psych. Reports*, 25, pp. 229-30.

8. Abramo, J. L., Lundgrew, D. C., and Bogart, D. H., (1978) 'Status Threat and Group Dogmatism', *Human Relations*, 31, pp. 745-752.

9. Rockeach, M., (1960) *The Open and Closed Mind*, Basic Books Inc, New York, p 5.

10. *ibid.*, p. 68.

11. Kohlberg, L., (1966) 'Moral Education in the School: A Development View', *School Review* .

12. Salters, J., McEwan, A., 'Doing Something Different: Integrated Parents in Northern Ireland', *Research in Education*, No. 49, May 1993.

6
Religious Faith and Integrated Schools
A Personal Perspective

Terence McMackin

There are a number of reasons why a study of integrated schools, certainly in Northern Ireland, should include a consideration of the religious faith dimension of these schools. Part of the reality in Northern Ireland is that religion has always been profoundly political. For the unionist community, much of their political sense of themselves has included their Protestantism; for nationalists, Catholicism has in an important sense been the most enduring symbol of their identity and separateness. The emergence of the integrated schools in Northern Ireland was itself prompted by the religious aspect of the difference between the two communities, most notably as represented by a system of separate schools, that is controlled (Protestant) and maintained (Catholic) schools.

Since the inception of the integrated sector the overall context in which the schools have developed has included a commitment to a Christian ethos. In the debate on integrated education, 'ethos' is often at the centre when the merits of different types of school are discussed. Ethos here is to be understood as meaning the all-pervasive religious or secular climate of a school. For some participants in the integrated education debate, perhaps principally those opposed to integrated education on the Catholic side, a religious faith dimension or the alleged lack of one, is the critical issue.

The present contribution to this debate attempts to give a personal perspective. It is personal because it seems reasonable to suggest that in a field as controversial as integrated education can be in Northern Ireland, it is not possible to approach its study completely 'value free'. Issues which arise in this area are not just engaged 'out there somewhere', but must also find more than an echo 'within' those involved. Questions about one's own ultimate allegiances and commitment can easily be stirred. Accordingly, in order that some allowance may be made for the writer's own values in this area it might be helpful to be explicit about the background and personal interest brought to this contribution.

The writer is a believing and practising Catholic, educated in Catholic schools, and would like to acknowledge at the outset a great debt to those responsible for his education. A teaching career in the Catholic sector spanned twenty years and included spells in a Catholic mission school in East Africa and two post-primary schools in Belfast. Since 1985 it has been spent in the integrated post-primary sector. The decision to move there from a Catholic school was grounded in a belief that integrated education is an important way forward for our divided society in Northern Ireland. Equally important was the conviction that if integrated education is to succeed there must be a meaningful presence of committed Catholic and Protestant staff as a support and witness for the two main traditions represented in integrated schools in the province.

Even given what must seem a solidly Catholic background, the faith perspective offered in this chapter is essentially personal, rather than denominational, although obviously still rooted in the Catholic tradition. It is my understanding of religious faith that while in the living out of a faith commitment, one's church or tradition and belonging to a faith community are important, Christian faith itself is in essence a personal relationship with Christ. Christ cannot simply be identified with any institutional church.

The chapter is not intended to be prescriptive. Two main tasks will be attempted: first to outline a model of what an integrated school can become when its ethos is informed by a faith dimension which is Christian. The model outlined is one which is both Christian in thrust and able at the same time to meet the essential faith requirements which Catholic parents in particular may reasonably look for in a school. Secondly, to outline the current reality of religious faith provision, especially for Catholics in integrated schools at post primary level. Finally, a brief attempt will be made to suggest some of the key issues for the future in the provision of a meaningful religious faith dimension in integrated schools, again with special reference to provision for Catholics.

An Early Christian Model

A valuable model for the integrated school which seeks to give expression to its Christian character is that of the early Christian community with its characteristics of fellowship, service, mission to the world and worship.[1] It is a model, too, which arguably meets the essentials of what Catholic parents in particular may seek in terms of faith provision for their children. (The notion of the Catholic school as 'a community of faith' is also central to the case put for separate

Catholic education.) Ideally it includes the following characteristics:

Fellowship The school will be open to children of all abilities, with each pupil respected and equally valued. There will be an emphasis on the quality of relationships among all in the school community. There will be no fear of differences. Rather these will be seen as a source of enrichment for all.

Service An attitude of service in the sense of developing sensitivity to the needs of others will be encouraged. A conscious attempt will be made to work on individual senses of denominational or cultural superiority. There will be an awareness of a responsibility to work for a more just world and a better deal for the developing world.

Mission to the world The integrated school will be conscious of its role in opening up new ground in Northern Ireland, exploring new avenues to reconciliation, seeking actively the fulfilment of Christ's desire for unity rather than disunity.

Worship Worship is always an opportunity to celebrate community. For Christians it is intended as praise of God. Ways will be found to enable individuals of each tradition to use their gifts of worship. There will be an awareness of the inherent power of symbols for pupils' understanding of life and a creative use of these in formal worship and in the school environment.

Current Faith Provision

Current provision for the specific faith requirements of pupils at post-primary integrated schools varies somewhat from school to school. What follows is an outline of the particular provision for Catholic pupils in one of the schools with which the writer is familiar, Brownlow College, together with the rationale for this provision. In this school parallel provision is made for the other denominations, (at present the Church of Ireland, Presbyterian, Methodist, Baptist) although the rationale in each case is obviously different. The agreed elements of the provision are set out as follows:[2]

1. The College affirms that the privilege and responsibility for handing on the faith to Catholic children belongs firstly to their parents and then to the parish community. Because the school also can have an important part to play the College is committed to ensuring that:

   (i) all Catholic pupils have Religious Education in accordance with the common programme agreed by the Christian churches and as required by the Northern Ireland Curriculum;

(ii) additional separate and specific Catholic catechesis is available in accordance with any particular guidelines issued by diocesan advisers to supplement the common programme;

(iii) Catholic catechesis will be taken by a Catholic specialist teacher of RE and any textbooks used will be those used also in Catholic schools in the diocese.

2. Because they are primarily responsible for the education of their children in the faith, Catholic parents will be fully informed of the content of the catechetical programme at the beginning of the school year. There will be opportunities also for parental involvement throughout the programme.

3. Each Catholic pupil will have the opportunity and will be encouraged to attend retreats, residentials and/or non-residentials, at a retreat centre during the school year.

4. There will be facilities for extra curricular activities both in line with pupil interests and with the maintenance and development of a sense of identity with the Catholic tradition.

5. A teacher with particular responsibility for Catholic pupils will be available on a day-to-day basis for guidance and as a support to pupils in any matters which are relevant to them as Catholic pupils at the College. This teacher will function as a lay chaplain.

A variation of the above is the presence of a team of one Catholic and one Protestant chaplain, as at Lagan College, operating together in many matters while each also provides a focus of identity for pupils of each tradition. In addition to this full-time team, there are honorary chaplains for the main denominations represented in the school. [3]

Future Faith Provision

The future of faith provision in integrated schools raises a number of important issues. In one way or another these issues are related to particular philosophical or theological presuppositions about the part the school should, or should not play in faith nurture. On the Catholic side, a key question in Northern Ireland is the attitude of the hierarchy to such matters as the appointment or approval of school chaplains (clerical, religious or lay) in integrated schools, and whether integrated schools can be trusted with any role at all in the faith formation of Catholic pupils. The following brief observations address this key question.

It is accepted Catholic teaching that for Catholics it is primarily the responsibility of parents to hand on faith to their children, in association, first, with the parish and then with the schools. Parents would be much better equipped to do this, and less inclined to leave to the school what is their prerogative, if some of the resources which up to now have been put into Catholic schools were channelled instead into adult catechesis programmes. Now that Catholic schools are being 100 per cent funded this should be much easier to achieve.

Joint Anglican-Catholic shared schools have existed in England since the early 1980s with the full approval of both hierarchies. Failure to get the churches in Northern Ireland to agree to similar joint provision has meant that integrated schools here are not church schools but rather lay Christian schools. As a result there has been an emphasis on a perceived need to 'normalise' relationships with the hierarchy, for example in terms of the appointment of priest chaplains. Desirable as this may be for pastoral reasons, from a purely Catholic perspective, it is not obvious that there needs to be for Catholic lay people an over-emphasis on 'normalisation'. Instead, the development can be seen as providing one avenue for the empowerment of Catholic lay people.

In practice, the Catholic Church has accommodated to the situation where a school is not Catholic but where the number of Catholics is large and it is deemed appropriate to establish formal links between the school and the parish clergy. To date, to the writer's knowledge, this has only happened in controlled schools at primary level; but the principle of pastoral care for Catholics at 'non-Catholic' schools is clear and is surely applicable in other situations at both primary and post-primary level, including integrated schools.

It is in the interests of all the churches to find ways to combat the real enemies of our society, which are violence, intolerance and a rampant materialism. Integrated schooling which entails conscientious and sincere provision for particular faith requirements, is to be valued alongside, and as an incentive to, whatever reconciliation among the churches is proceeding otherwise.

Integrated schools have a prophetic role in today's society – in the scriptural sense that having read the signs of the times, they seek to challenge people to explore a new way forwards, a reconciliation which must be the will of God. An appropriate scriptural model for those committed to integrated schools could well be the patriarch, Abraham, whose life witnesses to two key elements of religious faith - the elements of risk and journeying. Abraham risked everything and was prepared to journey to unknown lands in response to the divine call. For those involved in integrated schools there can also be risk, the journey to unknown territory. What must give encouragement is that the meeting place for those who risk and make the journey, the integrated school itself is, in a profound sense, like the Promised Land, a sacred place. 'The most sacred place on earth is where an ancient hatred has become a present love.'

Notes

1. See for example, Acts 2.42-47.
2. Extracted from Provision for Catholic Pupils, Brownlow College.
3. For details see the current prospectus of Lagan College, Belfast.

7
Making Integrated Education Work for Pupils

Colin Irwin

The last school I went to was a segregated school, it was all Protestant. If there were any Catholics no one knew about it. It was very strong about Protestant. My best friend had a cousin and she was a Roman Catholic. She really hated her. When the people in the class found out she got called names. In P7 most of the people supported Rangers. If you mentioned any other football teams they said 'Rangers is the best.' Since P1 I was there. Not until about P5 I found out that I was Protestant because I didn't know what religion was all about. But in P5–P6 we started to get to know more and more about religion. When I was in P7 we all used to say that we hated Catholics. My parents are both Protestant, they suggested Lagan College because it was integrated. My Grandad supports Rangers and he didn't really say congratulations for getting into Lagan College. When I got my results in my eleven plus I got a grade 2 which was a pass. They were all congratulating me for passing and everyone suggested Ulster Grammar School. My friends all went there because it is said to be a good school. In assembly it was always Protestant ministers for chaplain there was never no Catholic chaplains. When we were sending our letters away for what schools we wanted to go to I picked Lagan College and Ulster Grammar. When I told everyone I picked Lagan College they all laughed and said, 'Ah, imagine going to a Catholic school. Wise up they're all scums and you're going to turn out a scum.' But I never took any heed. Now at Lagan College all my friends are Roman Catholics and I couldn't care less. Now I just think there is no such thing as religion. I wish it hadn't been invented. I just look at it as if there is no such thing because I know that there is no difference between the two religions, Catholic and Protestant, because we are all human beings. And now at home people say, 'Very good for going to one of them schools,' and I say 'What schools? It is just the same as every other school. We have human beings for teachers, a proper school, we get taught the same way and educated the same

way.' But my friends say 'She goes to Lagan College and it's one of them Catholic schools.' But I don't care it's all the same to me.
(Protestant girl, aged 12)

Integrated Education and Social Theory

The concept of integrated education and the use of school policies to improve inter-community relations in divided societies is at least as old as the history of formal education itself. For example, in Ireland the first national system of education established in Dublin in 1831 was intentionally created to be non-denominational with the expressed 'hope that by learning to live together as children they would at least tolerate each other as adults.'[1] This point of view is supported by social theory which suggests that integrated schools can succeed when they are founded on a basis of equality and when they include the critical years that mark the transition from childhood to young adult. [2]

Conversely, the suggestion that segregated education is central to the process of social polarisation is given support by a study completed by Whyte[3] who concluded that of the mechanisms used to maintain social boundaries in Northern Ireland, the churches, the Orange Order, social ranking, residential segregation, separate education and endogamy, 'education divides the population into two communities more precisely than any other market which we have so far examined.'

The principal objection made against the social effectiveness of integrated education is that formal education can make little difference to the values and behaviour of individuals when compared to the socialising force of a child's community, represented for example by the child's family, peer group, neighbourhood, church, youth groups, etc.[4] However, this objection is not supported by the study of integrated and segregated schools in Northern Ireland completed by Douglas[5] who concludes that:

> The change in attitudes at the intergroup level found in pupils at an integrated school appear to be lost within 3 months of attending a segregated secondary school. One reason that could be given to account for this change of attitudes in such a short period of time is that it is due to social conformity. The children who go to the segregated secondary school from an integrated primary school may have to conform to a different set of social norms.

Perhaps the efficacy of the informal aspects of formal education in divided societies, such as the role of the school in the community and the establishment of peer groups, has been significantly underestimated by the critics of integrated education.[6] The idea that peer groups established in schools may have a significant influence on the development of a child's friendships and attitudes is not new. Greeley and Rossi[7] make the point that:

> Social scientists are ready to concede that a considerable amount of socialisation occurs in the school milieu, but they suggest that it takes place, not as a result of formal instruction in the classroom, but in the informal groups which grow up amongst the students.

If this is true, then schools like Lagan College may have the potential to produce a far more positive effect on the improvement of inter-community relations in Northern Ireland than Education for Mutual Understanding (EMU) alone, as the principal focus of EMU is on the more formal aspects of curricular reform.[8]

Research at Lagan College: The Student Population

Our area is quite mixed, however the Catholics do not mix with the Protestants. As a Catholic I know that there are Protestants in our area and I often see them regularly but do not talk to them. Often we would get involved in fights with Protestants and these fights are at their worst at very sensitive times such as the 12th of July. At nights we would walk about in groups not because we are looking for fights but for safety. Apart from at this school I would not have any Protestant friends. A lot of the trouble in our area is related to what football team you support and what school you go to.

If anyone finds out that you have got friends of the opposite religion you get called many things and most likely hit many times. School is like a different world where things like religion do not matter but when you get off the school bus you are back in Northern Ireland. Often when the police and army drive down the road some of the Catholics would hurl abuse and anti-British slogans while Protestants often would salute them and encourage them with slogans such as 'God save the Queen.'

At the primary schools which we went to we were never taught about the battle between King William and James in 1690 but we were told about the 1916 Easter rising. There are certain sections of our area which are Catholic and others which are strictly Protestant. The religion of these areas can simply be defined by looking at the pictures on the wall. While this strict segregation remains at schools, youth clubs and even streets there is little hope of peace in Northern Ireland. Many people fear that integration might only end up in worse violence, but Lagan College is an example that integration can work for both sides of the community. (Catholic boy, aged 14)

Belfast is a divided city that is predominantly Protestant. Some Catholics live in the more middle-class Protestant areas. However, very few Protestants live in the working-class Catholic areas, and the mixed areas are predominantly Protestant.[9] Given this reality simple probabilities predict that very few Catholics and Protestants will have friends in the 'other' community although the minority Catholic population will have more Protestant friends than Protestants will have Catholic friends.[10]

The founders of Lagan College deliberately sought to counter this unfortunate situation by creating a school environment in which Catholic and Protestant children would have an equal opportunity to make friends with each other. In an effort to maintain a student balance the charter setting up the college prohibited its enrolment from drifting beyond the outer limits of a 40:60 ratio. In practice Lagan College has been able to maintain a 47:53 Catholic/Protestant ratio; a 42:58 working-class/middle-class ratio and a 55:45 boy/girl ratio based on data collected in 1989. Definitions relating to religious denomination and social class can affect these ratios. In October 1989 the student population of 586 contained one Hindu and one Muslim while all the remaining students were 'labelled' as Protestants or Catholics in much the same way as each member of Northern Irish society is 'labelled' by their peers.[11] Social class was defined by the occupation of the parents. However, it should be noted that the occupation of both parents was used here. Had only the father's been used, as is common practice in many government surveys, then the percentage of working class would have been higher and the percentage of middle class lower than the 42:58 ratio recorded.

In 1989 students were transferred to Lagan College from 149 primary schools in the greater Belfast area. Owing to adoptions, divorces, deaths, remarriages, mixed marriages, or the lack of an appropriate primary school close to the parents' home, between one and two percent of the students that came to Lagan College from Catholic schools were Protestant while nearly fourteen percent of the children from Protestant schools were Catholic. These percentages are probably not representative of the percentages of minorities in sectarian schools in the Belfast area, but more closely reflected a requirement for secondary integrated education amongst Catholics and Protestants that found themselves outside the social mainstream of their respective communities. These percentages are now declining as the needs of these minorities are met. Of the 139 students enrolled into the new first year in 1990 only four were Catholics from Protestant schools while only one Protestant came from a Catholic school.

The Friendships of New Students

The first weeks at Lagan College were OK! But the first day was terrible because when I was leaving my house to get the bus I was very scared because I did not know anybody and I did not even know the school. But when the second day came it was a bit better because I knew a lot of people by then. About when a week come in I started to play football and basketball with my friends. Most of the pupils were right on, but a couple of them were not so pleasant because some of them hit me and a couple other of my friends. But I did not want to tell any teachers because I am not a squealer. And because I did not tell any teachers they stopped hitting me and started to play with me.
(Protestant boy, aged 11)

In September 1990, the new first year, just two weeks after arriving at Lagan College, were asked to list ten friends they played with outside school. They were also asked to list the school these friends attended. As it is known that almost none of the children at Catholic schools are Protestant and that only a small minority of students at Protestant schools are Catholic, it is possible to use this as a fairly accurate index of religious denomination. Of the 120 students included in this survey, 71 per cent listed no friends at all from the 'other' community. On average only 14 per cent of the friends of these children were from the other community and this percentage only rose to a maximum of 28 per cent for Catholics in Catholic schools when they were living in a predominantly Protestant neighbourhood.

It is clear from these results that the demographics of the student population of the school attended by a child in Belfast have far more effect on the choice of the friends of the child than the housing area in which they live. It follows that if children are to have an equal opportunity to make both Catholic and Protestant friends then sending children to mixed schools will provide a greater opportunity for such friendships to develop than simply living in a mixed housing area. However, creating the 'opportunity to make both Catholic and Protestant friends', in a statistical or probabilistic kind of way, is not the same as actually making friends. The question that must now be asked is whether or not the children who come to Lagan College, with their patterns of friendships shaped by the experience of a segregated primary school education, do make friends across the sectarian divide.

Changing Friendships

When I first came to Lagan College my first friend was Mathew. Then I got to know more people in my class. My best friends at the moment are Shawn and Mathew. My best mate Pat is a Catholic and Mathew is a Protestant. Pat has a motor bike and so do I. Pat has a Yamaha and I have a Kawasaki. I race motor bikes but Pat does not. Mathew likes skate boards. I used to like them myself but I have given it up now. Me, Pat and Mathew play together in the playground. There is not much to do in the playground except play basket ball. But I have not got a basket ball.

(Catholic boy, aged 11)

Every student attending Lagan College on October 10th 1989 was asked to list, from their tutor group, his or her three best friends, three other students they would like to have as friends, three they would invite home and three they prefer to work with on school projects. In order to prevent any discussion, the questionnaire was given to all the students at the same time. When this data was combined with the age, tutor group, religious denomination, social class and gender of the students, over twenty thousand observations were created that could be analysed from any desired point of view.[12]

When the actual friendship choices made by Lagan College students are separated to represent the changing friendship patterns of Catholics and Protestants, the trend shows a bias for the children to choose members of their own denomination in their first year. This bias changes to a slight preference for members of the 'other' denomination by the fifth year. A bias toward friendships amongst their own community, in the first year, leading toward more friends in the 'other' community in subsequent years, is expected and welcome. However a slight bias toward the 'other' community in the fifth year is surprising. Perhaps the fifth year, anticipating the use to which the questionnaire was to be put, biased their answers? However when only the responses for the choices of their three best friends is analysed for reciprocal friendships, namely when two students unknowingly chose each other, the same surprising result was reproduced.

Additionally, when the results are analysed for each of the four questions, the variations in the responses are more consistent with expectations. Namely, the choice of 'best friends' and 'take home friends' at Lagan College are slightly biased toward their own community, while the choice of 'wish friends' is biased toward the 'other' community. It may be important to note that some fourth and fifth year students refused to answer the question on 'wish' friends and occasionally remarked on their questionnaire that everyone in their class was their friend.

Given all these results I believe the observation that the fifth year students at Lagan College have a slight preference for friends in the 'other' community must be taken seriously and may represent the replacement of values that favour sectarian friendships with new values that encourage friendships to be created between the divided communities of Belfast. It may be speculated that these values could be introduced by the parents encouraging their children to make more friends in the 'other' community and by the school whose 'ethos' may encourage the children to make more friends in the other community. A combination of these, and perhaps other factors, is probably at work here. Either way, the role of Lagan College may be indispensable to this process in as much as it is able to provide a 'social opportunity' for the establishment of these new friendships and the expression of these social values.

Further analysis of the social relationships at Lagan College revealed a slight preference for working class friends by the working class and a very strong separation of the friendships of the boys and the girls. If all the Catholics in a tutor group were girls and all the Protestants were boys, very few friendships would be established between the two religious groups even if the tutor group maintained a 50:50 mix.

Providing this gender bias aspect of the group relationships at Lagan College is allowed for, it is possible to compare the degree of integration for each subgroup of the student population broken down by religion, social class and gender. The results were mixed. Amongst the Catholics, the working class had more Protestant friends than the middle class, and amongst the Protestants, the girls had more Catholic friends than the boys. The only firm conclusion that can be drawn is that there is little difference between Catholic and Protestant children, boys and girls, and middle-class and working-class children, when it comes to making friends across the sectarian divide.

Established Friendships

I am George, a Protestant from a Protestant area. My best friend is Patrick, he is a Catholic from a fairly Catholic area of Belfast. We met on our first day of school. He asked what religion I was and I told him. He told me he was a Catholic. I had never had a Catholic friend before. We are best friends now and we go into town on Saturdays but he is a bit scared to come to my house in case he gets beat up. But he is coming to my house for my birthday party. I have been to his house and I don't mind going his way. I have some other Catholic friends like Kevin and Brian.

(Protestant boy, aged 13)

My name is Patrick. I am a Catholic and I live in a fairly Catholic area. I met George who is a Protestant from a Protestant area on the first day of school in first year. I have also got a lot of other Protestant friends in the school, William and Jim and some more out of class. We all hang around with each other and sometimes go to town. Sometimes George comes to my house and sometimes I go to his house. We have a lot of things in common, us, we both like football. But he supports different teams to me.

I came to Lagan College to try and find something out about different religions and customs and also to make more Protestant friends. At the start I was a bit nervous because I had never really messed and played around with any Protestants before. But once I got to school and got to know them it was easy. Now I always play with them at school and bring them to my house sometimes. I am glad now that I came to Lagan College because if this school helps to end the troubles here I can say that I done my bit.

(Catholic boy, aged 13)

Using a very different statistical technique, the same data, from the same questionnaires, were analysed using a computer programme specifically developed to map social relationships within groups of school children. These maps were then discussed in interviews with each tutor group supervisor and year head. As the data had to be taken to Israel for analysis there was a six month delay prior to these interviews. This proved to be most fortuitous as it was found that the maps of the social relationships of the new first year had changed a great deal, and the tutor group supervisors were able to describe, in detail, how the patterns of friendships had been rearranged during the past six months. However, in comparison to the first year, the social relationships had changed comparatively little in the second to fifth years and were most notable when a student was moved, left, or a new pupil was introduced into a class.

Another obvious difference was found in the patterns of close, or reciprocal friendships that were relatively open in the first year and increasingly clustered, or closed, in later years. The tutor group supervisors, particularly those that had been with their students for several years, were able to give detailed information about the nature of these friendships. It became clear from these interviews that although initial friendships were influenced by a preference for members of their 'own' community, common interests and characteristics, such as sports, personality, academic pursuits and social activities, soon came to replace any residual sectarian bias as the primary foundation for the creation of lasting relationships.

In the fourth year, the social importance of the tutor group at Lagan College is diminished when the students start to specialise in subjects that are held in classes formed from the whole year. By the fifth year, the pupils have had a considerable opportunity to make many new friends, with whom they would share common academic interests. However, although the religious structure of these new groups could be quite arbitrary, the fifth year students showed little or no tendency to revert to sectarian patterns of friendships when asked to list their ten best friends from throughout the whole of their year.

When the results of this survey were examined in greater detail, it was found that approximately half of the students' friends were chosen from their original tutor group and half from the three remaining tutor groups in the fifth year. Further, when the friends chosen were ranked, from their first choice to their tenth choice, most of their best friends were from their old tutor group. Clearly, both quantitatively and qualitatively, friendships established during the first three years at Lagan College come to dominate the closest relationships found amongst the students at the school.

The Friendships of Past Pupils

Lagan College is a very important and different school from the rest in Northern Ireland. I think the majority of the pupils in this school like the atmosphere but there are several pupils in this school that have been brought up in a sectarian place and atmosphere. These pupils think that it is too late to change but it is never too late to change. Lagan College accepts this fact and they try to bring all different communities together and to be as one. My first friends at this school were Protestants but even then I didn't think about fighting with the opposite religion but unfortunately some others did. As the years went on I saw these people changing as so it didn't matter anymore. This is why I think there should be more schools like Lagan College in Northern Ireland because maybe then the people from both sides in this community could live together as one.
(Catholic boy, aged 15)

Some of the friendships established at Lagan College may well turn out to be friendships that the students will carry with them for the rest of their lives. This is probably true for most children at most secondary schools. However, it may be hoped that the lasting social effects of Lagan College would not be limited to simply just a few 'best friends' from across the divide. In an effort to explore this issue, I first met with a group of twelve past pupils attending a reunion at the ecumenical community at Corrymeela. In addition to listening to their views on the value of their years spent at Lagan College, I asked them to list anonymously their ten best friends by using their initials. When this was done I asked them to identify the religion of each friend. The results of this 'pilot study' indicated 33 per cent of the friends of the Catholics to be Protestant, and 40 per cent of the friends of the Protestants to be Catholic. In this group only one individual listed no friends from the 'other' community.

A second, larger, sample of past pupils was obtained with the use of a postal questionnaire that, in addition to the 'ten best friends' methodology, also requested information on the past pupil's gender, age and housing area. Of 270 questionnaires sent out, 92 were returned and analysed. As might be expected, those living in Protestant or Catholic housing areas had fewer friends in the 'other' community than those living in mixed housing areas. Males also tended to have slightly fewer friends in the 'other' community than females. In general, however, these past pupils, aged between seventeen and twenty, continued to have significant numbers of friendships on both sides of the divide.

But it must be remembered that this success in maintaining the effects of social integration amongst the past pupils of Lagan College is relative and needs to be put into comparative perspective. In a survey of Catholic and Protestant students at The Queen's University of Belfast,[13] only 12 per cent of the students' friends were from the 'other' community compared to 44 per cent for the Lagan College past pupils. It is interesting to note that only 14 per cent of the friends of the new first year students at Lagan College were from the 'other' community suggesting that both they, and the Queen's students, may be equally representative of the social relationships of Belfast residents.

When these same data are expressed as percentages of those with no friends in the 'other' community the results range from highs of 71 per cent, for new students at Lagan College, to 51 per cent for students who had been at Queen's University for less than two years. This compares to 8 per cent for the 12 past pupils surveyed at Corrymeela, and zero per cent for the Lagan College fifth year. By way of contrast 40 per cent of the students who had been at Queen's for between three and six years still listed no friends in the other community. Clearly the pro-social effects of an integrated secondary school education are significantly stronger than those of a mixed university. By the time the children of Northern Ireland reach university age, the best opportunity for social integration seems to have passed them by.

Integration and School Policies [14]

A lot of people run the College down, and really do hate the school and what it stands for. Others will listen to these people and accept their view. It is so stupid that this is happening because most of them have never seen or had any sort of experience in connection with Lagan. Lagan College is trying to do something about the problems within this country, helping the youth which is more than can be said about most other schools. From what I have seen so far it's worked. At my previous school I would come up against more rivalry in one week than I have come up against in two and a half years here. It is also stupid to think that both sides of the church want peace, but yet they preach during the mass that you shouldn't be sending your children to integrated schools and instead support your own. They are hypocrites and hold nothing other than pessimistic views of the school. They're hoping the College will fail, and its my belief that they will be proved wrong. The amount of support for the school is clearly evident in the number of parents who want their children to come here. This proves that there definitely is the support for the College to succeed.
(Catholic boy, aged 15)

All the studies reviewed here on the formation of individual friendships around common interests and personalities, point to one simple principle for increasing success. As children make the majority of their school friends in their tutor group, or school class, the opportunity to find a friend in the 'other' community must be made equal for the members of both communities. Ideally this requires a 50:50 ratio. However, as boys make friends with boys, girls with girls, footballers with footballers and computer hackers with computer hackers, etc., then it follows that in an ideally structured group of students, all these characteristics of the children should be equally divided between the communities that are the focus of social integration. Of course, in practice, this ideal classroom structure is impossible to achieve, although steps should be taken to ensure the closest possible match to the ideal.

The enrolment of the school should be balanced to make sure that an equal number of Catholics and Protestants are boys, girls, academically weak, academically strong, middle class, working class etc. Lagan College try to maintain an equal balance by all these criteria, and given their success this is to be encouraged. It may not matter too much if the school were all boys or all girls, or all academically weak or all academically strong, or all working class or all middle class, or any combination of these characteristics, providing each aspect of the school population is equally divided between Catholics and Protestants; but in practice, integrated schools should strive to maintain a balance in those aspects of the student population that they do have some control over, while remembering that a balance within each sex should be given the highest priority.

Because most friendships are made in the classroom, any balance that is achieved through enrolment should be reflected in, and equally distributed through, each tutor group. This can be achieved by carefully sorting and dividing up each incoming first year into balanced classes. Additionally, new students who arrive from time to time can be carefully placed to improve balance. Teachers responsible for tutor groups should be aware of the religious/ethnic background and the interests and social relationships of their pupils. When this knowledge is pooled with the leaders of the other tutor groups in their year, and with their year head, it is possible to imaginatively orchestrate improvements in integration. For example, if a tutor group contained two boys who were very close friends by virtue of their keen interest in football, and also happened to be Catholic, and if a new boy of the same age came to the school who was also a keen footballer, but happened to be Protestant, then clearly, introducing this new boy into this tutor group would expand the social possibilities for all three children. However, this can only be done when the religious denomination, interests and social relationships of the children are known.

Lagan College now has over 800 pupils and another 17 integrated schools have been set up. I believe the research reviewed here proves the social value of this type of education. Lagan College is successful because it was founded on a principle of equality that establishes a balance between the Catholic and Protestant students, staff, and governors. The principle of equality is also extended to the teaching of history, culture and the political views of both communities. In other parts of the world, where school integration has been forced, or where the curriculum has been biased to present the perspective of the dominant group, or 'paste over' an oppressive history, integrated education has not been so successful.[15] Indeed minorities in some societies have had their attitudes and status enforced by being a minority in a mixed school. Research and experience points to the apparently simple conclusion that integrated education is most effective when it is founded on the principles of freedom of choice, equality and openness in curriculum development.

The Rights of Peace Makers
Many parents do choose integrated education for their children for idealistic reasons or because their partner comes from the 'other' community.[16] However it

would be wrong to assume that in all these cases the parents' values and subsequent choice are necessarily a simple expression of a 'do good' attitude or family interests that are not shaped by the real needs of their child. Unfortunately most of the research completed on why children do go to integrated schools tends to focus on the parents' role in the decision making process.[17] However, when the children are given an opportunity to tell their side of the story we discover that their experiences and input are frequently as important as the contribution made by their parents.

I have been brought up in a neighbourhood both Catholic and Protestant. That is why I chose Lagan College.
(Catholic girl, aged 12)

I went to an integrated primary school. I did not want to change suddenly to a Catholic or Protestant school after spending four or five years learning to be integrated.
(Non-Denominational girl, aged 11)

I lived in Dublin for most of my life and went to a Church of Ireland primary school but it was integrated as most of the schools in the Republic of Ireland are... I found life very difficult when I first moved to Belfast as people automatically presume I was Catholic because I'm from Dublin. If I presumed everyone up here was Protestant I would most likely get hit. Going to Lagan did help me settle in and I'm glad I came here as it was the only school anything like Dublin!
(Baptist girl, aged 14)

Now people want to be friendly with people of the other religion and not always fighting over stupid things like religion. Sometimes it is the child who sees and understands and he wants to go to Lagan College. These children tell their friends how good and how much fun it is at Lagan College. So friends want to go to Lagan College.
(Protestant boy, aged 13)

I came to Lagan College because I wanted to see what it would be like working with Protestants. I thought that there would be a lot of fighting. But my friend told me there was not a lot of fighting and that both Protestants and Catholics get on well.
(Catholic girl, aged 13)

I am eleven years old. My Mum and Dad wanted me to go to Ulster High but I did not want to go so I told them that I wanted to go to Lagan College.
(Protestant girl, aged 11)

The United Nations *Convention on the Rights of the Child* gives children the right for their point of view to be taken into account when decisions are made concerning their well being.

> *Article 11.1.* States Parties shall assure to the child who is capable of forming his or her own views the right to express those views freely in all matters affecting the child, the views of the child being given due weight in accordance with the age and maturity of the child.

This convention also protects children from discrimination and seeks to promote understanding and respect for all ethnic and religious groups through the medium of education:

> *Article 2.2.* States Parties shall take all appropriate measures to ensure that the child is protected against all forms of discrimination or punishment on the basis of the status, activities, expressed opinions, or beliefs of the child's parents, legal guardians, or family members.

> *Article 29.1.* States Parties agree that the education of the child shall be directed to: (d) The preparation of the child for responsible life in a free society, in the spirit of understanding, peace, tolerance, equality of sexes, and friendship among all peoples, ethnic, national and religious groups and persons of indigenous origin.

Unfortunately these rights are frequently broken in Northern Ireland where choosing integrated education can be thought of as a revolutionary act that threatens the status quo of a divided community. Parents who choose integration may be subject to discrimination and threats. They are often seen as traitors and the children who go to integrated schools can also fall victim to these social pressures by providing a focus for the bigotry endemic in the adult world that surrounds them.

I went to a Catholic primary school. Across the road was a Protestant school. It did not matter to me about Catholics and Protestants. When I was in P6 we were told all about religion. My P6 teacher did not agree on having a school for both Catholics and Protestants. It was coming time for me to do the 11 plus. The teacher asked me what school I would like to go to. I said 'Lagan College.' Then the teacher started asking me all these questions. The teacher said 'Why do you not want to go to a Catholic school?' I replied 'just because that's where I want to go and my parents want me to go.' When my results came out I had passed my eleven plus. My teacher asked our class again what school do you want to go to. There was me and three others that had said they were going to Lagan College. Then the teacher took us out of the room. He said to us 'What are you going to Lagan College for?' When I was in P6 and P7 I always got chased because I was Catholic and called Fenian. So our teacher would say it would be worse at Lagan College because it was mainly Protestant.

(Catholic girl, aged 12)

The area in which I live is mostly Protestant. There are very few Catholics, maybe two or three, and it is not well known. If Catholics come to the estate they would get chased and a group of Protestants would start a fight. Even if you are Protestant and are suspected of being Catholic a fight may be started. This is not all the time. Sometimes if a Catholic came to visit a Protestant friend nothing would be said. If I brought a Catholic friend to visit I would maybe change their name, because even though nothing might not be said I wouldn't like to take a chance. It can annoy me because I would like to bring people from school without changing their names etc. As I go to Lagan College some people think that I am Catholic and taunt me. It doesn't really worry me. People say I should change schools and not to mix.

(Protestant girl, aged 13)

Although the 1960 *UNESCO Convention against Discrimination in Education* provides for separate religious schools, attendance at such schools must be voluntary and access to all types of schools, which would include integrated schools, cannot be restricted:

> *Article 2 (b).* The establishment or maintenance, for religious or linguistic reasons, of separate educational systems or institutions offering an education which is in keeping with the wishes of the pupil's parents or legal guardians, if participation in such systems or attendance at such institutions is optional...

> *Article 1 and 1(a).* For the purpose of the Convention, the term 'discrimination' includes any distinction, exclusion, limitation or preference which... has the purpose or effect... of depriving any person or group of persons of access to education of any type at any level.

The system of segregated education in Northern Ireland contributes to the perpetuation of prejudice and social conflict in Ulster, while integrated education increases cross-community understanding and friendship. Unfortunately, in the face of opposition from local community leaders, the churches and education boards, the Northern Ireland Office and Department of Education have failed to provide every child in the province with a real option of attending an integrated school.[18] This failure represents a breach of the human rights and fundamental freedoms of the children of Northern Ireland and should not be tolerated by an international community that is now expressly concerned with peace building through the medium of education. Children dream of peace. It is our moral duty and international obligation to give them every possibility of realising their ambitions.

Go to the sky, look down, you'll see a large blue green planet, focus, click, find a continent, focus, click, find a country, focus, look down. You see Ireland, more specifically Northern Ireland. The troubles have swamped the land. Close your eyes. Imagine in your mind's eye you see a land. It is a beautiful land, it is perfect— WAIT! what is this? An army. You focus your eyes on it. It is the troubles, they spread and kill. Stop. Fast-forward fifty years. Stop. Play. Look. You see the same land. Is it? It does not look like it, but it is. It has been swamped by the troubles. There are no more places to run, no more refuge. The light at the end of the tunnel has gone out, forever. The End.

Wait. The light has been rekindled. It is only small but growing stronger. Open your eyes. What do you see? A school. It is just one but it takes children from the troubles, from both Catholic and Protestant regions and teaches them, draws them together. They learn to understand each other, they make friends.

But can they heal the wound?

Only time will tell. The End.

(First year student)

Notes

1   Akenson, D., (1970), *The Irish Education Experiment: The National System of Education in the Nineteenth Century*, Routledge and Kegan Paul.

2   For a detailed discussion of the theoretical issues see Irwin, C. J., (1992), 'Integrated Education: From Theory to Practice in Divided Societies', *Prospects, UNESCO Quarterly Review of Education*. Vol. XXII, No.1. UNESCO, Paris.

3   Whyte, J. H., (1986), 'How is the Boundary Maintained Between the Two Communities in Northern Ireland?', *Ethnic and Racial Studies*, Vol. 9, No. 2.

4   Greeley, A. M. and Rossi, P. H., (1966), *The Education of Catholic Americans*, Aldine

Press, Chicago; Salters, J., (1970), *Attitudes Towards Society in Protestant and Roman Catholic Schoolchildren in Belfast*, M. Ed. Thesis, Queen's University of Belfast; Russell, J., (1974), 'Sources of Conflict', *The Northern Teacher*, 11, 3.

5   Douglas, S. E., (1983), *Differences in Group Identity and Intergroup Attitudes in Children Attending Integrated or Segregated Schools in Northern Ireland*, thesis submitted to the Department of Psychology, Queen's University of Belfast.

6   For a more detailed discussion of these issues see Irwin, C. J., (1991), *Education and the Development of Social Integration in Divided Societies*, Northern Ireland Council For Integrated Education, Belfast, and Irwin (1993).

7   Greeley and Rossi (1966).

8   For a more detailed analysis of all the research reviewed here see Irwin (1991).

9   Boal, F., (1982), 'Segregating and Mixing: Space and Residence in Belfast', in F. Boal and J. Douglas (Eds.) *Integration and Division: Geographical Perspectives on the Northern Ireland Problem*, Academic Press, London.

10 Keane, M. C., (1990), 'Segregation Processes in Public Sector Housing', *Geographical Perspectives on the Belfast Region, Geographical Society of Ireland Special Publications, No. 5*, Ed. P. Doherty. Geographical Society of Ireland.

11 Cairns, E., (1987), *Caught in Crossfire: Children and the Northern Ireland Conflict*, Syracuse University Press.

12 For a detailed discussion of the methodological problems associated with this research see Irwin (1991).

13 Spencer, A. E. C. W., (1982), 'Integration and Segregation in the N. Ireland Educational System: Lagan College and its Context', *Queen's News*, November 1982, Queen's University of Belfast.

14 For a more detailed discussion see Irwin (1991, 1993).

15 Wright, F., (1991), *Integrated Education and New Beginnings in Northern Ireland*, Corrymeela Press, Belfast.

16 McEwen, A. and Salters, J., (1992), *Integrated Education: The Views of Parents*, School of Education, Queen's University of Belfast; Morgan, V., Dunn, S., Cairns, E. and Fraser, G., (1992), *Breaking the Mould: The Roles of Parents and Teachers in the Integrated Schools in Northern Ireland*, Centre for the Study of Conflict, University of Ulster at Coleraine.

17 Cairns, E., Dunn, S., Morgan, V. and Giles, M., (1989), 'Attitudes towards integrated education in Northern Ireland: the impact of real choice', *Education North*, 1, 2, 20-23, and McEwen and Salters (1992).

18 Irwin, C. J., (1992), 'Integrated Education: A Moral Issue', *First Call for Children*, UNICEF, New York, October, and Irwin (1993).

8
A Whole Attitude of Mind
Teaching in Integrated Schools

Grace Fraser

Since Lagan College opened in 1981, much attention has been focused on the parents who became involved in establishing this and the other planned integrated schools which were to follow. Parental input was high and there can be little doubt that the schools would not exist had it not been for the founder parents, whose vision of a better future for their children and the community led them to invest long hours of hard work before the opening day. Most parents understood that their support for their new school would not stop here, that this would in fact be a beginning, not an end. Integrated education was a fragile plant which had to be nurtured, not left to survive one way or another. At the same time, parents knew that much of the task which lay ahead would fall on those appointed to teach in the new schools. Seldom must teachers have had to carry such an enormous responsibility. [1]

In 1989 the Centre for the Study of Conflict at the University of Ulster was funded by the Economic and Social Research Council to carry out a two year study of the roles of parents and teachers in the planned integrated schools in Northern Ireland. This chapter is based on its findings about the people who were teaching in the new schools at the time of the study – who they were, why they entered integrated education, what they felt about the experience of teaching in an integrated school, the nature of their relationship with parents and, lastly, their concerns for their own future and that of integrated education. [2]

Those who teach in the established system of schools in Northern Ireland, that is to say, in either the maintained or the controlled schools, have for the most part been educated in one or other of these kinds of school, so that their professional careers are mostly spent in an ambience with which they are familiar and comfortable. Teachers in integrated schools do not usually have this advantage and it will be a few years before there is a significant number who have themselves attended such schools. Of those who came to the integrated schools, few, even from amongst the experienced teachers, had taught children from both Protestant and Catholic communities. Most had been 'reared' in Northern Ireland, had been trained there and had always worked there. A small number had worked outside, either in Great Britain or abroad, and had returned here. A few came from outside. It is possible to suggest that the proportion of teachers with experience of working outside Northern Ireland is higher in the integrated schools than in other schools. That this was particularly true of the principals is in itself an interesting finding which underlines the difficulties facing teachers wishing to break free of a system of education in which they themselves were a part. The fact that the new schools still had to prove themselves viable also acted as a restraint. The effects of the small but steady and successful growth of integrated education on applications for posts in the integrated schools, especially at the senior level, will be interesting to observe. In terms of their background, then, most teachers in integrated schools were scarcely dissimilar to the rest of the teaching force in Northern Ireland. Given this, facing a classroom of Catholics and Protestants on their first day proved just as novel an experience for the teachers as it did for the children sitting in front of them. Integration was something that both had to learn and work at – from scratch. Few came to it ready-made.

The decision to work in an integrated school was not therefore one which any teacher, either new or experienced, took lightly. It was clear that their motivation was something which deserved closer scrutiny. Interviews revealed a variety of reasons for making this choice, teachers often suggesting that they had been influenced by more than one. These fell under four main headings, ideology, religion, education and professional career.

The majority of those interviewed were deeply committed ideologically to integrated education. This was something which they shared with those parents who had set up the schools and which served as an inspiration to their work. Teaching was a 'practical' way of countering what they considered to be wrong with segregated education and, for them, was always better than just 'speaking out against it'. There was considerable concern that, like many of them, most people educated in Northern Ireland met members of the 'opposite side' informally on comparatively rare occasions, if at all. Mutual understanding was not encouraged by such an environment. No one thought that integrated education would solve such problems overnight, but it could make a positive, long-term contribution to improving relations between the two communities. The decision to take up a position in an integrated school was a huge commitment for the teachers, for, as one parent commented, 'they were putting their careers on the line'. Parents who were considering integrated education as an option for their children could not fail to be impressed. From the same parent, 'this was convincing'.

The opponents of integrated education have frequently attacked the schools over the question of their teaching of religion, accusing them of 'watering down beliefs'. Such polemics have a variety of origins, some having little to do with religion, others deriving from simple ignorance of what is actually being taught. [3] By implication, those who taught in these schools were not persons of deep religious commitment. Of the teachers interviewed, many cited their Christian faith as a strong, often primary, reason, for moving into integrated education. This was closely allied to ideological motivation, for segregation seemed to them to cut across both boundaries of philosophy and belief. Some teachers had had to endure criticism at the private as well as the public level, even from their own clergy, which was particularly hurtful.

It would have been surprising if education had not featured among the reasons offered by teachers for making the move into integrated education. The new schools were not only about children; they were also for them. The needs of the child were considered to be central. A child who was 'valued' would in turn 'value' others. In previous teaching posts, some teachers had chafed under what they felt was a stricter, more formal environment emphasised by the selection procedure then in place. 'I was unhappy about teaching in a system where the school appeared to be run for itself, rather than for the children.' This does not mean that other schools were not 'child-centred'. Such comments reflect the experience of those teachers who felt that the new schools would have a better chance of affirming such an ethos. The newness, the possibilities and the challenges on offer attracted senior teachers, especially those who became principals, for amongst them were a number for whom integrated education also provided an opportunity to put these kinds of long-held view into practice, for the first time within a sympathetic milieu.

Teachers also took up posts in the integrated schools for reasons of career. In some cases, these were people who believed that they were never likely to be promoted because of their 'attitudes'. For others, it would have been a case of 'waiting to fill a dead man's shoes'. Given the difficulty of finding a permanent teaching position here, younger teachers had applied for this post among others. Such a degree of realism does not imply a lack of commitment to integrated education. It was clear from interviews that teachers took this very seriously, with the younger ones 'growing' into the ethos of the school. Importantly there was a small number who moved from fairly senior posts to the new schools for the precise purpose of fulfilling this ideal. What is important to remember is that when these people were interviewed , the planned integrated schools were still in the position of having to find funding to keep going until, and also after, grant maintained status came through. Teachers recalled the stressful experience of wondering whether there would still be a job and/or a salary at the end of the month. Not even a move to a promoted post could guarantee tenure. For everyone, it was a leap in the dark. Our findings revealed few regrets.

In the Classroom

What was it like to teach in an integrated school? Was it the same or different from teaching in segregated schools? As all schools are in the business of education, one would expect teaching in the integrated schools to be similar in a number of respects. This was quite true. The daily routine – lesson preparation, marking, maintaining classroom control and attending to general administrative duties – still applied. The differences lay in the overall aims of integrated education which governed the school and 'permeates all attitudes – to parents, the curriculum, even inter-staff relations'. It is perhaps worth reiterating the newness of this experience for most of the teachers. No teacher training institution had prepared them for what now confronted them. They had to learn on the job. This was not easy. 'Conscious of the need to be different' and uncertain about what to expect, some worried if they did not *feel* different.

As regards the overall curriculum, teachers said that having both Protestant and Catholic children in front of them made them much more aware of how and what they said in class. This happened more at the secondary level than the primary, as one would expect, when the use and perception of language by children is more sophisticated, and applies particularly in interpretive subjects like literature, history and religious education. For primary teachers, the last posed particular problems. Faced with having to plan a syllabus which would do justice to both Protestant and Catholic traditions, teachers admitted, not surprisingly, to a fair degree of ignorance about the 'other side'. The kind of support which could have helped transcend these difficulties, was only too often absent. For the most part, teachers were left to their own devices. This had a positive side effect – staff had to depend on each other for help. Significantly, when principals and senior staff attended a conference during the first year of the project, religious education dominated discussions. This was a measure of the concern which teachers had with 'getting it right'.

One major difference which was mentioned by all teachers was the amount of time they had to devote outside of the classroom to the new school, particularly at the beginning, when schools were still in the process of being established. Teachers found themselves involved in a daily round of meetings during and after school hours, solving problems of resources and accommodation, curriculum planning and management structures, often in close cooperation with parents. Much of this was unfamiliar territory which had to be mapped out with care and sensitivity in line with the aims of integrated education. Principals tended to carry the heaviest workload, especially those in the primary schools where they were also teaching principals. As a researcher attending some of the meetings with parents and teachers, I never ceased to be impressed by the stamina of all concerned. New organisations often acquire a certain momentum of their own, as people work hard together and become buoyed up with the enthusiasm of achieving their goal. The question one has to ask is whether such commitment on the part of teachers is sustainable in the long term when the 'honeymoon' period is over. At a time when teachers everywhere are confronting extra workloads imposed by frequent curriculum changes and LMS, this remains an extremely relevant issue.

The planned integrated schools have a commitment to maintaining a religious balance between the two communities. This covers the school roll, management structures, parent bodies and teaching and ancillary staff. Problems can arise from the application of this principle in practical terms, particularly with regard to the appointment of teaching personnel. At the beginning, when schools were opened, staff numbers were small and often the only promoted post was that held by the principal. As the roll expanded, more teachers were required, including those who would hold promoted posts, for example, that of vice-principal. The convention appeared to be that if the principal was a Protestant, then the vice-principal should be a Catholic, and *vice versa*. If this did not happen, the balance was upset and appointments were skewed thereafter. Either way, teachers' expectations were affected as was their place in the 'pecking' order. Inevitably, some found this rather discouraging. A frequently unsympathetic public was not slow to discover such anomalies. When advertisements for teaching posts in the integrated schools appeared in the press, comments were sometimes made to the effect that 'there is no point in applying, because they want a Catholic/ Protestant...' Was this a case of the schools shooting themselves in the foot? Hopefully, as the schools continue to grow and staff numbers correspondingly, there will be no need for such exactitude.

Parents and Teachers

Parental involvement is a basic tenet of the integrated education movement in Northern Ireland. For some parents, their relationship with the school began as founders and expanded into a continued involvement as the school developed. For others, their connection began when they enrolled their child. Parents participate at all levels of management. Their role is recognized as indispensable; it is in no way an afterthought. Witness the following extract from the educational aims listed by Hazelwood College :

> To develop an open system of school organisation, emphasising
> the partnership and interdependence of parents, pupils and staff. [4]

What we have here is a deliberate attempt to establish a new kind of relationship between parent and school, and, at the heart of it, between parent and teacher. Writing it into the constitution of schools was one thing; doing it was another. Teachers traditionally have had a great deal of autonomy, though in recent years this has been much subject to erosion. Accountability is a fairly recent concept in education. Too often parents had visiting rights and little else. Integrated schools view this kind of negative, one-way relationship as totally unproductive for the child's education. Parents and teachers ought to cooperate in the best interests of the pupils. But neither parents nor teachers knew exactly how this concept could be translated into practical terms. This has meant that no two schools have approached parental involvement in the same way. When *Breaking the Mould* was published, early in 1992, the research team felt that all the schools in the survey were still striving towards a model of cooperation and that this was 'likely to be a long process'. [5]

Parents and teachers have not begun from the same starting-point in this process. Because there is little tradition of strong, pro-active parental involvement in the established systems, parents in the integrated schools have considerable expectations of what can be achieved if a determined group of parents and teachers are enthused by the same ideals. Compared with the norm, it can only be better. Teachers, of course, are already involved in the schools – they work there. Their job is the basis of their professional standing. What would an input by parents mean? How would they be affected by it? Would it stop outside the classroom door or come inside? Would parental involvement be a euphemism for parental interference?

In our research parents' and teachers' expectations differed. Some parents were content to have a fairly low level of involvement, attending meetings and visiting staff only when necessary and usually only when it concerned their own child, while others saw their input in more global terms, participating on the committees of parent councils and on the boards of governors. Among the latter group were also parents who expressed the desire to have some say in curriculum planning and teaching methods. Teachers welcomed the idea of closer cooperation with parents because they saw it as potentially beneficial to the children they taught, but some were concerned that this would impinge on their professionalism. Inevitably this led to a certain amount of line-drawing. In the primary schools where parents possibly feel more confident about their role, teachers sometimes found parental involvement threatening. One teacher had even been accused by colleagues of 'siding with parents'. At the secondary level, the roles tended to be reversed, perhaps due to the greater size of the school, increased number of staff and a more specialised curriculum.

Each of the schools in our study had a number of formal mechanisms for cooperation between parents and teachers. These included the various structures where both would be represented, but the main body to which all parents could belong, the parents' council, occasionally had a very vague, unstructured relationship with the teaching staff. Some teachers did not know whether or not they were welcome to attend; others waited until formally invited to come. This could even apply to the principal. [6] As schools continue to grow, both the parent group and the teacher group change and are supplemented. A few founder parents and teachers felt that the 'new' parents and 'new' teachers could not always be counted upon to share the enthusiasm of the original founding group. This may or may not be true. The late Frank Wright considered that 'favourable financial incentives' such as those contained in the Education Reform (NI) Order (1989) which offered integrated schools full salary and running costs from the start, would prove detrimental because, in future, schools would 'leapfrog the growing experience' of parents and teachers working in close concert to get them up and running and that this would serve to store up 'concealed conflicts'. [7]

What is certain is that, at the time of our research project, some parents' councils were beginning to find it hard to maintain numbers. If parents were losing interest, was it because, as one parent complained: 'It seems to be run much like other schools now. The role of parents has become normalised.' Some parents were very uncertain about what their role vis-a-vis the school should be and blamed teachers for not offering 'active encouragement'. Teachers sometimes felt that reticence prevented parents from getting 'more out of their relationship with the school'. But many parents were fulsome in their praise of how they were treated by the teaching staff and described this as totally different from their previous experience of parent-teacher relations. Such a range of comments reflects the variety of experience which was found in the schools at the time of our study. Clearly, it will be up to each school to pursue its own model of parent-teacher cooperation in practical terms and in its own way, provided neither group proceeds only along parallel tracks.

Looking Forward

The planned integrated schools have continued to grow both during and after our study. We were anxious to know what teachers felt about their own future and that of the schools. In addition, since the publication of our report, a new category of integrated school has arrived on the educational scene, the controlled integrated school, those which have opted to become integrated within the controlled system. At the moment these are very few but their arrival also raises a number of questions relevant to teachers.

The teachers whom we interviewed expressed a number of concerns about the future, some career-related. There are usually two avenues of career advancement open to teachers. One is to remain with one's present school in the hope of an internal promotion; the other is to move to a more senior position in another school. But were the same options open to those who taught in the integrated schools? The first option is complicated by the need to maintain a religious balance among all personnel, teaching staff included. Continued growth in numbers on the school roll does help to increase and accelerate promotion among staff, but, although the schools have continued to develop, their internal expansion has not yet been sufficiently rapid to have a major effect. Similarly, although new schools continue to open, this is not happening fast enough to make the second option – moving to another integrated school – really viable. There is perhaps a third possibility. If they wanted to, for career or perhaps other reasons, could a teacher move from an integrated school to a maintained or controlled school? At the time of our fieldwork, most teachers in the integrated schools regarded this as an extremely doubtful possibility. 'I have burned my boats', the stock, if rather gloomy, response to this question, undoubtedly constituted a realistic appraisal on their part of their chances of moving out of integrated education. Other research on attitudes among other principals to the integrated schools, indicates that this could be a fairly accurate prediction[8], although it is probably still too early to say whether or not an 'integrated' teacher can count this out as a career option. Teachers also pointed out that in their time in the integrated schools, they had had access to many opportunities to enhance their own professional development and that invaluable experience of this kind 'ought to stand someone in good stead in interviews in other schools'.

But did they want to move 'out'? The enthusiasm and commitment of teachers was always impressively genuine. Most accepted the situation for what it was and got on with the business of teaching. Younger teachers, especially those in their first permanent post, did not worry too much about the long term. More senior colleagues had often chosen to move from a permanent, sometimes more senior post, for strong ideological reasons and were happy to be where they were. If there were worries, they were more immediate, concerning the ethos of the schools. What, for example, did it mean to be an 'integrated' teacher? Many were coming to terms with the fact that it was more than just 'contact'. There was anxiety about becoming 'normal'. Even so, one of the few teachers to have experience of both maintained and controlled schools made a perceptive comment which mirrors what many teachers seemed to feel. She had no desire to return to either system after having taught in an integrated school. A move of this kind, she said, would involve 'major rethinking' on her part because 'teaching in an integrated school is a whole attitude of mind'. At the same time, there was regret that such experience, both of mutual understanding and professional development, was unlikely to be shared with other teachers in other kinds of schools if hostile attitudes forced the integrated schools into virtual separation from other parts of the educational system.

In the future it is possible that new groups of teachers will join the integrated 'stable' if the number of schools converting to integrated status increases. An essential point to remember is that although these now have 'integrated' status, they are not 'planned' in the sense that schools like Lagan College or Bridge or the Hazelwood Schools were planned, i.e. from the beginning. They are schools which have 'become' integrated. All the implications of this important distinction are not yet known, but some may be hinted at. The opportunity to begin from scratch is absent; instead schools will have to begin anew but with existing staff who were appointed to the school before its change of direction. There is an opportunity here for experienced staff from the planned integrated schools to share their expertise and, sensibly, this is already being done in at least one school through secondment. These new arrangements will demand a high degree of sensitivity from all concerned. 'Born-again' environments can be hard on the uncommitted and unconvinced – teachers or parents – though 'opting in' must be easier for the latter than the former. All those who want the experiment to be successful, will have to work together, utilising the familiarity of existing relationships and the excitement of being involved in something new to set the pace and ease the way. As for the rest, to paraphrase President Clinton in a recent seminal speech, they have got to play the hand they were dealt. [9]

Writing up of our research was completed early in 1991. Since then, new 'planned' schools have continued to open at a faster rate than before, encouraged by supportive legislation as well as by the success of existing schools and the support of the umbrella body NICIE. There is also some slight movement towards change in the controlled sector. But as far as teachers are concerned, some of the issues which concerned them before remain to be resolved. Those who were 'in at the beginning' are now more secure in their employment and this is certainly more attractive to teachers thinking of making the move into integrated schools. But internal advancement or moving to a controlled or a maintained school must still be problematic. Parental involvement, a term which *Breaking the Mould* considered much over-simplified and misunderstood, has sometimes taken on the aspect of a nettle which all schools, not only the integrated schools, must now grasp. Both parents and teachers, but especially teachers, have to be aware of the mutual benefits of partnership. The horrendous workload which might have been expected to decrease as schools became viable, has not gone away as staff, especially principals, have exchanged one back-pack for another, this time loaded with the National Curriculum. In the midst of all this, 'integrated' teachers still have to stop and think about where they are, why they are there and what they are trying to do. If they fail to do this in a consistent way, then the schools may fall far short of their original objectives. This prompts the question: If this is what all teachers should be doing anyway, what is the difference? The difference lies in what is at stake. For 'integrated' teachers, it is what makes maintaining their commitment to integrated education, and coming to terms with what this demands, their most important priorities.

Notes

1. Wright, Frank, *Integrated Education and New Beginnings in Northern Ireland*, (1991); see also chapter 15.
2. When the project began, there were eight planned integrated schools – two secondary and six primary. During the course of the research, this number increased to ten and finally twelve. Given the time-scale of the project, it was not possible to undertake an in-depth study of all of them. It was decided that three schools – two primary and one secondary – should be looked at in this way, while, at the same time, as far as possible, maintaining an overview of the other schools. Information was obtained by the

Research Officer from semi-structured interviews with teachers and parents and from attendance at meetings. The final research report, *Breaking the Mould,* was published by the Centre for the Study of Conflict in 1992.

3. Morgan, V., Fraser, G., Dunn, S., and Cairns, E. (1992) 'Views from Outside – other Professionals' Views of the Religiously Integrated Schools in Northern Ireland', *British Journal of Religious Education* , 14, 3, p. 169-177.

4. *Hazelwood College Prospectus* (1990) p.8

5. Morgan, V., Dunn, S., Cairns, E., and Fraser, G. (1992) *Breaking the Mould*, p.76.

6. Morgan, V., Fraser, G., Dunn, S. and Cairns, E. (1993) 'A New Order of Cooperation and Involvement? Relationships between parents and teachers in the integrated schools', *Educational Review*, 45, 1, p. 43-52.

7. See chapter 15.

8. Morgan, et al. 'Views from Outside.'

9. Clinton, W. Speech to Congress, 17/2/93, *Time*, 141, 9, p.21.

9
Parental Involvement in Integrated Schools

Trevor Parkhill

Each of the fourteen primary and four secondary integrated schools set up since the early or mid 1980s has owed its establishment and formative development to the vision and perseverance of parents. Whether created out of the joint ambition of a group of parents to begin a new planned integrated school, or a 'normal' school which has now opted for grant maintained integrated status, the initiative is very much that of parents. The transformation of the ideal into a practical reality has taken many forms. All of them have involved dedicated work, ranging from cleaning out long-deserted buildings, as in the case of the Hazelwood schools which began life in the same premises in September 1985, to helping and encouraging other groups of parents also considering setting up an integrated school.

The same two rather sterile observations about integrated schools being the domain of middle-class parents and, more recently, that parents of mixed marriages are more likely to send their children to them, have been parroted many times. The truth of the matter is rather different. Several surveys have looked closely at the characteristics of integrated schools. (Indeed, one of the features of being parents in an integrated school is that you sometimes feel you know what it must be like to live in a goldfish bowl, so many studies are undertaken on the subject.) What they have found is that parents of children at integrated schools reflect every socio-economic and most religious groupings in Northern Ireland. Their most identifiable common characteristic is a broad acceptance of the value of providing their children with an educational environment where they can encounter, in a regular and non-hostile way, children of their own age from a different religion. In other words, making the choice to opt out of the accepted system of voluntary grammar, maintained or controlled schools, and placing their children in integrated schools, is a significant commitment by the parents of the 3,500 children now attending integrated schools.

A more subtle criticism which has sometimes been voiced is that parents who opt to support a recently-established integrated school in preference to a well-established and possibly more convenient state or maintained school may be jeopardising their children's education in the fulfilment of their ideals. It is indeed a consideration uppermost in the minds of most parents. But the fact is that official Department of Education inspection visits to integrated schools have commented in the most favourable of terms on the quality of teaching and range of educational opportunities available in the schools. The reports are now published and available to the public. Their conclusions are a source of reassurance, particularly to parents who through their parent governors have been closely involved in the selection and appointment of staff for the schools.

Parental Influence

This is an aspect of parental involvement in which integrated schools can claim to have played an innovative role. The Education Reform Order 1989 gave parents a recognisably more influential say in the administration of schools. All schools have representatives of parents on their boards of governors. But for integrated schools, this represents more of a continuation of previous practice than is the case in most state-controlled or maintained schools. Parental representation has been crucial in the foundation of integrated schools and is also accepted and welcomed in the running of the schools. Indeed the proportion of parents on integrated school boards is higher than in any other sector, with a minimum of three parents in grant maintained integrated schools compared with two for other schools. The lead taken by integrated schools has been no small influence in bringing about this important change in parents' relationship with their children's school.

The emphasis of recent political developments in education has not only been in the direction of greater parental involvement but also in making schools more accountable to parents. For example a quorate general meeting, at which a report of the school's activities and progress is presented, must be held annually. In this respect, government and integrated sector thinking have been more or less along the same lines – even if the rationale of each is very different. The *Citizen's Charter for Northern Ireland* proclaims in its *Charter for Parents* section 'greater parental involvement in decisions about the education of children and more freedom of choice'. Official encouragement of this trend may be seen, for example, in new provisions enabling civil and public servants to claim time off to carry out governor's duties, such as interviewing for posts. This too corresponds with the higher profile that parents have in integrated schools.

It will be interesting, however, to read the results of the studies that will surely be carried out on how effective these new moves have been in providing parents with a greater say in controlled and maintained schools. The National Association of Head Teachers has asserted that parents do not want to be involved in conducting the business of schools. Although initial surveys suggest that this could be the case, it would not be unduly cynical to suspect that this is also a way of saying that schools do not welcome parents becoming too involved. Generally, it is only a small group of parents in any one school who devote the time and energy required for effective involvement. However, the constructive part that parents have played and continue to play in integrated schools in close cooperation with the schools' management teams may, over the longer term, stand out as one of the most distinctive characteristics of the integrated schools movement.

Balanced Representation

An important condition for integrated schools which is not written in to the 1989 Education Reform Order is that there should be an equal balance of Roman Catholic and Protestant parent representatives. This should be commensurate with the overall balanced intake of a planned integrated school which normally operates a 60:40 per cent band: in other words, the school population must not comprise more than 60 per cent of one tradition or less than 40 per cent of the other.

Apart from parent representatives, governors are also elected specifically to represent the two main traditions. In Hazelwood Primary School, for example, the representative of the Roman Catholic tradition on the board is involved in the important and sometimes delicate arrangements for the first Holy Communion of children, usually in P3. Normally in maintained schools, all pupils make their first Holy Communion together in the parish church with which the school is associated. In integrated schools, in the Belfast area of the Down and Connor diocese, parents must make their own arrangements with their local priest as the collective celebration of this sacrament has not yet been permitted by diocesan authorities. The individual ceremonies therefore take place over a period of several weeks, usually on Saturday mornings. One of the roles of the governor representing the Catholic tradition on the board and of the Catholic parent governor is to provide support for teachers and parents in this important stage in the development of the child's faith.

The value of parental involvement is recognised by integrated schools and is explicitly detailed in the schools' prospectuses. Parents are made fully aware of how they can make contact with the school, both officially and unofficially, primarily via their child's teacher or their parent-governor (whose name and telephone number will be in the prospectus). They are also made aware of their responsibility in partnership with the school of ensuring that their child benefits from all the educational facilities and opportunities which the school can offer. This includes making sure that attendance and punctuality are regular, that a suitable amount of time each evening is spent on homework and that standards of uniform are maintained. But it is more than just a businesslike contract: parents are positively welcome in schools and every opportunity is taken to make use of their skills. Workshops are held for parents on aspects of the curriculum that are new, such as Education for Mutual Understanding, Cultural Heritage and Health Education, and even on how they should be aware of the widespread danger of solvent abuse and how they might detect it.

The structures are in place for parents to feel very much part of the school in a clearly non-patronised way. Amongst the contributions that parents offer to the school in Hazelwood Primary, for example, are services such as acting as classroom assistants and superintending on buses at home time or on educational trips during the school day. At secondary level in Hazelwood College, computer and desk-top printing facilities and a 'drop-in' room are used by parents. In this way they are seen to be, and feel themselves to be, part of the work of the school.

This approach is a natural extension of the child-centred philosophy which permeates integrated schools, a characteristic which has drawn positive comment from DENI inspection visits. For parents who have been educated in the decidedly more old-fashioned secondary/grammar school system of the 1950s and 1960s, it comes as something of a shock to hear pupils and teachers address each other in first name terms. In my son's first week at Hazelwood College, he was chosen to represent the school in an athletics event. The teacher, Barney Gadd, strove heroically to raise a team of five from the small number of pupils enrolled in those early days. At the end of the race, I asked my son to say cheerio and thanks to Mr. Gadd. 'Cheerio and thanks, Barney,' came the reply, with no trace of self-consciousness. As I slunk away, I was left wondering whether I would adapt to this new order. In fact, adaptation comes quickly, once you realise that this sort of familiarity is more likely to breed respect than contempt.

Parents' Council

This educational generation gap could well account for the apparent reluctance of parents to take too close an interest in parents' council affairs. The council is a forum which parents can attend and at which they can raise issues which are exercising them at the time. At Hazelwood College, parents' council meetings on a range of topics of common concern, including an explanation of what exactly Cultural Heritage is meant to be and seeing the architects' early plans for a new building, have all attracted sizeable audiences in excess of fifty. But issues such as fund-raising and even a talk on 'What is parental involvement?' have been sparsely attended. Explanations are plausible, including unreliable means of communication, particularly the note at the bottom of the schoolbag syndrome, in which a note is produced to the parent days after the event it announces has taken place.

Perhaps the name 'council' is in itself off-putting; there are grounds for calling it the parents' forum, in any case. It may be inevitable however that, even though more pupils are attending integrated schools, their parents' councils are no more successful than those in other schools in attracting significant numbers to plenary meetings. Even though parents have taken the step of sending their children to integrated schools, they are (understandably) primarily concerned with their children's own education, rather than with the broader issues. Certainly parents' nights, at which interviews are held with teachers on the children's progress and aptitudes, are fully attended and often continue until 11 p.m. and beyond. Nonetheless, it is surprising that a consideration of the creditable aspects of parental involvement in integrated schools should also acknowledge that one of its key areas – the parents' council – only merits a half-term report of 'could do better'.

As educational developments continue, it is clear that the concept of parental involvement is more and more likely to assume the proportions of parental responsibility. Parents will be obliged to take a more active interest in their offspring's education, whether or not their inclination is to 'let the school get on with it'. Parental involvement is already crucial in helping children cope with the strictures of the new pressurised curriculum at all of Key Stages One to Four. A regime of regular testing is being established which will require much closer parental monitoring than would have been expected in the past. In matters of school discipline, parents are also required to be the guarantors for the good conduct of their children if there is persistent misbehaviour. Such behaviour at secondary level in integrated schools leads to a contract being drawn up, to which the school, the pupil and the parents are parties. These are aspects of parental involvement which, sooner or later, will be widely observed.

This sombre scenario, however necessary, jars rather with the overriding sensation of excitement, apprehension, doubt and determination that continues to be experienced by the groups of parents who band together throughout Ulster to provide their children with as good an education as they deserve in a planned integrated school. But when the euphoria of the early pioneer days has settled, the realisation sets in that running a school, any school, in the 1990s is very much like running a business in which teaching and ancillary staff, parents and pupils are partners. Hard work, negotiating skills, and the almost indefinable sense of purpose which is commented on by the many visitors to integrated schools, are all required to maintain the momentum. The object is to provide the best learning opportunities in an environment where Roman Catholic and Protestant are well placed to understand each other, respect the other's traditions and points of view, and come to realise that they share more than divides them. And that is why the parents became involved in the first place.

10
Building on the Founding Principles
Managing Change in an Integrated School

Charles Graham

The purpose of this chapter is to document some of the practical problems and many positive elements encountered by the principal of a newly established integrated school in Northern Ireland. It will investigate some of the conflicts that result from the philosophical background to the concept of integrated education; and the need for constant adjustment and review in a situation of rapid change and growth in terms of numbers. I hope it will shed some light on the difficulties arising from the need to maintain a religious balance in terms of both children and staff; and some insight into how the perceptions of those not involved can exacerbate socio-religious tensions. Given the personal involvement of the writer, what follows is to a large extent based on observations on first hand experience. Many unresolved tensions exist outside integrated education and it is hoped that the chapter will help to bridge the gap between the varied perceptions of integrated education held by those involved and those who are not.

Foundations
Bridge Primary School in Banbridge was established in 1987 with an enrolment of 75 pupils and a teaching complement of three. It was agreed to appoint a part time teacher in order that the principal could be relieved for administrative duties and planning. At the time of writing (some five years later) there are 210 pupils enrolled, with plans in the pipeline for the development of a new purpose-built school that will accommodate up to 435 pupils.

As with all integrated schools the project began in premises unsuited to the requirements of today's educational system. Yet, in the months and weeks leading up to the school opening, the degree of parental support (a feature of integrated education) was evident. Teams worked incessantly to transform a large residential dwelling into a school of three classes. There was the spirit of a crusade because Banbridge was to have a viable alternative to the established systems which had done little over the years to promote an understanding of 'the other side'. It was being established not by any department or body but by ordinary concerned and committed parents, Protestants and Catholics, together. The atmosphere was highly charged and relationships and friendships were established with people who did not share the same religious sympathies and who otherwise would probably never have met.

As the school has grown there has been a conscious decision to broaden this platform of common understanding among the children and to enhance their own specific culture and traditions. It is an ongoing challenge that is accepted by all involved, bringing very clearly to the fore the real purpose and nature of Education for Mutual Understanding (EMU). To a greater or lesser degree this cross-curricular theme is taught in all schools; but within the integrated sector it is a cross-curricular theme with no 'time out'. It pervades the entire climate and ethos of the school and opportunities to promote and extend it are constantly sought.

The prospectus of our school refers to the need to promote good relationships among both parents and children alike. Such are the structures of management, that parental support and assistance have been encouraged continually throughout the school's development. There have been seminars and frequent invitations to attend evening meetings. A parents' council meets monthly and there are regular sub-committee meetings of the various management groups.

Change and Conflict

There is an innate irony however, in the fact that conflict has been manifest in the development of at least some integrated schools, certainly ours. Conflict has been frequent, particularly initially. Sometimes it has been destructive, but it has also led to the development of a strong cohesive unit. The word conflict itself invites feelings of suspicion, doubt and fear, and while it is and has been potentially harmful, its potential for harm can be minimised. In our particular situation there has been a realisation that concerns have been vocalised by very honest and committed individuals with contrasting points of view. It has often been uncomfortable, but in retrospect one must say that it has been both healthy and expected.

While the integrated schools have evolved from an almost embryonic state, those outside the movement may have naively attributed conflict to the personalities involved. But this is to label the disciples of integrated education as clearly as those from the 'other side'. In the early days integrated schools were very much a shot in the dark and people waited and watched in anticipation to see if they could sustain independence. Each school was dependent on a substantial but limited input of finance from trust funds. The schools were jointly managed by a small nucleus of teachers and a very much larger parent body. Once established, this survival of the school was itself dependent on internal development, change and growth. Conflict was inevitable.

Everard and Morris, in *The Self Managing School*, refer to conflict as occurring whenever or wherever change is anticipated or proposed. [1] In this school change has occurred in almost every aspect of school life. For example, staffing levels have risen in each successive year and new members of staff have had to be initiated into the 'ways' of the school with its management structure of governors, directors, and highly involved and motivated parent body or parents' council. Considering this high degree of involvement, internal organisational conflict has been inevitable. Personal stakes have often been high and the potential for personal destruction has been fierce and sometimes even vicious. Inevitably therefore there have been victims. A perceived democratic distribution of authority has threatened conventional methods of management; and attempts to marry the theory and practice of integrated education have not always been successful.

The movement generally appeals to people's sense of justice and belief in the theory that we are all equal. In reality the political situation in Northern Ireland has not been developed on such principles, and suspicion has consequently been an ingrained aspect of the persona of the Ulster citizen, which is unlikely to change simply because a new type of school has opened – even if it is a school that challenges these old established and entrenched perceptions. Ultimately therefore, conflict has been necessary in order to dispose of suspicions and scepticism. It has been healthy although it has often not been seen to be so at the time. The absence of conflict, say Everard and Morris, may denote an abdication of responsibility or lack of interest; and if we accept this valuation the degree of conflict in our school has been a positive influence. At the same time there have been casualties. Frustration and threats to individual egos may have led to entrenchment and a vehement personal stance that has impeded negotiation and even discussion. In such instances, progress has been arduous. Conversely, the identification of problems has often led to discussion, resolve and heightened self-esteem as well as progress towards predetermined goals and objectives.

A point in case has been the sub-division, or sub-structuring, of the governing body. The composition of 16 members with possible co-opted members has often made negotiation and consensus difficult. Although the delegation of limited responsibility to sub-committees, has meant an increase in their workload, it has also made for more structured and more professionally executed meetings. Meetings of the full board are now bi-monthly as opposed to fortnightly and all matters are more harmoniously and reasonably despatched. Initial conflict meant that pressures were intense, which is possibly why Peter McGaffin in *Schools Under Scrutiny* [2] writes that he does not look back with great relish on the growing pains, as he refers to them, of starting and developing a new integrated school.

The concept of change is a very influential factor in the development of a planned integrated school. Like a wheel, its force is felt more at the hub than at the periphery. Initially, change was rapid and was felt most acutely by the teaching staff. Those on the fringes and less involved managerially did not feel the full thrust. The pace of change could not have been sustained and when it eventually slowed those other than teachers may have felt that development was becoming slower than anticipated and that their input was not as much required as previously. This is not the case and every effort must be made to continue well directed parental involvement in all integrated schools.

Change must be managed, although the questions of how and by whom have never really been answered. Should change be managed and directed by governors, senior management or parents? There is no definitive answer, but it may be worthwhile considering the nature of change in relation to the nature of integrated schools. Firstly, change is an inevitable and integral part of each school's growth. It affects the way people think. It provides experience and expects both mistakes and advancement. It affects people's emotions and perceptions. It is possible for change to alter the school almost out of recognition and in our case this is a very real possibility, with an anticipated future intake of about 450 pupils, a move to a new green field site, changes in status and new teaching staff. Yet what hasn't changed and what will never change are the basic beliefs and principles upon which the school was founded: beliefs and principles that were established by the pioneers of integrated education and later enhanced by such groups are ACT and NICIE as well as by our own teaching staff and governors.

Within an integrated school it is an unwritten requirement for all involved to expand their perceptions and change their attitudes. Circumstances change and people must adapt accordingly. Not to change is to court failure, disappointment or even resentment. It must be said that while progress has been made, some have withdrawn either their services or their children from the school because of an inability to come to terms with rapid change or a realisation that their perceptions are not in tandem with the majority.

Parental Involvement

It is my opinion that part of the reason for such apparent diversity of perception is that some aspects of the underlying philosophy of integrated education have not, even as yet, been fully explained, defined or appreciated. This can be illustrated with reference to the concept of parental involvement. In general it is a noble and potentially strong aspect of all our schools. But it can be controversial and potentially destructive. The constitution of each school requires that there shall be a parents' council, whose function is to assist the principal and governors and advise them on matters of concern to parents. However there is no guidance on how the parents' council should be structured. Each parent is automatically a member; but because of the intrinsic nature of the schools, with their dependence (particularly in the early years) on parental input, the status of the parents' council is much more than that of either the parents' association or parent teacher association in other schools. Unfortunately, because of the lack of direction in this field, meetings of the parents' council, to which the principal and teaching staff may or may not be invited, have on occasion degenerated into arguments that have only deterred parents from further attendance or involvement. (Conversations with principals in other schools suggest that the function and level of support from parents' councils varies dramatically. While in some schools it is strong, in others it is not. One described the parents' council as 'an ineffective body with no real input into the school.') The general consensus has been that this does constitute a grey area. Nobody is sure of the role the parents' council and this makes for controversy and concern.

Spencer, an early proponent of parents' councils wrote: 'The more interest and involvement the parents have in their children's education the more effective the school will be as a formal socialising agency.'[3] This is undoubtedly so as numerous schools have proved. However, in an educational environment of almost constant change, parents as well as children require education and direction and this must necessarily emanate from within the school. This point was mentioned by Her Majesty's Inspectorate in the 1977 Report *Ten Good Schools* in which the best establishments were seen as 'places designed for learning: they take trouble to make their philosophies explicit for themselves and explain them to parents and pupils. The foundation of their work and corporate life is an acceptance of shared values.' Undoubtedly parents can and do influence schools.

That input is welcome and expected. Yet it is essential that those who influence schools externally (parents, governors, departmental bodies) and those who direct from within (principals and teaching staff) harmonise their efforts and conceptual values. Fortunately, the presence of NICIE has done much to alleviate the frustrations that were very real and powerful in the early years.

Our initial year was very much a make or break period. Everyone was anxious and there were many natural tensions and frustrations. For the teachers, it was essential to determine what the integrated curriculum meant and how it might affect the overall philosophy and ethos of the school. A document was drawn up by the Bridge staff team without the benefit of previous professional experience of integrated teaching or methods. While its preparation demanded a considerable degree of time and energy, particularly from the principal, this document has formed the essence of all that has henceforth been taught in the school. Its completion also assisted in placating an anxious body of sponsors and parents. However, it was probably a very positive inspection early in 1988 that did more than anything to relieve the gradual but constant build up of anxiety amongst governors and parents.

Religious Balance

The founders of integrated schools and those who pioneered their introduction were very much idealists. In their quest for equality the question of balance came to the fore and balance is expected in all integrated schools. It exists amongst pupils in as much as a religious balance is maintained, and this is again reflected in the composition of the teaching staff, governors and directors. In Bridge Primary School we have always been acutely aware of the need for balance; but it is an emotive and sensitive issue and one which has presented problems in various forms.

Visitors to our school have always been welcome. Their religious affiliations are not always relevant; but in some instances they are. In defining the roles of clerics and pastors within the school, we could have been seriously disadvantaged were it not for the presence and commitment of a Roman Catholic nun who visited us and remained teaching voluntarily for the best part of a year. Her presence along with that of Church of Ireland, Methodist and Presbyterian ministers helped to bring to the children a healthy appreciation of their ministry as they attended assemblies or spoke to children in their classes. The children believe that these continuing visits demonstrate interest and concern. They also provide opportunities to discuss the different aspects of Christianity. Furthermore, children come to appreciate that these human beings have something very real and worthwhile to offer them and the community at large.

However, while we have had visits from Roman Catholic priests from England and America, we have had no visits whatever from local Roman Catholic clergy who accommodate children and parents only by meeting those of them preparing for sacraments outside school. This policy of non-attendance is detrimental on two accounts. Firstly, it detracts from the sense of balance that we promote in an attempt to strengthen cross-community harmony. Secondly, it illustrates to those of us who are aware of this deliberate non-participation an unwillingness by the Catholic Church to be as concerned as I believe it should be for those members of its flock who have deigned not to choose Catholic education 'per se'. This would appear to be the general trend throughout, although there are exceptions.

Balance is also a serious consideration in terms of intake. Before 1991, over-subscription for places at our school meant that we were able to adhere strictly to a predetermined and widely accepted balance in pupil numbers. From September 1991 onwards there has been a possibility, albeit slight, that children may be refused admission, not because we are oversubscribed, but because of our agreed policy on balance. Unfortunately the Education Reform (N.I.) Order 1989 has not categorically defined the constituent forms of balance in integrated schools. But planned integrated schools do maintain that balance should not be more than 60:40 in either direction. The simple reason for this is that it necessarily follows from the underlying philosophy of integrated education as the coming together of children from the two major traditions, Protestant and Catholic, within an educational setting. Within such a context it is important that schools strive to maintain a balance in their numbers. Without balance there is the likelihood of suspicion and anxiety.

Even with a healthy balance difficulties are possible, as has been experienced in our school. In our first year when a great deal of effort was given to the preparation of six Roman Catholic boys and girls for the reception of sacraments, some Protestant members of our school community felt that a precedent for imbalance was being created in our inaugural year. (Such is the psyche of we Ulster people, suspicion is almost inbred!) However, through discussion this perception of imbalance was amended. When taken seriously integrated education forces people to face issues and confront prejudices they might not otherwise acknowledge.

In much the same way as with enrolment, so too must a sense of balance be maintained amongst teachers; and such principles beg to ask whether or not integrated education is fundamentally undemocratic in its philosophy. It has often grieved me that young men and women who are keen to secure a post at an integrated school may have their chances seriously diminished because of their religion. This is discriminatory and yet the constitution of each integrated school states that balance should exist in the staffing ratios, on the governing body and in the ancillary and administrative staff as well as in pupil enrolment. The argument used against the integration movement here, however, that the best person for the job may be neglected is rather specious. Consider maintained schools. Within such establishments would the best person for the job be a Protestant? It is very unlikely. Or, in controlled schools, would the best candidate be a Roman Catholic? The answer is the same. Some years ago when I attended an interview for a senior position in a primary school, I asked at the conclusion of the interview what my chances were in view of the fact that my religion was not that of the school's general philosophy. I was told that an appointment would be made in keeping with the religious ethos of the school. In integrated schools it does not happen this way, although positive discrimination is imperative to ensure a balanced staff. In point of fact, schools are one of the four areas exempt from the Fair Employment legislation. Nevertheless, I believe that integrated schools must state in their advertisements that they require either a Catholic or a Protestant if and when that is what they do require. Such practice does demonstrate a sense of strong conviction that will, I believe, assist the growth of integration in Northern Ireland.

Views from the Community

People not involved have a number of misconceptions about integrated education. In their research on how the integrated schools are perceived by other professionals, *Views from Outside*, the authors, Morgan, Fraser, et al, identify a degree of suspicion and unease about integrated schools.[4] Two major misapprehensions appear to have persisted since the first school opened in 1981. One is the argument that they are elitist, more suited to middle-class aspirations. It is felt that they appeal mainly to one small sector of the community which transferred children from other local schools and consequently incurred a measure of resentment within the community.

Unfortunately integrated schools could not have opened without attracting and drawing children from other quarters. In our own instance, children with only one or two years of primary education remaining, were withdrawn from other schools and sent to Bridge Primary. But it was not intended to imply that the established sectors could not provide for the academic welfare of these children. Rather, that this new form of education requires a commitment that can only be realised and appreciated through total support. In our first year there were two such children in P7 and four in P6. (Many others waited in the wings to see if the school would succeed.) But I would be very reluctant to ascribe a social label to any of those six children. They were a mixed bunch with only one identifiable common element. Each was a child of parents whose evident commitment and energy was harnessed to support and develop our school. Incidentally, one was a glazier, another a farmer, one a dentist, one a labourer, one a health visitor and another an insurance agent.

The origin of this misperception that integrated schools are middle-class and/ or elitist may be realised if one looks at the founders of the movement or at the schools themselves. By and large, they have been intellectuals with middle-class backgrounds: teachers, lecturers, lawyers, accountants, engineers, etc. But the concept would not have come to fruition had it not been for their skills, enterprise and acumen. Our school has grown considerably over the past few years and presents the same social structure as would be expected in any other primary school in any provincial town.

Another major concern, or opinion, expressed from the outside is that we are neither one thing nor the other. We are 'wishy-washy', uncertain of our direction, attractive to those of 'mixed' marriages, an emasculated attempt to breach the religious divide with watered down policies that accommodate only the non-committed. This 'opinion' is, I feel, a weapon that has been used to detract from the natural growth of the schools and dissuade people from registering their children. Religion is a serious component of integrated education and the Christian ethos is strong in Bridge Primary School. Staff, Protestant and Catholic alike, are chosen partly because they have a commitment to their own faith. As a Christian school we would subscribe to the notion that we are all the children of God; and none more so than the children themselves. We are constantly changing and struggling in our daily lives (or should be!) to attain a greater affinity with Christ. For some this is done through Protestantism; for others through Catholicism. But the teachers in our school are aware that part of their duty is to encourage a response to faith whatever 'side' the child belongs to; and this is why we ask parents to state categorically the religion of their child on entering school. The term 'Christian' is not sufficient. Teachers realise too, that it is their duty not to proselytise or to exaggerate differences. Yet they have a realistic appreciation that differences do exist. We do not proclaim Christianity at every opportunity. It is neither necessary nor realistic. What is important is that we acknowledge all forms of Christian worship and attempt to promote a greater understanding of them. While we do therefore recognise differences, our underlying philosophy stems from the attempt to create brotherhood and sisterhood between young children of different religious perspectives while affirming the strength of their parents' religious convictions. We believe that this should occur in all towns in Northern Ireland, for despite claims to the contrary, the divide does not simply exist in inner city or ghetto areas. Resentment and misunderstanding is not confined to the extremists. There is a fear in many schools of acknowledging, let alone embracing, the other side; a fact realised through attempts to establish links with schools of either tradition for the enhancement of Education for Mutual Understanding.

It has not been possible in this short chapter to identify all the problems we have encountered, or all the emotional 'highs'. However, from a managerial perspective, all the experiences have been fulfilling and enriching. None would have been realised without the support and understanding of an equally committed family, nor without the support of a committed senior management team and a body of governors, whose involvement has now given each of them a deep insight into teaching generally and a greater understanding of the inherent strengths and potential weaknesses of integrated education.

Notes

1. Everard, B. and Morris, G. (1991), *The Self Managing School: Effective School Management,* Paul Chapman, London.

2. McGaffin, P., 'The Development of an Integrated School', in *Schools Under Scrutiny,* Caul, L. (ed), Macmillan Education, 1990

3. Spencer, A.E.C.W., 'Arguments for an Integrated School System', in *Education and Policy in Northern Ireland,* 1987.

4. Morgan, V., Fraser, G., Dunn S., and Cairns E., (1992) 'Views from Outside – Other Professional's Views of the Religiously Integrated Schools in Northern Ireland', *British Journal of Religious Education,* 14,3 p 169-177.

11
The Transformation Option
Part i – Integration and Institutional Change

Chris Moffat

The aim of this chapter is to explore some of the issues which arise when a school from one of the segregated sectors in Northern Ireland seeks to become integrated. Brownlow College was the first school to be recognised officially as 'controlled integrated'. Its 'transformation' is by no means complete, but some of the lessons which have been learned are worth recording. The first part of the chapter looks at the process of change from the point of view of a member of a pro-integration community group which actively supported the transformation; the second, from the point of view of a member of staff of the school.

Many people are sceptical about the idea that a school, from whatever 'side', can become integrated in any realistic or meaningful sense. Institutional change is difficult in schools at the best of times and there are few precedents for it in Northern Ireland.[1] Moreover, parents who have worked hard together to create new integrated schools are cautious; supporting the idea of integration is not the same thing as being committed to making it work. But Brownlow may not be typical. Much of the initial impetus for change came from parents, many from outside the school. The experience of new integrated schools suggests that clear cross-community parental support is required for schools to have the necessary sense of purpose to achieve change. Both these conditions seem to have existed in Brownlow.

The initial legislation which created 'controlled integrated status' was the Dunleath Act. Originally sponsored by All Children Together in 1978, it sought to provide an opportunity for trustees of Catholic maintained schools to share the management of a controlled 'state' school with existing Protestant representatives on the board of governors of the school. The initiative for change had to come from the Protestant side, however, and other aspects of inter-church, as well as inter-communal cooperation, were not addressed in the act. For instance, change required 75 per cent support from parents at the school, but other potential parents from the minority community were not consulted. These limitations and the churches' and area boards' lack of interest in joint school management became clear when the act was invoked in the case of Throne, a Belfast controlled primary school which was facing closure. No Catholic governors were appointed either by Catholic trustees or the area board, and predictably the school failed to attract cross-community support.

The possibility of parents having more say in the development of integrated schools came with the Education Reform Order 1989. The Conservative government wanted to give wider expression to 'parental preference' and choice. In the Northern Ireland context, this made it easier for schools to be set up or transformed on the initiative of parents. Both controlled and voluntary schools could in theory seek recognition as either controlled or grant maintained integrated on the basis of parental demand expressed as a simple majority in favour in a parental ballot.

But the Education Reform Order procedure did not deal with the process of change itself or provide any guarantee that such schools would remain integrated. Nor did it provide a very clear definition of integration. The law only requires that integrated schools are 'likely to be attended by reasonable numbers of both Roman Catholic and Protestant pupils' (Art 71(8)). For controlled integrated schools, the Dunleath assumption of joint church management was retained in the Order. However, the requirement that RE provision and collective worship should remain undenominational was dropped – an important concession.

Parents who have founded new integrated schools have insisted on much stricter requirements for recognition. The NICIE *Statement of Principles* has evolved over several years out of the experience of trying to make equality a practical reality. Though the requirements of 'balance' and other principles of integrated education were developed primarily for newly established schools, they are just as relevant to schools wishing to become integrated. Their message to existing schools is that transformation is not merely about conforming to purely statutory requirements, but about reassuring parents of both traditions of the capacity of a previously mono-cultural segregated school to become genuinely integrated. The scale of change envisaged in the idea of the transformation is considerable. Given the nature of Northern Ireland society, it is likely to involve some degree of conflict.

Parental Action

The demand for integrated education in the Portadown/Brownlow/ Lurgan area grew out of an association of parents from both sides of the community. Members of the North Armagh Group for Integrated Education (NAGIE) shared a desire for an alternative to segregated schooling for their own children and supported the principle that the option should be available as of right to all parents who wanted it. During a recruitment drive for potential parents and pupils for a new integrated secondary school, however, the group was approached by the principal of a local controlled secondary school, Brownlow High School. He argued that members of NAGIE should consider sending their children to the school as it was committed to catering for the needs of each pupil regardless of religion or cultural identity and had a significantly mixed intake. Around 20% of pupils were Catholics and there were also a number of other religious and national minorities.

Not everyone in the group was persuaded by the argument; the very fact that the membership included parents and teachers connected with other secondary schools in the area made a clean break with all existing school systems by far the most attractive option. But at the time there was no government funding for new integrated schools and voluntary trust funds were already over-stretched. After much discussion a majority voted to suspend the campaign for a new integrated secondary school for a year, to give the state school a chance. Though it was recognised that the school could not change overnight, the group wanted to see evidence of a very clear commitment to the same principles of balanced structure, organisation, management, enrolment and curriculum that the new integrated schools had adopted. Anything less would fail to inspire cross-community confidence in the school.

The first step was for Brownlow to make a formal application for controlled integrated status under the Dunleath procedure, by then part of the Education and Libraries Order 1986. The next, as far as NAGIE was concerned, was for the school to demonstrate its willingness to work with the group to draw up a programme of changes which would convince potential parents that Brownlow would become genuinely integrated. The programme eventually agreed with the board of governors and accepted as necessary by the majority of staff included:

(a) the establishment of a management structure with balanced representation from both the Catholic and Protestant communities and other viewpoints and a clear commitment to the principle of integrated schooling;

(b) agreement on the need for a balanced intake of pupils, preferably as close as possible to a 50:50 ratio, but not less than 40:60 either way;

(c) commitment to the principle of balanced staffing and agreement over staffing policies to ensure steady progress towards balance;

(d) implementation of a review programme to ensure that the structure and curriculum of the school adequately reflected the needs, interests and aspirations of all within it;

(e) commitment to parental involvement in the school and to comprehensive, child-centred education.

In the short term it was also agreed:

(f) to establish a joint NAGIE-Brownlow liaison committee to review and monitor progress;

(g) to take steps to secure the appointment of an additional senior member of staff, if necessary with funds raised by NAGIE;

(h) co-option of a NAGIE member onto the Brownlow Board of Governors.

Local Parental Demand

Early in its campaign NAGIE had commissioned a survey of the demand for integrated education in the area in an attempt to persuade the Southern Education and Library Board of the need for the planned provision of integrated schooling. The board had shown no interest in the results, but the survey helped to clarify the relative strength of support for a 'transformed' Brownlow as against a hypothetical new integrated school.[2] The findings confirmed what other surveys had found: between one and two thirds of parents supported shared schooling; more Catholic parents than Protestant were supportive; but overall considerably more would support it than would consider it for their own children.[3] Support was highest in central Craigavon where the Brownlow school was situated. Here half of parents stated a definite preference for sending their children to an integrated school, suggesting that the new town was a much better potential site for an integrated school than the more polarised communities of Lurgan and Portadown.

However the survey also revealed that both central Craigavon and the school itself had an image problem, even with integrated education supporters. One fifth of parents said they would definitely consider supporting an integrated Brownlow, the same as would consider a completely new integrated school; but only one third of these (6% of the total sample) were keen on the Brownlow option. This translated into a potential enrolment after five years of a minimum of 215 and a maximum of 650 pupils. It was clear that transformation of Brownlow would not be a soft option.

In the event it took more than three years before the Brownlow governors could even make an official application for controlled integrated status. The Department of Education delayed granting permission for a parental ballot for almost a year. When it was eventually announced it was opposed by local Orange Lodges and Unionist and DUP members on the local Craigavon Council as well as by others less obviously hostile who objected to the government's apparent determination to override locally elected bodies.[4] A ballot was eventually held in February 1989. However, in the face of fierce political pressure it was declared void on a technicality and the result, although thought to be within a few points the 75 per cent required, was never announced.

A second ballot was held the following June. This coincided with the local council elections and Unionist politicians lost no time in making further political capital out of it. Despite the unhelpful political climate, an encouraging majority of 63% of parents at the school said they would continue to send their children to Brownlow if it became integrated. However, this was not the three quarters required under the 1986 Order and the proposal lapsed.

This setback posed a dilemma for members of the North Armagh Group who were keen to see definite plans for an integrated school. But a majority were persuaded that it was worth continuing with co-operation and support for another year. The commitment shown by some of the Brownlow parents and teachers and their readiness to stand up to the hostile campaign by unionist politicians had impressed the group. Moreover, a few NAGIE members had already decided to enrol their transfer-aged children at the school in the forthcoming year and they were keen see practical plans to develop a genuinely integrated curriculum.

A Brownlow-North Armagh Group liaison committee was set up and met regularly throughout the period, exploring in particular the possibility of securing funds to employ an additional senior Catholic teacher at the school. It was felt that this would increase confidence in the ability of the school to revise its curriculum and management structure. A curriculum subcommittee was also set up to run a series of public seminars, inviting teachers from a range of schools (including Brownlow) to discuss how they handled such subjects as history, religious education, Irish/Ulster Studies, sports and community relations and the 'hidden curriculum'. These meetings and other joint social events helped to strengthen personal relationships between parents in and outside the school.

The implementation of the Education Reform Order in 1989 gave an unexpected opportunity for the school to renew its application for controlled integrated status under the new procedure for recognition which required only a simple majority in favour of change in a parental ballot. The Brownlow governors' proposal to run another ballot was opposed again by local Unionist councillors, one of whom by this time was a governor of the school nominated by the area board. He orchestrated a campaign to oppose 'the sacrifice of a state school' and its 'take-over by unelected parents', and also attacked the motives and competence of the staff and principal of the school. Despite this, 45 per cent of parents voted in favour of change – not enough for the school to proceed with the proposal, but a creditable achievement in the circumstances.

Many thought this was the end of the Brownlow option. But there was an unexpected initiative to revive the application by parents within the school. The new Order included provision for a petition signed by at least 20 per cent of parents of children at the school to request a further ballot. A very committed group organised a petition and a ballot third time round produced a result of 60.5 per cent in favour of change. Out of 260 who could have voted, 133 voted for, and 87 voted against.

Structural Change

This positive vote made it possible for the school to formally announce the process of change which had in fact already begun. A Brownlow Support Group was set up to bring together all the groups interested in the development of the school. The anti-integration campaigners had predicted that the change would result in a mass exodus of existing pupils. But in the event, only one child was removed to another school.

A number of major problems still remained. The school was now meant to be 'managed in a way that would make it likely that it would be attended by reasonable numbers of both Roman Catholic and Protestant pupils'; but the legislation provided no clear mechanism for achieving the balanced management, staffing and curriculum which would make this possible. 'Controlled integrated status' depended on a degree of cooperation between the churches that had not previously been demonstrated. It also required responsible involvement by the education board, in particular in making appropriate appointments to the board of a controlled integrated school.

The reconstitution of the board of governors for Brownlow showed that neither the board nor all the churches were necessarily willing to do this, and the issue became a major focus for conflict during the school's first formative year. Parents at the school elected four parents to the new board and had no difficulty in choosing two to represent the Catholic tradition and two to represent the Protestant traditions as specified in the NICIE *Statement of Principles*. A similar balance was achieved in the nomination of two teacher representatives on the board. Three of the Area Board's possible four nominees, however, were people drawn from the Protestant tradition, two of whom had been leading activists in campaigns against the move towards integration.

Supporters of integrated education saw such appointments as a deliberate attempt to prevent precisely the kind of changes which would be necessary for the school to work towards balanced staffing and enrolment, and hardly a gesture that would signal a spirit of reconciliation to potential parents. In the event, a number of formal complaints persuaded the Department of Education to intervene. The area board was directed to 'take reasonable steps to satisfy itself that the persons it proposed to choose for appointment appear to have a commitment to the continuing viability of Brownlow College as a controlled integrated school.' After some hesitation the board agreed to nominate two Catholics and two Protestants. There are still worries, however, about how it will exercise its powers in future nominations.

The mechanism for securing joint church representation on the board of Brownlow also revealed weaknesses in the statutory provisions for a controlled integrated school. As expected the nominating trustees of local Catholic maintained schools chose not to take up their right to make nominations to the Brownlow board and, under the Education Reform Order, the default power of nomination reverted to the area board. In this case the Southern Area Board sought informal recommendations from local integrated primary schools and the Northern Ireland Council for Integrated Education before eventually making satisfactory nominations. But supporters of integrated education felt that would have been more appropriate if the legislation had given formal rights of nomination to local integrated schools and trusts in the first place.

Issues for the Future

From the beginning the most important issue for the North Armagh Group when confronted with the prospect of working with Brownlow rather than starting a new school from scratch, was the question of how a so-called 'Protestant' school could move to a position of genuine curriculum balance and equality of esteem for the two traditions amongst the staff and other structures of the school. Equally important, given the non-involvement of the Catholic Church, was that of convincing the school of the need to create opportunities for the Catholic community to become involved in the spiritual life of the school. These were daunting issues for a group of ordinary parents who had no formal status or professional standing, let alone the right or the wish to impose their views on others. But both were and are crucial in sustaining the confidence of supporters of integrated education in the school.

An important factor in this respect, has been the secondment of an experienced and committed Catholic teacher from Lagan College, made possible by a generous grant from the Halley Stewart Trust in response to a request from the North Armagh Group. Even in a small 'Protestant' school one additional senior Catholic teacher does not contribute much to 'balance'. But it has provided the essential professional expertise and lay witness for denominational instruction and pastoral care for Catholic pupils. If it is at a sufficiently senior level, it can also ensure the representation of Catholic views in curriculum and planning decisions. More importantly in a school that is ready for change, like Brownlow, the right person can act as a catalyst and give much needed leadership in exploring how Christian ideas of reconciliation can be incorporated into the relationships and values of the school.[5]

Such a development was crucial for Brownlow – not least in sustaining cross-community confidence in the school. But it would not have been possible without a sizable sum to cover a senior post for an initial two or three years. The very fact that a so-called 'state' school must resort to charitable funds for this important stage in creating an integrated ethos, raises questions about the strength of government commitment to facilitating the transformation of existing schools to integrated status. In practice, the voluntary principle may give supporters of genuine integration a sense of continuing involvement in the process of change; nevertheless lack of resources will remain a continuing problem for Brownlow and for any other schools considering transformation. DENI sets aside considerable resources for other forms of education reorganisation, such as school amalgamations; there is a strong argument for similar levels of support for integration developments.

For Brownlow, another problem could be the link which the label 'controlled' implies. Grant maintained integrated schools have sufficient autonomy to ensure that their 'ethos' is relatively protected from political interference, and their commitment to power-sharing is backed up by the explicit rules contained within the NICIE *Statement of Principles*, which in particular emphasise deep parental involvement. By contrast, power-sharing on governing bodies of 'controlled' integrated schools is much more open to outside pressures. Nomination rights are held by religious and education boards with no specific commitment to power-sharing and their nomination procedures are not open to public scrutiny. Without clear rules there is no guarantee that integrated schools which remain under board 'control' will be able to protect and maintain an integrated ethos and curriculum. And parents will worry that their concerns about tokenism on issues like staff appointments or admissions, will be ignored or ridiculed.

It remains to be seen whether the Brownlow experiment can be repeated in other schools and communities. In some respects its situation provided a unique opportunity for transformation. Even though Craigavon had failed as a new town, it had not become a traditional, inward-looking community. There was some mixing of pupils at primary school level. Both sides of the community had many experiences in common and good cross-community relations reflected this shared experience of good times and bad.

Another positive factor is that North Armagh is one of the few areas in Northern Ireland which has a non-selective system. Although controlled and Catholic maintained secondary schools in the area are completely separate, all are (or were) comprehensive, at least up to 14 plus. In a selective area there would not have been any obvious potential school for transformation and a forced choice between grammar or secondary would have brought out suspicions of a hidden agenda of middle-class exclusivity – not the least of the social factors underlying communal mistrust. In a context where an all-ability ethos is accepted as the norm, transformation of an existing school had a less disruptive effect on inter-school relations than it would have in a selective area.

Given the Northern Ireland political climate and suspicions about 'social engineering', it may be inevitable that the legislation must maintain the fiction that the development toward integration within an existing school is a natural process which is merely confirmed by a formal change of name. The experience of Brownlow is that it is more complex than this. Institutional change is a long and often difficult process which almost invariably entails conflict. Such conflicts are not just, or even mainly, between the two 'sides', but bottled up within each communal stronghold. Although Brownlow College is not fully integrated yet, it has gone a long way towards meeting the wishes of parents who wanted genuine integrated schooling for their children. It has shown that parental action can help to overcome the divisions which lock institutions into the past and blight people's hopes for the future.

Notes

1. Cathcart, H.R., 'The Politics of 'No Change' ' in Caul, L., (ed) (1990) *Schools Under Scrutiny*, Macmillan; Dunn, S., (1986) 'The Role of Education in the Northern Ireland Conflict', *Oxford Rev*, Vol 1; No 3.

2. *Integrated Education: A Survey of Parental Demand*, The Coopers and Lybrand Report, Nov 1989.

3. Fortnight/ Sunday Times Survey of Northern Ireland (1973) *Fortnight* no. 62. Northern Ireland Attitude Survey in Brown E.M.(1983), *Nation, Class and Creed in Northern Ireland*. Fortnight/RTE survey of political opinion in N. Ireland, *Fortnight*, no. 178, Oct/Nov 1980. Fortnight/Irish Times Poll, 1986. Standing Advisory Commission on Human Rights, *Seventeenth Annual Report*, 1991/2.

4. *Lurgan Mail*, 9.3.89, 'Board chief declines to meet council'; *Portadown Times*, 17.3.89, 'Council gives mixed schools a caning'; *Portadown Times*, 24.3.89, 'Council to meet education chief on mixed schools'.

5. *Portadown Examiner*, 23.4.92, 'Brownlow College on the Way to full Integration'. See also *NAGIE newsletter No 5*, March 1992.

Part ii – The Transformation Process Viewed from the Staffroom

Errol Lemon

In the first part of this chapter the process of change at Brownlow was looked at from the point of view of a pro-integrationist community group. This second part deals with the process of change as it unfolded, from the point of view of a member of staff from within the school. I write from the perspective of a member of the senior management team in the school, staff representative on the board of governors when the process was first inaugurated and as someone committed to the concept of integrated education. It should be borne in mind that at the time when the integration issue was under debate, the staff was, and continues to be, subject to all the pressures associated with the introduction of the Northern Ireland Curriculum and other aspects of the Education Reform Order. The broad strategy was therefore left up to the board of governors, the headmaster, NAGIE, and the senior management team, with teachers recruited to assist with specific tasks as they arose.

The Board of Governors

At a board of governors meeting in September 1987, came the first official mention of integration. The headmaster informed the meeting that he had been approached by members of the North Armagh Group for Integrated Education with a view to ascertaining the attitude of the school to a possible change in status. In their first newsletter the group had claimed that they had already 80 committed families representing up to 135 potential pupils, achieved after one public meeting and minimal advertising. In this way the myth was launched that integration was, in its conception, an extra-school phenomenon; and this was used later to deflect criticism from the board of governors who could claim that they were merely responding to reasonable requests from outside the school. In fact, of course, conception requires two parties and had NAGIE not received a sympathetic response from the headmaster when they first approached him nothing more would have been heard of the matter. This point alone indicates the pivotal role of the headmaster in the subsequent developments.

The headmaster revealed his thinking on integration in relation to the school in an interview in May 1988 in the NAGIE *Newsletter*:

I personally think integration is the way forward for Brownlow. The ethos of the school has been basically Protestant and we presume those Catholics who attend the school at the moment find nothing offensive in this and certainly there has been no demand for change from them. However, there may be in the wider community a number of Catholic parents who, if they could see more recognition of their aims and aspirations, would be willing to send their children to the school. We are aware that many of the parents of children at the school at the moment would be opposed to any form of official integration. Presumably they have no objection to the mixed school concept otherwise their children would not be here, but they balk at the idea of fully-fledged integration. As an integrationist committed to respecting all points of view I must acknowledge their fears but ultimately, if the school does become fully integrated they will have to search their consciences and decide whether they will still send their children to us. For our part we will endeavour to allay their fears as we believe they are based on a fundamental misunderstanding of what an integrated school is.

With parental choice becoming law we, if we become integrated, will be offering parents another alternative within the state system... At the moment integrationists have no choice. In the day-to-day running of the school and in the way we care for each child we don't see a need for many changes. When we visited Lagan College what struck us was how similar it was to ourselves in so many respects. However if we go integrated there are bound to be alterations in the ethos of the school and in the academic and extra-curricular activities.

We have accepted the principle of a balanced staffing and management. We are aware of the bad image the Brownlow area has and we know that much of this is not within our control to alter. We know we have a good school with many achievements to our credit.

The headmaster at the governors' meeting in March 1988 had been able to report that 'a majority of parents had replied affirmatively to the Governors' survey of parental opinion with respect to possible integration at the school.' To initiate the process at Brownlow, however, was not the responsibility of the board of governors as a whole but rather the four people nominated by the transferrors or superseded managers of contributory controlled schools. In practice Brownlow had opened in 1973 and was not a transferred school in this sense. Nevertheless it was these four individuals who could block the whole process at the starting line by voting 'No'. Aware of their power in this respect and using arguments of a pro-democratic nature rather than pro-integrationist as such, all four, including two Protestant clergymen, one Church of Ireland and one Presbyterian, voted 'Yes.' This was a particularly brave decision on the part of the latter two men as they were both aware by this stage that there were elements within their own churches bitterly opposed to integration.

The board of governors thus passed on the request to initiate the procedure for a change in status to the area board. To give some idea of the pressures on the school and the way myths about cultural identity became entwined in the debate, I turn briefly to the way the change was perceived by opponents of the possible move towards integrated status. Once it was revealed that a staff ballot on integration had produced a 'significant majority in favour'[1] and that the reaction of the Board of Governors had been 'not unfavourable', the battle for the hearts and minds and the votes of the Brownlow parents was well and truly joined. Both the local and the Belfast press published attacks on the integration plans by Craigavon DUP councillors and others.[2] It was claimed that the parents were not fully aware of the implications behind the venture and that:

> While it is true that the majority of the staff voted in favour of the new idea, it must be pointed out that there is a division at senior staff level, with many teachers only voting in favour rather than risk the possibility of losing their jobs.

It was argued that if the proposed changes went ahead, it would undoubtedly mean that new teaching staff appointed in the future would be Roman Catholic, to make up an even balance. It would mean in fact discrimination against Protestants as: 'It will involve the introduction of the Irish language and Gaelic culture into the school curriculum which I am sure goes against the grain of many parents.'

A letter to the local newspaper carried this argument further: 'This new venture is being encouraged by the ecumenical movement and the Alliance Party, but according to reports does not seem to be getting a favourable response from the Roman Catholic Church. It has claimed it does not support integrated education. Surely this defeats the whole purpose of mixed schooling.'

The Mid-Ulster District of the Independent Loyal Orange Institution demanded: 'What evidence is there that pupil numbers would significantly increase with integration?' They expressed concern that the only state school in Brownlow would be 'sacrificed' without adequate research as to the benefits and suggested that 'the pressing necessity is for an exact definition of an integrated school,' pointing out that there was nothing to prohibit a Roman Catholic from attending a state school. The Order seemed to have already made up their minds about integration as they claimed: 'What makes the integrated school movement different is, in fact, its process of indoctrination of the pupils and the propagandist intention.' What they further wanted to know was: 'Who will safeguard the interests of the Protestant pupils?'

The debate was taken up at a Craigavon Council meeting, where the first ballot proposal was discussed. A DUP Councillor alleged that an attempt was being made to 'de-Protestantise' the school and turn it into a 'semi-Roman Catholic' one. A motion condemning the Brownlow ballot was passed by eight votes to nil, the two SDLP members and one Workers Party member at the meeting earlier having left. This was a pity as it would have been interesting to see how they would have responded to a claim made when the motion was seconded, that 'ecumenicism and communism were behind this sinister move.'[3]

Curriculum and Culture
How far these claims were justified, has to be evaluated in the light of the background to Brownlow's move towards integration. The school had always been mixed with the Catholic numbers varying between 15 and 20 per cent. Until then there had been no overt recognition of this fact. Indeed it was the arrival of a number of Vietnamese boat people that first stimulated thinking about the problems facing a school with a multi-cultural intake.[4] One result of this was the

development of Multi-cultural Education in the junior school which dealt specifically with Third World issues of a political, social, economic and cultural nature.

When the idea of integration was first mooted consideration was given to the effect this might have on the curriculum, and as a gesture of intent it was decided to introduce Irish as an option in the junior school. This has been operating for three years now and it is interesting to note that nearly three-quarters of the children studying it are Protestants.

There was an on-going programme of cross-community contacts which fitted in well with the aims of Education for Mutual Understanding. The school had developed strong links with a Catholic high school in Portadown and had arranged joint residentials, ski, water sport, charity events, quizzes and educational visits. I participated in a joint water sports holiday to the South of France. However, I would tend to agree with others[5] writing of such breaks, that 'the Pleasant Interlude with Interaction' works in the personal arena, but changes wrought do not always stand up when group labels again come to the fore.

An area of the curriculum often seen as contentious is history. I am Head of History. Our syllabus had always tried to strike a balance between local, provincial, national, European and world issues. In the junior school one term per year was taken up with local history, a particular interest of mine. It could be defined as cultural heritage stressing the shared elements in our background. A topic on Irish history was studied each year which almost invariably examined diverse elements in our culture such as the Plantation, the Williamite wars and the Famine. We took the Ireland 1906-1972 option in GCSE and the local history coursework element we studied was the Lady's Day Riot in Lurgan in 1879 during which the police shot dead two Home Rule demonstrators. This offered the opportunity to study a contentious event from differing viewpoints. We faced the problem common to all schools in studying Irish history; that of finding good quality, balanced textbooks suitable for schoolchildren. I have never had any difficulty teaching contentious issues such as the origins of the present troubles — not at least in terms of pupil reaction. There are no real problems in incorporating much of this material in the School Designed Units which are emerging from the History Programmes of Study.

One of the features of considering the issue of changing status, however, was that the school began to examine its assumptions in relation both to its overt and hidden curriculum. What messages were being sent to Catholic parents by a system which failed to differentiate between Catholics and Protestants, which though theoretically non-denominational, was essentially Protestant in ethos and practice? As a controlled school, Brownlow had provided religious education in line with statutory requirements. A number of pupils, specifically Muslims and Jehovah's Witnesses, had exercised their right to opt out. Muslims were allowed time out of class on Fridays to attend prayers at the local mosque and a member of the Jehovah's Witnesses community came in each morning to take their assembly. (Incidentally they have been amongst the most firm supporters of integration.)

Catholics had never exercised this right and had attended non-denominational assemblies and timetabled RE classes without any apparent embarrassment; and there was a largely unspoken assumption that this acquiescence indicated acceptance. But such negative acceptance was very different from the kind of positive participation expected from all denominations in a genuinely integrated school.

If there was to be parity of esteem between the two main religious groups then it was clear the status of Catholicism within the school would have to be enhanced to the point where it was given equal billing with Protestantism. That this process would be a contentious one became clear when even the introduction of the shorter form of the Lord's Prayer in assembly was taken as evidence of a 'Romeward' trend in the school. Nevertheless it was decided to press on with changes which would enhance the position of Catholics within the school.

Lessons in Democracy

In relation to Brownlow High School it was easy to make the accusation that the only reason for opting for integration was to avoid redundancies and possible closure. Indeed these very accusations came increasingly to the fore in the anti-integrationist campaign.[6] It would be foolish to deny that this was not a factor in the decision, but to suggest it was the only one or even the dominant one would be equally facile. The headmaster was relatively new to the school at the time and had long been committed to the idea of integrated education. He felt that the situation in Brownlow indicated that it was well placed to become the first controlled integrated school in Northern Ireland. As well as a moderate percentage of Catholic pupils in the school, community relations in the area were good, there was a readiness within the school to innovate and the staff were almost unanimously in favour of the change. The decision to continue the attempt to move towards integration had not been taken lightly; parents had been consulted at every stage; contacts had been made with Lagan College and other integrated schools and several 'Baker Days' had been set aside to explore the implications of the change.

The story of the battle to change the status of the school in itself goes some way to refuting the claim that the motivation was purely selfish. Although professionally and temperamentally the staff were reluctant to get involved in the ballot campaign they were fully behind it and were confident that the majority in favour of integration would eventually win the day. The first ballot was declared void on a technicality and the second failed to get the required 75% majority. However, a change in the legal position shortly afterwards meant that in future a simple majority would be sufficient. All we felt we had to do was sit still, turn the other cheek to the hostility of the anti-campaigners and the ballot box would see us through.

The third ballot however taught us we should have had more respect for the power of propaganda. To our chagrin and dismay even though we needed only a simple majority under the new legislation, we lost narrowly on a low turnout. There was much disappointment and soul searching over what had gone wrong. Clearly we had been over-confident. The positive results in the first two polls had lulled us into a false sense of security. The anti-integrationist campaign had clearly got through to some people at least and the moderates, possibly getting impatient with the number of polls, had abstained.

Parent representatives on the board of governors felt strongly that since the new Education Reform Order provided for a petition, one should be organised. They set about collecting signatures and within a week had 58, well over the 20 per cent necessary. There is not room to describe this fourth ballot campaign except to say that we, i.e. the pro-integrationists, amongst whom were numbered the staff (all but one) the governors (all but one) and the parents who had signed the petition, realised that merely re-running the ballot would not be enough. We resolved to learn by our mistakes. We would have to make a more determined effort to get our views across and take the opposition on head-on, not let them win the argument by default, and, given the potential ballot-fatigue, do all in our power to ensure there was a good turn-out of voters.

As the request for the ballot had come from the parents, we felt it important that they were seen to be the main movers behind the new tactics and that the governors as such should take a back seat. An ad-hoc committee consisting of parents sympathetic to integration and the headmaster was set up and a plan of campaign was mapped out. The opposition was led by the DUP and by the member of our board of governors for whom the anti-integration cause had become a personal mission. Inevitably, as this was the fourth ballot campaign a lot of the old arguments were re-cycled.

The eventual positive result in February 1991 was greeted with considerable satisfaction in the staff room if not elsewhere. But we had always known that if we went integrated some parents would withdraw their children. The question was how many? That 87 parents had voted against the proposed change compared to 133 in favour was certain, but by the end of the summer term 1991, only one pupil had officially requested transfer to another school and this was the child of a parent who had received considerable publicity in the local press for his opposition to the change. In our election campaign we had sought every opportunity to re-assure these parents, and it was to this theme I returned in an interview with the local paper:

> To those parents who voted 'No' we have a particular responsibility. It is the continued presence of their children in the school that we believe would make it genuinely integrated, in that it would reflect a broader spectrum of opinion than a school made up of only pro-integrationists could show... We would ask these parents to give us a chance and re-assure them that changes made would be gradual and optional in contentious areas... all this fits in with our concept of what an integrated school ought to be — not a dilution or melting pot, but an institution characterised by openness and intellectual curiosity about the stimulating variety of human culture.[7]

'Planned' Integration

The crucial question in all this is how does an integrated school differ from a non-integrated school? One of the unexpected problems which Brownlow faced, even from some of its supporters, was the suggestion that the school would not be truly integrated because it would not be a 'planned' integrated school. However, it would not be 'planned' only in the sense that it was not 'originally' planned as an integrated school. If anything, even more 'planning' was required to effect a change in status that would satisfy recognised criteria in relation to the definition of integration.

A criticism levelled at existing 'planned' integrated schools is that they are middle-class institutions catering for the converted and are therefore really effecting no change in society. None of these criticisms can be applied to Brownlow. The immediate catchment area is almost entirely working-class and there would be in the school – at least in the first few years – a number of pupils not philosophically committed to integration. To convince such pupils and their parents that educating Catholic and Protestant pupils together can be successful is surely a much more desirable form of integration than that which already exists – the difference being between teaching people to swim and providing a pool for those who can already swim.

A direct consequence of the change for Brownlow has been in the school's social role. Integrated schools differ from non-integrated in their concern for preparing the children for life in a pluralistic society. The distinction may be blurred somewhat now the Northern Ireland Curriculum and in particular the cross-curricular themes of Cultural Heritage and Education for Mutual Understanding have come on stream. But integrated schools are at an advantage over mainstream schools in that they have, as it were, a captive audience representative of the two main traditions within their walls and are able to pursue a kind of internal EMU. If current research proves to be accurate, this will be more effective in breaking down barriers of mistrust than the occasional encounters of external EMU can hope to achieve. This notion has considerable implications not only in terms of curriculum design and syllabus content but also in relation to classroom organisation and teaching methodologies, as well as extra-curricular activities.

Implicit in the notion of preparing children for life in a pluralistic society are the concepts of tolerance and respect for the views of others. There may be some question begging here in that it is not clear how integrated schools would react if pupils were intolerant and disrespectful of others. It might be argued that such individuals are unlikely to attend integrated schools in the first place and that therefore the problem is not likely to arise. Brownlow, however, has had to give serious consideration to how it would face this problem if it arose.

In fact it has arisen more immediately in the board of governors. A vigorous anti-integrationist campaign conducted by a school governor representing the area education board who promised to remain on the integrated school board to ensure it would not be inundated with 'Gaelic culture' certainly tried our principles of tolerance and mutual respect to the limit. Louis MacNeice described him well:

> The hard cold fire of the northerner
> Frozen into his blood
> The fire of his basalt
> Glares from behind the mica of his eyes.

Faced with such breadth of opinion on the board, another governor was prompted to say: 'Would you go on picking a player for your team who consistently and deliberately attempted to score goals for the opposition and who sought to have every goal you scored disallowed for some obscure infringement that existed only in his biased imagination?' But the presence of such individuals can be useful in that they help focus the mind on what one means by toleration and respect and where one would place the parameters.

It has had the effect of making the school more aware of the ethical problems associated with the idea of social engineering. Those who tend to support integration are by definition liberal in their attitudes with a distaste for manipulation of any kind however well intentioned. Brownlow staff like those in any other school exhibit the full range of professional types and on the matter of integration would range from those who would see it as being sufficient that there was a balance within the school and rely on the hidden curriculum of day-to-day contact to do its job, to those who would advocate a much more interventionist approach, requiring pupils to overtly confront the problems of a divided society. The dilemma is that in seeking to break the mould of exclusiveness they may have to resort to methods not far removed from the indoctrination techniques they find so objectionable when used by the segregationists.

Another vexed question for Brownlow is that of balance. Brownlow started off with an 85:15 imbalance in favour of Protestants pupils and with only one Catholic member of staff. Clearly if the school is to be successfully integrated many more Catholic pupils than Protestant pupils will have to be recruited over a number of years. There are practical difficulties here apart from, but related to, the official opposition of the Catholic Church. For example it does not seem likely that the school will be welcomed in the local Catholic primary schools which liaise with a reputable local Catholic comprehensive or other nearby Catholic secondary schools. But the presence of integrated primary schools in the area has begun to make a difference, and the projected first year intake for 1993 is 30% up on the previous year, with twelve primary schools contributing, including a number of Catholic ones.

Balancing the pupils and balancing the staff are related problems as far as Brownlow is concerned and the solving of the former would contribute greatly to the solving of the latter. If numbers increased new staff would have to be recruited and this would give the opportunity of recruiting more Catholics onto the staff, notwithstanding the difficulties inherent in policies of positive discrimination.

One direct consequence of integration for Brownlow has been an enhancement of the status of Christianity in the school. The school prospectus indicates that as a Christian College, Brownlow aims to be Christian in ethos, ensuring through the Northern Ireland Common RE programme, regular worship and extra curricular provision, that our pupils learn together and experience together those values and beliefs which are common to all Christians, while also providing for the pupils of those parents who require it, a separate and specific programme of denominational care. The school will also welcome and facilitate the clergy of all Christian denominations represented in the college.

While this higher profile for the Christian outlook might bring it more in line with the relationship between religion and education in maintained schools and assist the school in attracting Catholic pupils, it may be that it has quite a different effect on those who either have no religious beliefs or who espouse the concept of secular education. Perhaps the idea of integration itself, and the perceived personal and social benefits that follow from it are powerful enough to overcome any misgivings any particular interest group might feel in relation to the compromising of their beliefs.

Notes

1. *Portadown Times*, 8.1.1989.
2. *Belfast News Letter*, 14.1.88, 'Integrated college plans slammed'; *Lurgan Mail*, 14.1.1988, 'Division amongst senior staff, says Biggs'; *Lurgan Mail*, 21.1.1989, 'Republic Culture feared'.
3. *Lurgan Mail*, 18.3.1989, 'Council gives mixed school a caning'; *Belfast Telegraph*, 24.3.1989, 'Talks on plans to integrate school'; 5.4.1989, 'Alderman slur claim'.
4. Kernaghan, E., D.A.S.E. Dissertation, *An examination of the provision made for non-English pupils in a Northern Ireland school*, Queen's University, Belfast.
5. Trew, K. *Project Children 1987 Evaluation*, Department of Psychology, Queen's University, Belfast. See also Trew. K., 'Evaluating the impact of contact schemes for Catholic and Protestant children', in Harbison, J., (Ed.) (1988) *Growing Up in Northern Ireland*.
6. *Lurgan Mail*, 24.1.1991; 'Say No to Integrated Schooling says Concerned Parents of Craigavon Circular'.
7. *Lurgan Mail*, 21.2.1991.

12
Shared Governance
Maintaining Shared Participation in Integrated Schools

Alan Smith

The most important feature which distinguishes integrated schools today from earlier attempts to create mixed schools is that the impetus for their foundation has come from parents. The motivation has been pragmatic rather than political or proselytising and it has been important for the schools not to become identified with traditionally powerful or partisan groups in society. Instead, credibility and trust have come from a community development process involving parents from different traditions working toward a common goal. This chapter looks at this process and in particular at how it has contributed to the distinctive ethos of integrated schools. Essentially this ethos includes the principles of parental involvement, the acceptance of the need for structural safeguards to encourage a sense of joint ownership by the two main cultural traditions in Northern Ireland, and shared Christian values.

Community Development
Typically the initiative has come from a small number of concerned parents meeting informally and discussing the possibility of an integrated school in their own area. This has led to further meetings and tentative plans drawing on the previous experience of parents from other areas. Gradually the group has expanded and through discussion become aware of the need to make a conscious attempt to reach and involve people from both sides of the community. At some point a public meeting in the local area will take place to announce plans and gauge public support. Difficult decisions have to be made concerning basic principles, a school site, premises, staffing, enrolment and finance. All these potentially expose any lack of solidarity within the group – or confirm and strengthen the sense of common purpose and commitment to the distinctive characteristics of an integrated school.

There are no short cuts to the process of community development and the need for people to develop the trust and confidence in each other which leads to joint decision-making. It is highly significant that most groups have adopted consensus models of decision-making. Rather than go straight for the divisiveness of a vote on contentious issues, members have accepted the need to listen to the diversity of opinion and, where possible, make decisions without a vote. This may mean that the views of some individuals must bow to the wishes of the overall group, but the consensus procedure allows it to be recognised and acknowledged. Some schools have persevered with this principle more than others. The more passionate argue that the need to vote is an inverse measure of group cohesion, but practical pressures also have a bearing. It is easy to understand how a consensus procedure, which inevitably leads to protracted discussion, takes its toll in terms of stamina and emotional energy. Nevertheless, consensus decision-making remains more than an aspiration for integrated schools and has been incorporated into the written constitutions and schemes of management of most.

Parental Involvement

The high level of parental involvement in founding integrated schools generates a strong sense of shared ownership amongst parents, and it is no surprise that it has been carried over into many of the formal structures in the schools. The first schools were set up as limited companies managed by boards of directors, a significant number of whom were elected by parents in annual general meeting. In the early days it was mainly parents on these bodies who interviewed, appointed and employed teachers. Even now with government funding and recognition, it is not unusual for roughly half of the governing body to be parents.

Most integrated schools' constitutions and schemes of management secure a prominent place for parents in many other areas. Most, for example, have a clause which states that the school should:

> promote and protect the rights of parents to be involved in the
> decision-making and community life of the school, while respecting
> the role of staff as professional teachers.

One way that this is achieved is through membership of the school's committees. Most schemes of management specify that committees or sub-committees established by the governing body should contain at least one teacher and one parent, thus providing an effective way of involving parents who are not governors.

All integrated schools also provide for a parents' council or parents' association which is part of the institutional structure and not simply an appendage, formed or disbanded at the whim or prerogative of the principal (as is a common perception in Northern Ireland). The parents' council is not only concerned with social and fund-raising activities but also provides a forum for parents to raise issues concerning the school and its development. Experience and success in operating a parents' council has been varied. Some have been more effective than others in bringing issues to the attention of the governors. Some are highly organised and have drafted their own constitutions. Others have been more *ad hoc*. But in general, experience has shown that parents are willing to participate when opportunities are provided.

In this sense, integrated schools are no different from other schools which grapple with the issue of organising parental involvement effectively; but it means they must come to terms with a variety of forms of parental involvement. Although it may not appeal to all parents (or teachers), access to decision-making and management roles is as important as participation in the social life of the school and interaction with teachers concerning an individual child's education. As recent research has shown[1] high levels of parental involvement have important implications, particularly for teachers; but it is likely that integrated schools will continue to be at the forefront of attempts to understand how diverse aspirations in this area might be achieved in practice.

An equally important issue for parents is how the ideals of the founding group can be sustained and reflected in decisions made by future groups of parents involved in management. The institutions of church and state do not have the same degree of influence over the ethos of integrated schools as their maintained and controlled school counterparts. It is the founding parents and their successors and teachers within the schools who have most influence. But while this may make integrated schools both more autonomous and responsive, it can mean that they are more susceptible to the ebb and flow of different parental commitments. Parents are a transient population. In this respect the involvement of supporting trusts, and latterly of NICIE, have served to guard against the possible erosion of important founding principles. But founding parents have also been concerned to ensure that new parents themselves understand and accept the importance of their responsibility for the future of the schools – hence the importance of strategies to involve them in induction processes to explain how the school functions. The evolution of integrated schools however cannot avoid a healthy tension between concerns to maintain certain basic principles and the aspiration that the schools should be responsive, participatory and democratic institutions.

Supporting Organisations and Trusts

Whilst each school grew from a group of parents, legal considerations dictated that the parent group should not own the school premises if it wished to receive grant-aid at a later date. Thus the first formal structures associated with the early schools were charitable supporting trusts. At one time it looked as though each new integrated school might have its own supporting trust, but it was also recognised that there were arguments for limiting the number of supporting trusts to a few geographical areas. The most widely accepted view was that they should coincide with the five education and library boards, although in most cases the interests and energies of the supporting trust groups proved to be considerably more localised.

In broad terms, the role of the supporting trusts in relation to the first schools was: first, a property holding function, which in some cases involved acting as landlord, receiving rent and being responsible for capital development of a school until it was viable and in a position to apply for grant-aid to purchase premises itself; and second, a trusteeship role, seeking to ensure that the founding principles of each school were not ignored in future development. This role was exercised largely through the right of trusts to make appointments to integrated schools governing bodies.

In practice success in fulfilling these functions has varied. A number of people involved with the support trusts were not parents of school-age children, so their nomination to the governing bodies of integrated schools added a valuable perspective when issues preoccupying the parent group threatened to dominate more general issues of school board discussion. Questions, however, have been raised about the composition of area trusts and their trusteeship role regarding the ethos of integrated schools. The initial membership of the trusts was inevitably drawn from people declaring an interest in establishing an integrated school in a particular area. In this sense the trustees were self-selecting. Qualifications for trusteeship were to be committed, willing to act and to be there first. Initial attempts were made to set up democratic associations to elect and replace trustees, but the mechanism proved cumbersome and difficult to operate in practice. Another option, whereby existing trustees nominated their successors proved more efficient, but is open to the criticism that it can lead to a 'closed shop' which is self-replicating and unresponsive to new ideas. Critics argued that this model of trusteeship merely replicates patronising structures which already exist elsewhere in the education system. The compromise, which the later trusts adopted, was for trustees to be directors of a limited company, elected at an annual general meeting.

Since the introduction of grant maintained integrated status, the responsibility of trusteeship for the integrated ethos of the school has devolved onto the 'foundation governors' within the integrated school governing body. Thus the main formal role of the supporting trusts has been diminished. Strictly speaking, foundation governors now decide on their own replacements, but for most schools, consultation with an area trust is a continuing practice, and in some cases it is a non-statutory but accepted principle that a number of the foundation governors are appointed by a trust. The continuing debate within the integrated schools movement about the issue of trusteeship highlights the absence of social institutions within Northern Ireland which parents can look to with confidence to protect principles of integration.

The Northern Ireland Council for Integrated Education (NICIE) grew partly out of a recognition of the need to ensure that the principles of integrated schools become anchored to stable and durable structures and that their interests are adequately protected and represented within overall arrangements for the administration of education. The stimulus which initially brought the treasurers of all the trusts and schools together however, was a recognition of a common interest in coordinating funding. A meeting was jointly convened by All Children Together and the Belfast Trust for Integrated Education leading to a series of negotiations to agree on a constitutional framework which eventually led to the emergence of NICIE as the body representative of most schools and supporting organisations involved in integrated education. The three functions of NICIE are: (a) the creation of a representative forum for debate and policy development; (b) financial co-ordination; and, (c) support for parent groups and existing schools. It is made up of representatives of its member organisations, comprising integrated schools, supporting trusts and an association of teachers in integrated schools. These in turn elect representatives to serve on the Council's executive body where they are joined by appointees from the Department of Education.

NICIE contributes to maintaining the distinctive characteristics of integrated schools in three main ways. Firstly, it has drawn up a *Statement of Principles* to which member organisations subscribe and acceptance of which is a condition of membership of NICIE. Secondly, it has an advisory, and in the case of some schools, a direct role in nominating representatives to the integrated school governing bodies. Thirdly, it is consulted increasingly by statutory bodies and receives requests to provide representatives to serve on professional bodies and committees on educational matters.

Constitutional and Structural Safeguards

Each new integrated school was founded as a company limited by guarantee with the board of directors acting as school governors until the school becomes grant-aided by government. The school constitution is comprised of the memorandum and articles of association of the company which founded the school. The memorandum states the main principles by which the school should operate. It is here that the integrated nature of the institution is identified and commitments to parental involvement and a Christian ethos are enshrined. The articles of association define membership of the company and how it operates. When a school becomes grant-aided, an agreement is drawn up with the Department of Education to specify the composition of the board of governors and the rules and procedures for the control and management of the school. This agreement is known as the 'scheme of management' and in most integrated schools is linked to the founding documents so that the governing body is constrained to act in accordance with them. These documents have been designed to ensure that, in so far as it is possible, there is equal participation in the life of the school by members of the two main traditions in Northern Ireland. Specifically, there are clauses which require equal representation from both cultural traditions in the management, staffing and enrolment of the school.

One of the most important safeguards to equal participation in the life of the school relates to the composition of the board of governors. It is the constitution, (memorandum and articles of association) rather than the scheme of management, in most schools which requires that 'at least 40 per cent of the governors are of the Catholic tradition and at least 40 per cent of the Protestant tradition'. It is argued that if schools are not seen to have this sort of 'proportional representation' within the governing body they are unlikely to secure confidence within the local community or to meet the statutory requirement under the 1989 Education Reform Order to use 'best endeavours to ensure that the management, control and ethos of the school are such as are likely to attract to the school reasonable numbers of both Roman Catholic and Protestant pupils'. For the same reason most schools accept that it would be inappropriate for clergy to sit on governing bodies, especially if nominations are not forthcoming from all denominations.

Securing shared participation has meant finding a combination of nominating procedures and electoral formulae which do not constrain parents and others to simply opt for members of their own cultural group when determining the composition of governing bodies. Simple majoritarian or 'first past the post' concepts of democracy throw up contradictions and inconsistencies within institutions which seek shared government. In consequence, integrated schools have evolved complex procedures to secure an appropriate balance on governing bodies. They depend upon a consensus that governance should be shared by representatives from the different cultural traditions which the school serves. It is a pluralist concept, underlined by the fact that school government is not restricted to representatives from the Catholic and Protestant communities alone. Shared governance is therefore a fundamental principle, not just an aspiration and consensus on this issue is actively reinforced during discussions in the early development of schools.

Maintaining Shared Participation

Within grant maintained integrated schools, the election of teacher and parent governors to governing bodies is conducted in the explicit knowledge that equal representation from both cultural traditions is sought. Elections are generally prefaced by careful explanations of voting procedures and the rationale for seeking equal representation. Teacher governors are elected by their professional colleagues and in most schools the small size of the staff means that discussion can take place within the staff group before any formal election takes place. Often this means that staff will take into account the expectation that both traditions should be represented and arrive at a collective agreement about who the teacher governors should be without the need for a vote.

The election of parent governors can be more complex, partly because there are more positions to be filled and partly because the elections involve a larger, more diverse electorate. Chairing such elections can be a daunting task. Again, considerable explanation of the voting procedures and of the rationale for equal representation is required. Where the need for equal representation is stated explicitly, experience has shown that it is understood implicitly in the way people vote. Candidates normally have an opportunity to say something about their background before an election and thus can decide for themselves whether to identify with any religious or cultural tradition, or none. Voting for a larger number of vacant positions can be simplified by conducting a ballot for each vacancy in turn, enabling voters to see who has been elected as each place is filled one at a time, as is done in some schools. Such 'sequential voting' offers parents greater control over progress toward equal representation. If the principle of equal representation is accepted as desirable, sequential voting can also encourage parents to vote across traditional voting lines as well as for candidates from their own tradition. However, the system is also open to abuse by cliques within the electorate if they are large enough to vote in one of their own candidates for each vacancy (images of middle-class, cross-community alliances).

Other forms of voting system have been used in the election of parent governors in integrated schools. One is a system of proportional representation similar to that used in local council elections which usually secures a fairly even spread of cultural traditions, but can also have less predictable results. Another is a system which places all the candidates' names on one ballot paper and gives each voter the same number of votes as there are vacancies. The requisite number of candidates at the top of the poll then fill the vacancies. In terms of achieving equal representation between cultural traditions this can turn out to be a bit of a lottery. Finally, all schools can experience difficulties in finding candidates for vacancies, in which case a certain amount of persuasion is usually necessary. Integrated schools are no different in this respect from other schools, particularly as all governors are being given increasing responsibilities and it is becoming more difficult to find people willing to serve on any governing body.

Apart from elected members, both the 'foundation governors' and the Department of Education have power to appoint governors. The initial appointments are crucial in the case of foundation governors if there is to be equal representation from the start. It is also important to appoint people who are committed to integrated education and understand the rational for equal representation in future appointments. This responsibility falls to the original organising group or members of the company which set up the school. Thereafter, foundation governors themselves appoint replacements to any vacancies which occur within their number, although as has already been mentioned, many schools accept the nominations of a supporting trust. This means that it is important that foundation governors give earnest consideration to their successors. People who are only mildly sympathetic to integrated education can leave the school particularly vulnerable for the future because of the way in which foundation governors replicate themselves.

The Department of Education also has power to appoint governors to integrated schools, but legislation places no requirement that it should balance the two main cultural traditions. So far, this has not proved to be a problem and in most cases when making appointments the department has been sensitive enough to take into account the integrated nature of the school. Indeed, the department has an opportunity to play a constructive role by bringing about more balanced representation where this has not been achieved already. However, recent experience of insensitive and inappropriate appointments to integrated schools by area boards is a reminder that times change, as do governments, and that a clearer definition of the department's statutory responsibility for acknowledging the need for balance would be preferable.

It can be argued that the whole concept of balanced representation in the government of integrated schools is artificial, that voting procedures are cumbersome and that the 'electorate' in the school is not representative of the extreme views encountered in the wider society. Such criticisms may be valid up to a point, but it is difficult to see how any institution which sets out to cater for the needs of diverse groups can retain credibility without such arrangements. Within the limited context of school management, integrated schools provide rare examples of how shared responsibility and joint decision-making can work in practice.

Staffing

The achievement of equal representation from the two main cultural traditions, amongst staff as well as management of integrated schools, has been seen as potentially more controversial. All schools in Northern Ireland continue to be exempt from the Fair Employment acts; however, it is ironic that what the legislation strives to achieve throughout the community should cause concern to be expressed about what integrated schools do in practice. Catholic maintained schools have argued that the religious ethos of their schools, and the needs of Catholic pupils, require the employment of Catholic teachers. A similar, though unstated, approach is adopted in practice in much of the controlled sector. Segregated teacher training and traditional recruitment patterns for teaching vacancies reinforce the effects of exemption from the fair employment legislation, and give little incentive for teachers to cross the barrier between the two sectors. However, many people, and even those who are unsympathetic to integrated education, accept that the viability of an integrated school would be in question if all the staff came from the same cultural tradition. Therefore any controversy is more about how to achieve and maintain equal representation within the staff, than about the principle itself.

The difficulties and sensitivities surrounding equity and employment issues are, however, matters of concern for the whole community. There is an important distinction between commitments to equity within integrated schools and within the wider society. Integrated schools are committed to a clear concept of equity. In practice this means aiming to maintain staffing levels within a 60:40 balance and to secure minimum levels of participation from both communities in the institutional life of the school. Despite the fact that the latest Census indicates that there will soon be roughly the same number of people within both traditions in Northern Ireland as a whole, there are wide variations in different areas. It has therefore been suggested that the achievement of balanced representation in employment on a wide scale is unrealistic, and the aim should be to reflect the demography of the local area of the employing institution. This means that a balance of the two communities might be as wide as 90:10 and would be considered 'reasonable' and acceptable if it reflected the local demography. However, integrationists maintain that integrated schools could not function if one community were as predominant or under-represented as this, and thus insist on a stricter definition of staffing balance.

The great advantage which new integrated schools have when making initial appointments is that they begin with a clean sheet. They have usually attempted to achieve a balance within the overall staff, although the most visible posts are obviously teaching positions. (Achieving representation from both communities within the ancillary staff can be a problem, particularly if the school is located in a segregated housing area. The lower salaries involved with ancillary staff can restrict the distance which people are willing to travel to work because of transport costs.) For a new school, teaching appointments normally begin with the principal. Once this post is filled it becomes clearer what attributes should be sought in other candidates. Priority may be given to candidates whose experience would provide a breadth and diversity to the curriculum, including those with particular strengths in denominational religious education or a background and knowledge of different cultural traditions. This makes it more likely that teaching staff will be drawn from different cultural backgrounds, but does not guarantee balance. Thus, although unconstrained by fair employment legislation, some integrated schools have nevertheless found it appropriate and necessary to adopt 'fair employment' strategies including, for example, targeting recruitment advertisements at an under-represented cultural group.

Equally sensitive issues arise once a school has been established and natural turnover of staff occurs and questions of promotion and posts of responsibility come into play. Opinion is divided about the extent to which equity should be pursued at these levels. On the one hand it may involve unacceptable forms of positive discrimination. It is not clear that teachers would be comfortable with the notion that their personal career advancement might have to take second place to the principle of equity between cultural traditions. They are not immune to the anxieties generated by living in a divided society and are as susceptible as the rest of us to notions that members of 'the other community' are being advantaged.

When schools are small, achieving strict equity, for example, in promotions may in any case be impractical. One the other hand, the overall aim of equity and balance require schools to face up to their obligations. When schools are larger there is more room for adjustment between individual and communal equity.

In practice, the emphasis within the wider society on reducing employment differentials means that issues about maintaining equity, although not yet a priority, will become more important. Employment practice within the integrated schools provides a useful insight into the sort of question which arises once broad equity is established. The issues are delicate and often controversial, but must be faced. The schools have few precedents to draw on so it is important that they receive sympathetic support from other organisations which are grappling with fair employment issues.

Enrolment

Integrated schools are committed to maintaining roughly equal numbers of pupils from the two main cultural traditions in Northern Ireland. To achieve this, they try to operate within a broad band whereby pupil enrolment from either tradition does not fall below 40 per cent, or rise above 60 per cent of the overall pupil population. This arrangement is related to a phenomenon known as the 'tipping point', a term coined in the discussion surrounding desegregation of schools in the United States during the 1960s. The notion of 'tipping' described a critical point (often put at 40 per cent) when the proportion of black students tended to precipitate a mass withdrawal of children of white parents, leaving an all-black school. In the United States the 'tipping point' argument was used to slow the pace of desegregation and avoid 'white flight'. But the concept was contentious and not always supported by the evidence.[2] In Northern Ireland there have been examples where a similar phenomenon has occurred. In a few cases where controlled schools have reached a roughly equal number of Catholic and Protestant pupils, enrolments have eventually become predominantly, or exclusively, Catholic. Integrationists argue that this has happened because the schools had no mechanisms which helped them sustain a roughly equal enrolment and arrest the demographic drift.

Grammar schools and some controlled secondary schools provide the other examples of a potential mixing of pupils from 'the other tradition' in enrolments. However, in most of these cases there is a tendency to exaggerate the size of the minority group within the overall school population (usually between 5-20 per cent); and because the relative size of the group from the 'other tradition' rarely changes it poses little threat either to the institution or to members of the majority group – in other words, the 'tipping point' is never exceeded. Minority group members who have been pupils in this sort of situation often comment that there is little imperative for the school to take account of their needs, and a common experience for pupils seems to have been that they become 'invisible' or 'conceal' their identity to avoid attracting attention.

It is for such reasons that integrated schools in Northern Ireland are explicit about the enrolment levels they seek from each tradition, although in practice, it has not been necessary in most cases to operate strict quotas to maintain between 40 and 60 per cent of both traditions. Often, monitoring procedures to reassure the management body are sufficient. Monitoring each year's intake may simply involve a question on the initial application form, in which parents are asked directly to indicate their cultural background or religious affiliation – unlike the monitoring forms used for Fair Employment monitoring, which infer religious affiliation from the school a person attended. Many schools have an open-ended question which allows individuals to define their identity in their own terms, others press a little harder by providing predefined categories. (Usually the rationale for monitoring is explained to prospective parents in some detail. Although some parents might feel uncomfortable initially, integrated schools have begun to develop approaches which are explicit, but sensitive.) In practice the schools are dependent on the goodwill and understanding of parents in operating monitoring procedures. A response is not compulsory and a child could not be refused admission if such information is not provided.

Usually monitoring is carried out by an admissions committee (a sub-committee of the board of governors as required in most schemes of management) using information from application forms. Each school has evolved its own way of dealing with complex and difficult questions, such as whether it is the identity of the parent or the child which is most important, and how and whether the background of both parents should be taken into account for a child with a parent from each tradition. (Some parents nominate a religious affiliation for their child, others indicate that the child has a 'mixed' background. In general such marriages are seen as a positive contribution to the school.) Although the underlying purpose of monitoring is a serious one, an ability to see the humorous side has helped defuse issues such as the distinction between English and Irish Catholicism or how to categorise some of the more exotic cultural backgrounds – both potentially divisive matters in Northern Ireland. The fact that up to 20 per cent of the places are also available to the children of parents who may come from neither cultural tradition, who subscribe to no Christian denomination, or who have no religious faith, also means the school is more 'open'. Monitoring is never clear cut, however, and where there is no pressure on places, the admissions committee can operate in the knowledge that the process is about reassurance of a broadly diverse and representative overall pupil population, rather than a means of labelling individuals.

Where problems arise, it is usually for one of two reasons – because one tradition might exceed 60 per cent of the overall pupil population, or where there are more applications than places available. When combined, these are particularly difficult to handle. Maintaining a balanced enrolment seems to be easier in areas where there is a majority Protestant population. When one group threatens to predominate, an initial course of action might involve speaking to parent groups within the under-represented community – the school's equivalent of affirmative action measures. Where a school is not oversubscribed parents from the over-represented community might be encouraged to 'match' their child's enrolment by making contact with a parent from the under-represented community. This has the additional advantage of encouraging cross-community contact between adults; however, there is a limit to how far it can remedy a significant imbalance.

The government's policy of 'open enrolment' which allows parents to express a preference for the school they wish their child to attend, has made admissions and enrolment decisions more difficult for integrated schools. Every school is now assigned a maximum enrolment number based on the physical capacity of the school, and an annual maximum admissions number. Schools are required to draw up admissions criteria to be applied when the school is oversubscribed. Parents can appeal to a tribunal if their child is refused a place at their chosen school, and they feel the admissions criteria have not been applied fairly.

The problems these pose for integrated schools highlight a potential conflict in legislation, since the Education Reform (NI) Order identifies an integrated school as one which is 'likely to attract reasonable numbers of Catholic and Protestant pupils', but nowhere specifies what might count as a 'reasonable' number. Theoretically, an integrated school could find that applications for places in a particular year all came from one cultural tradition. Under open enrolment it would have to accept them, up to the maximum enrolment number. At present an integrated school's only recourse is to include a general condition in its admissions criteria that the integrated nature of the school should be taken into account when places are being offered, but this too has problems. Schools have no legal protection if a parent argues that their child has been refused a place at the school on the grounds of religious affiliation. A possible defence for the school would be that the admission of the child would take the numbers of one cultural tradition past the 'tipping point', however it would be difficult to sustain the view that one extra child could cause a significant change in ethos. Clearly, however, at some point the enrolment of the school will inevitably drift toward an imbalance which most integrationists would consider unreasonable.

Underlying this problem is an issue about the rights of an individual in relation to the right of an institution to maintain a particular ethos. The issue has been recognised by the Standing Advisory Commission on Human Rights as a special aspect of individual rights in communally divided societies. The Commission is of the view that: 'There is a strong basis for permitting integrated schools to use religious affiliation as an express basis for admission for the maintenance of a reasonable balance of Catholics and Protestants within the schools. A similar exemption should be adopted when the general exemption in respect of the employment of teachers under the Fair Employment (N.I.) Acts is reviewed.'[3]

Integrated schools are keen to see legislative provision which would both sustain the rights of individuals and protect any integrated institution from destabilising litigation. Meanwhile, the operation of enrolment policies by integrated schools is dependent on the goodwill of parents and their appreciation of the integrated ethos which the schools are trying to achieve in practice.

Christian Ethos

It has been claimed that the integrated schools which have emerged to date have only been possible insofar as they are prepared to adopt a Christian ethos – reflecting the fact that the overwhelming majority of people in Northern Ireland define themselves in terms of a Christian religious denomination and would wish their schools to reflect this. The 1991 Census shows that 88.5 per cent of the population declared membership of a Christian denomination (38.4 per cent Roman Catholic, 21.3 per cent Presbyterian, 17.7 per cent Church of Ireland, 3.8 per cent Methodist and 7.3 per cent other denominations usually considered to be Christian).[4] In practice the integrated schools have attracted parents who have a range of perceptions on the issue of religion and schooling.

Within the parental population of integrated schools there is undoubtedly a substantial representation of practising and deeply committed Christians from different denominations, whose early involvement had a significant influence on foundation principles. Typically, an integrated school's constitution will include the following:

The school will provide a Christian rather than a secular approach, aiming to encourage Catholic and Protestant children to explore and value their own particular Christian tradition but so as to encourage the education together with them of children of other beliefs, cultures and traditions.

A number of factors are involved in these aspirations. Some schools emphasise a common, core religious education programme which focuses on Christian values and beliefs. In some cases this also involves comparative religious studies which contrast Christianity with other world religions. Most schools prefer not to separate children for religious education, but all have responded to the expectation of many Catholic parents that the school will help with the preparation of their children for the sacraments of First Communion and Confirmation. Sometimes this has meant separate classes within the school day for specific denominational instruction, whilst for others such preparation takes place before or after normal school hours. An indication of solidarity which generally exists within the whole school community, is that all usually join in the celebration of these religious events. Parents have been disappointed, however, that the churches have not been more supportive. Some schools have wished to appoint denominational chaplains and it has been hurtful, particularly for many Catholic parents, to find that their church in particular has been most uncooperative. Despite this, it is clear that the religious education provided by integrated schools is acceptable to many committed Christians of different denominations.

Many parents would perceive integrated schools to be *inter-denominational* institutions in the sense of a positive commitment to religious practice. Others may perceive integrated schools as *multi-denominational* in the more passive sense that, whilst not participating actively in religious worship themselves, they would wish for their children to gain some insight into the variety of practice within the Christian tradition. Other parents within integrated schools recognise that they have been brought up in a society which is largely shaped by Christian values, but take the terms 'Catholic' and 'Protestant' to be descriptive of cultural background rather than religious affiliation. These parents are probably most comfortable when religion is treated as a social or cultural phenomenon and would therefore wish the schools to be more *non-denominational* or *multi-cultural* in character.

It has been suggested that the Christian ethos of integrated schools is unlikely to attract people of other faiths. The criticism is understandable, but rather naive given the demography and political realities of Northern Ireland where religious minorities comprise less than 0.5 per cent of the population (including 972

Mohammedans, 742 Hindus, 410 Jews, 319 Bahá'ís, 270 Buddhists, 230 Sikhs and others in the 1991 Census). Parents from these traditions and also those amongst the 59,234 (3.7 per cent) in the 1991 Census who said they had no religious denomination and the 114,827 (7.35 per cent) who left all questions on religious denomination blank, have perhaps become accustomed to their needs coming a poor second to those of the two main traditions in Northern Ireland. But this does not mean that their needs can be ignored. Integrated schools have taken a small, but significant step in recognising that other faiths and philosophical viewpoints exist within society and have declared a commitment to take account of their needs. It is important, however, for all educational institutions to accommodate growing diversity within society. In this respect, the common core RE syllabus which has been recommended for all schools and which has a Judeo-Christian focus with scant recognition of other world religions, is a disappointing indication that our society needs to find a way of overcoming a reluctance to look beyond our own traditions.

Integrated schools have been remarkably successful at creating institutions which are neither denominational nor secular. They have succeeded in meeting the expectations of practising Christians from different denominations whilst avoiding the offence which is caused by assuming that children from other faiths and none can be ignored. Probably the single most influential factor in this respect has been an awareness of the political sensitivities of inter-church co-operation. While integrated schools have gone to considerable lengths to welcome the involvement of clergy in a pastoral role, most have maintained that it is inappropriate for clergy to be involved in management structures. Many clergy appreciate the distinction and, even if different denominations were equally represented on the governing body, historical precedents caution against the involvement of clergy in the management of integrated schools for the foreseeable future.

Prospects for the Future
The future direction of parental involvement may hinge on whether the first generation of parents are able to pass on a commitment the founding principles and how successful they are in creating a partnership with teachers in shaping the integrated ethos. It will be important that the schools find mechanisms which maintain relationships between existing and new parents, and between parents and teachers. The creation of non-teaching posts with a remit to facilitate interaction and communication between parents, the school and the wider

community, could be one way to facilitated this, although there is no evidence that any of the existing schools see it as a priority.

The most contentious issues are likely to remain the structural and constitutional safeguards at the level of management, staffing and enrolment and whether they are necessary or sustainable. In many ways they are artificial, but they do appear to ameliorate the lack of trust between members of the two main traditions in Northern Ireland. Without them, our social institutions appear to drift quite easily towards segregation. The very artificiality of constitutional safeguards may be the feature which creates an awareness that our society is in fact plural. Such checks and balances may only become unnecessary as confidence grows that discrimination is no longer significant.

The future development of integrated education will depend on how strong the current dynamic for change within our society is. The 1989 Education Reform Order, which introduced measures to support the development of integrated education was a turning point for integrated education, principally because it added a statutory dimension to what had, until then, been a voluntary process. The transition to government support brought welcome recognition and some funding; however, it also brought new challenges, particularly with regard to future development. Grant maintained integrated status introduced as part of the Conservative government's policy of encouraging schools to 'opt out' of local authority control, had the effect in the case of integrated schools of moving them a little further away from the notion of a voluntary school than had been the case initially. GMI status seemed to lie somewhere between a voluntary maintained and a state controlled school. Integrated schools were motivated to seek GMI status because it offered 'day one' recurrent funding and the possibility of 100 per cent capital funding (a distinct advantage over 85 per cent funding as a voluntary maintained school) and, more significantly, statutory recognition for the concept of an 'integrated' school. However it also fuelled the notion that integrated schools were a 'third sector', somehow associated with the political philosophy which generated the 'opting out' policy and unconnected to local educational administration.

Controlled integrated status, the second, alternative form of integration which the Order introduced, has also raised difficulties. For those schools which opted for controlled integrated status, having originally been founded by parents as a voluntary maintained school, there was a certain loss of control as the composition of the governing body changed and the protective link with a founding trust and parents was broken. For schools transforming from controlled to controlled integrated status, this is also a problem, quite apart from the process of change itself (which is much more complex and demanding of resources than the government has generally been prepared to acknowledge). Such schools have an association with the local education and library board has been shown to lead to difficulties over nominations to the governing body. Yet despite this, controlled integrated status remains a challenge to the whole society about the extent to which the ethos of a social institution can transform to serve the whole community rather than a single tradition.

The provision of government funding for NICIE as a central, representative body which can also assist the development of integrated schools has revived old questions about how integrated school projects should be initiated. NICIE has come under some pressure to undertake centralised, strategic planning and development, but this has been resisted on the grounds that integrated schools should emerge in response to an expressed need from parents in a local area. The current review of arrangements for education administration in Northern Ireland, has also raised questions about the balance between voluntary and statutory development and local and central control over the underlying principles of integrated schools. The interplay of these priorities is likely to influence the overall ethos of NICIE itself, although experience suggests that the tension could be constructive.

The immediate future for integrated schools looks secure. Relative to the overall system, the number of schools is small, but growing steadily. The most pressing issues seem to be practical and strategic, rather than philosophical. They concern how we can get to the point where no parent can say their child has been denied the opportunity of an integrated education because a school is not available locally. This aspiration will only be limited by the energy of parents and the availability of resources, but equal choice in education will only become available once all types of school are allowed to flourish to their maximum potential. It seems reasonable to expect that each new integrated school should open in purpose-built premises, as their controlled and maintained counterparts have done before them, although it seems that government still needs to be convinced that it should budget for expansion rather than containment.

Notes
1. Morgan, V., Dunn, S., Cairns, E. and Fraser, G. (1992), *Breaking the Mould. The Role of Parents and Teachers in the Integrated Schools in Northern Ireland*; Agnew, U., McEwan, A. and Salters, J. (1992), *Integrated Education: The Views of Parents*, Queen's University, Belfast.

2. Weinberg, M. (1977), *Minority Students: a research appraisal*, Washington DC, U.S. Department of Health, Education and Welfare, pp. 264-267.

3. Standing Advisory Commission on Human Rights (1990), *Religious and Political Discrimination and Equality of Opportunity in Northern Ireland,* Second Report, London: HMSO, Command 1107 Para 6.23)

PART 2

The Future Integrated Education Agenda

13
Multi-Denominational Schools in the Republic of Ireland

Áine Hyland

This chapter attempts to give an overview of the development of multi-denominational schools in the the Republic of Ireland. It looks at the historical development of primary education in Ireland and discusses the background to the setting up of multi-denominational schools, the issues faced by the individual schools and their present position. It briefly addresses a number of related issues: the indirect role which the setting up of these schools has had in encouraging and developing an attitude of self-help, creative enterprise, and community in people who might previously have felt marginalised; in contributing to a more embracing sense of Irish identity; in helping adults as well as children to develop skills in conflict-resolution; and in helping to develop a sense of democracy, and in women particularly, of empowerment. The chapter also explains the role and activities of Educate Together, the co-ordinating committee for existing and prospective schools. The multi-denominational sector still faces key problems in its development; the conclusion suggests how the forthcoming White Paper and educational legislation in the Republic might help to overcome these problems.

The Evolution of Primary (National) Education in Ireland

When the national school system was set up in 1831, its main object was 'to unite in one system children of different creeds'. The National Board was 'to look with peculiar favour' on applications for aid from schools jointly managed by Roman Catholics and Protestants. While some of the schools aided by the Board in the early years were jointly managed, the main Christian churches put pressure on the government to give aid to schools under the management of individual churches.[1] This pressure was so effective that by the mid-nineteenth century, only 4 per cent of national schools were under mixed management.[2] The main principle of nineteenth and early twentieth century primary education in Ireland was that schools should offer 'combined moral and literary instruction and separate religious instruction'.[3] While the National Board set down the curriculum for moral and literary instruction, the patron determined the form and content of religious instruction in the schools under his patronage. The rules for national schools in the Republic to the present day state that 'no pupil shall receive or be present at any religious instruction of which his parents or guardians do not approve'[4] and also 'that the periods of formal religious instruction shall be fixed so as to facilitate the withdrawal of (such) pupils'.[5]

The principle of mixed education remained the keystone of the national school system from 1831 to 1965. However in practice by the beginning of the twentieth century the national system had developed in such a way that virtually all schools were under denominational management. In this respect, the Irish system of national education was fundamentally different from Great Britain where 'parallel' systems had evolved, allowing denominational schools to exist side by side with local authority controlled schools.[6] It was also different from Northern Ireland in that there was no legislation underpinning primary education, as there was after 1922 in the north. Virtually all national schools were under the patronage and management of either the Catholic or Protestant churches, apart from a Jewish national school which was also recognised and funded by the state in the 1930s.

The rules for national schools were revised in 1965. The preface to the new rules stated: 'In pursuance of the provisions of these Articles (42 and 44.2.4.) the State provides for free primary education for children in national schools and gives explicit recognition to the denominational character of these schools'.[7] It is difficult to understand how articles 42 and 44.2.4. could have been construed in this way. No cognisance was taken of the fact that not all national schools were attended exclusively by children of the same denomination. Neither was there any provision made for parents who might not wish their children to attend denominational schools, although the rules quoted Article 42.4. of the 1937 Constitution of Ireland which recognised 'the rights of parents, especially in the matter of religious and moral formation'.

The publication of a new curriculum in 1971 added a further complication to the situation.[8] Although widely welcomed for its many innovations, the new curriculum encouraged the integration of both religious and 'secular' subjects. The official teachers' handbook specified that this integration should embrace all aspects of the curriculum[9] and justified it in the following terms: '...the separation of religious and secular instruction into differentiated subject compartments serves only to throw the whole educational function out of focus... The integration of the curriculum may be seen... in the religious and civic spirit which animates all its parts.' Taken together with the rules of 1965 this created a new situation. The state now formally recognised the denominational character of the national school system and made no provision for, nor even adverted to the rights of those children whose parents did not wish them to attend exclusively denominational schools or to receive religious instruction within such schools. It had removed the requirement for teachers to be sensitive to the religious beliefs of 'those of different religious persuasions'. Parents were still allowed to opt their children out of religious instruction, but the rule became inoperable since religious and secular instruction would now be integrated. Even if religious instruction were separately timetabled, it could be assumed that a specifically denominational ethos would 'permeate the school day'.

The Dalkey School Project

There was a growing interest in education in Ireland in the 1960s and early 70s. In 1967 free secondary education had been introduced and there was considerable public debate about educational issues generally. Vatican II had encouraged involvement by the Catholic laity in what had traditionally been a clerically dominated church. Some Catholics argued that 'a fairly strong case (could) be made from the reading of the documents of Vatican II for the introduction of integrated schools....'[10] The troubles in Northern Ireland had erupted afresh and after 1969 many Irish people were anxious to break down barriers between Protestant and Catholic on the island of Ireland.

In some areas of Dublin, growing numbers of families from a Catholic tradition began to send their children to local Church of Ireland schools, perhaps because they felt that the ethos of such schools was less pervasive than that of Catholic schools. One such area was the village of Dalkey in south Co. Dublin. The local Church of Ireland national school became increasingly popular and the enrolment began to increase. By 1974 it was a five teacher school with over 180 pupils on rolls.[11] Parents and teachers would have liked the school to continue to grow and its de facto multi-denominational nature to be endorsed. However, the school manager, (the local Church of Ireland rector) was unwilling to go along with parents' wishes. Subsequently the Department of Education directed the manager to restrict enrolment to the existing capacity of the school, and in a letter indicated that future enrolment should be decided on the basis of the denominational character of the school.[12]

This letter set on record unambiguously the enrolment implications of the 1965 rules for national schools. It also had other implications. If a Church of Ireland national school was unable to accept 'other children' and if the parents of these children did not wish them to attend the local Catholic school, the state saw no reason to make provision for them within the national school system.

The Dalkey School Project was set up in 1975 as a result. Its focus was the commitment of those who wanted the option of schools within the national school system, which would be multi-denominational, co-educational and under a democratic management structure, and which would have a child-centred approach to education, as indicated in the recently introduced new Primary Curriculum (1971). The strategy of the new organisation was to work to get one school into the system first, rather than to argue the principle at national level for many years to come.[13] The task confronting the project was formidable. The national school system had been undisturbed for over 100 years. There was an established equilibrium between the Department of Education, the churches and the Irish National Teachers Organisation, the only teacher union representing primary teachers in the Republic of Ireland. There was a price for the churches' control of education; they provided sites for schools and they paid the local contribution towards the capital and running costs of their schools. The state paid the salaries of the teaching staff, the larger share of the capital costs (averaging 85%) and an annual capitation grant (currently £33 per pupil per annum) towards maintenance costs. The Dalkey School Project realised that the entry fee for any new partner into the network would be high and that it would have to fund-raise on a very large scale if it was to succeed in setting up a school.

Political support for multi-denominational education within the national school system began to emerge around the mid 1970s. The then leader of the Fianna Fáil party, Jack Lynch, expressed support for a multi-denominational school on a pilot basis[14] and the Labour Party had consistently supported the idea. Individual Fine Gael T.D.s and local councillors had also indicated support, although Richard Burke, who was Minister for Education at the time was hostile.[15] During the years 1975 to 1978 the Dalkey School Project was involved in protracted correspondence with the political parties and with the Department of Education, while simultaneously building up its membership, establishing the extent of local support for a school,[16] organising fund-raising activities and searching for suitable premises.

In June 1977 a general election was held. When Fianna Fáil came to power, they delivered on their pre-election promise of support and the Education Minister

John Wilson instructed Department officials to enter into discussions with the Dalkey group. In September 1978 Dalkey National School was opened in temporary premises in Dun Laoghaire. There was considerable difficulty in procuring suitable premises and in obtaining planning permission from the local authority.[17] Some administrators at both local and central levels seemed to have difficulty in accepting that a multi-denominational school could be a valid part of the national school system.[18] However, many departmental and local authority officials were very helpful.

The Dalkey School Project operated in temporary premises for six years, while negotiations and planning for a new permanent purpose-built school continued. During this time it grew from 80 to more than 300 pupils, and from three teachers to ten. When the new building was opened in 1984 by Gemma Hussey, Minister for Education, all the political parties were represented, including former Taoiseach, Jack Lynch. The task of starting the first multi-denominational school in the Republic had not been easy. There had not been a great deal of overt opposition to the movement, but on occasions, it surfaced, as in 1978 when an organisation called the Council for Social Concern, launched an attack claiming in a circular that: 'Atheistic interest in the Dalkey School Project is clear. Ireland's system of education is denominational by Constitutional guarantee... We submit that there is no need for such a school as this which can only be divisive. It can only be hostile to religion in an age when it was never more needed.'[19]

Apart from the time and energy expended on the project, the financial costs had been substantial. The local contribution towards the cost of setting up the temporary premises, the cost of the new building and the cost of purchasing the site was in the region of £150,000, all of which had been raised by voluntary contributions and by various fund-raising events. In addition to these costs, the school management provides the local share of current costs every year.

The Growth of the Movement

Other groups with similar aims to the Dalkey School Project were also active. A second school was opened in Bray, Co Wicklow, in 1981 in pre-fabricated classrooms. As at Dalkey, the enrolment increased rapidly and within five years the school had outgrown its temporary premises. After some difficulty, the project acquired a site outside the town and in 1990 a purpose built, eight classroom school with room for remedial teaching, a school library and a school hall was formally opened by the Minister for Education, Mary O'Rourke, T.D.

The North Dublin National School Project was set up in the early 1980s. In 1984, the group negotiated a lease with the Board of Works for an empty model school building in Glasnevin and opened as a national school in September of that year. Like Dalkey and Bray, it grew rapidly and within a few years most of the playground space had been used up by pre-fabricated buildings. Since 1987 the project has spent considerable time and energy in trying to find a site on which a new building might be erected. But acquiring a site is not easy in an area close to the city centre where land is exorbitantly expensive. Meanwhile, in spite of its unsuitable premises, the school has to turn away almost as many pupils every year as it can accommodate.

No new school opened between 1984 and 1987 but a number of other projects began to develop and a committee – Educate Together – to co-ordinate the existing groups and support new groups was established. While the first three schools had been set up in the greater Dublin area, the next phase of development occurred outside Dublin. Between 1985 and 1987, four projects were set up and became associate members of Educate Together – Waterford, Cork, Sligo and Kilkenny. A further project was set up in the South Dublin area in 1985, supported largely by parents of children who could not be accommodated in the Dalkey School Project. Unfortunately, the Waterford and the South Dublin groups became inactive by 1986 and 1988, respectively. While they both had viable pre-enrolment numbers and had met regularly for two years or more, they had failed to find a premises and became disillusioned.

Sligo, Kilkenny and Cork were more successful and in 1987 all three projects succeeded in opening a school. They managed to do this despite new and more restrictive 'regulations' introduced by the Department of Education, which applied to multi-denominational and all-Irish schools, but not to denominational schools. The new regulations (not included in any rule book or circular but cited in letters from the Department to the new projects) [20] created a situation which was arguably in breach of the Constitution of Ireland. They stated that multi-denominational national schools, if recognised, would have temporary or provisional recognition only in the early years (an unspecified period) and during this time would not be eligible for any capital grants. This meant that at the stage when the schools would be growing most rapidly and would have to spend money on refurbishing and furnishing temporary premises, no capital grants would be available.

Falling birth figures in the Republic had also begun to affect overall enrolments in national schools and it was becoming clear that in the coming decade there would be surplus accommodation in national schools throughout the country. The government seemed to be reluctant to recognise further national schools, even though the lack of multi-denominational schools for parents who wanted them for their children could be deemed to be 'in violation…of (their) conscientious and lawful preference'.

Sligo was the first project which had to face the additional obstacles placed in the way of new multi-denominational schools. A request for sanction to open a school in a disused glass factory was turned down by the Department on the grounds that there were empty classrooms in a local Catholic national school. The same excuse was used to refuse permission to erect pre-fabricated classrooms on a site which the Vocational Education Committee was prepared to make available. The project's efforts to lease empty classrooms from the trustees of a Catholic national school failed because the Church was not prepared to negotiate with them. When Senator O'Higgins raised the matter with Minister Cooney, he said there was nothing he could do about it.'This is the system we have. I have no power to twist the arm of any school board and say they must give these people their spare space.'[21]

It was now becoming clear that the official tripartite lease of a national school building to which the Minister for Education was a party, gave only limited powers to the state.[22] The Minister had no control over the use of national school buildings, financed primarily from the public purse, even when practically empty or unused and required by a multi-denominational school.

A change of Minister, with the appointment of Mary O'Rourke to the Department of Education in spring 1987 was, however, an important landmark in the growth of the sector. During her Ministry to the end of 1991, seven new Educate Together schools were set up. Minister O'Rourke spoke in support of the sector on many occasions during that period. She launched the Educate Together Charter in Galway in 1990 and visited all ten schools in her official capacity. She also made an important policy decision in 1990 when she announced that children attending multi-denominational schools were entitled to the same school transport benefits as children attending denominational schools.[23] This was a very significant breakthrough and has meant that many children living outside a two or three mile radius but within travelling distance of a multi-denominational school have been allowed since 1980 to avail of subsidised school transport.

In spring 1987 Minister O'Rourke intervened directly on behalf of the Sligo School Project to get agreement from the Board of Works to lease to the project some pre-fabricated buildings. Despite early projections that parental demand in

Sligo might result in a four or six teacher school, demand has been much greater than anticipated. The school quickly outgrew its temporary premises and further prefabs have had to be provided. At the time of writing the school has more than 260 pupils on rolls and employs eight teachers. The longer term accommodation prospect is however unclear, even though the nearby Catholic national school is now completely empty.

In September 1987, Kilkenny and Cork School Projects also opened in temporary premises. Like the other schools, the Cork school grew rapidly, putting pressure on very limited accommodation. The Kilkenny School Project opened in a newly built complex owned by the Scouts and Guides. There are now 260 pupils and eight teachers in the school and new permenant premises are required.

The recognition of the Ranelagh Multi-Denominational National School came about in quite a different way and involved taking over the patronage of the school from the Church of Ireland.[24] The Church was supportive and agreed to transfer its title to the site and buildings to the new association. The school has continued to develop since 1991. There are now five teachers and the policy is to continue a phased growth until it becomes an eight teacher school in 1997, although the site of the school is cramped and the premises in need of renewal. The Department of Education however has not yet sanctioned a new building and has indicated that it would favour the use of empty school buildings in the general vicinity.

A group of parents in the Limerick area in July 1986 planned to open a school in 1988, but a number of premises which they tried to secure fell through.[25] Late in 1988 the Red Cross in Limerick agreed they could lease part of their premises. In September 1989 the school opened with 56 pupils and two teachers. It doubled in size the following year and grew to a five teacher school in 1991. As a result of the direct intervention of the Minister, space was secured in an empty Employment Exchange building for additional classrooms, though the school was still without a playground. Like other Educate Together schools, permenant accommodation remains a problem.

The South City School Project was formally constituted in July 1987. At the suggestion of the Department it sought to lease empty classrooms in primary and post-primary schools in the south city area; but its approaches to more than 30 schools with some empty space, proved unsuccessful.[26] The most disappointing refusal involved an empty, relatively new national school building, vested in the St. Lawrence O'Toole Diocesan Trust (which holds all property owned by the

Catholic Archdiocese of Dublin). Despite letters to the Department, the estate agent and the solicitors for the Diocesan Trust, indicating that the project was interested in acquiring or leasing the building, South City School Project was unable to prevent the private sale of the premises.

Subsequently, early in 1990, the group located a Church of Ireland school in Crumlin, only one room of which was being used by the single-teacher Church of Ireland school. The local Select Vestry agreed to rent two classrooms to the South City Project and in September 1990 the school opened with two teachers and about 50 pupils. It soon filled all the available space and there was great concern about the future despite the very many empty classrooms and large empty buildings in the area. A recent tragic fire which burnt the whole building to the ground has placed a shadow over future plans.

The North Bay National School Project was set up in 1988 and included some of the parents who had failed to get a place for their children in the North Dublin National School Project. They were eventually successful in obtaining a block of classrooms, through the direct intervention of the Minister, Mary O'Rourke, in a large former Catholic national school building in Kilbarrack then owned by the Department. Their accommodation is the most satisfactory of all Educate Together schools to date. If this solution could be replicated in other areas, the sector would grow much more rapidly and multi-denominational education would be accessible to families who seek such education.

New Groups

There are four further associate members of Educate Together which have not yet found premises in which to open a school. These are Galway, North Kildare (Celbridge), Dingle and Terenure. The first three have been active now for three or four years. Galway has become particularly frustrated in its search for suitable premises. In 1991 and 1992 the situation looked hopeful – they had identified possible accommodation for a school. But each time, problems have arisen and the current situation is not encouraging. A request to the former bishop of Galway, Dr. Casey, who was Patron of all Catholic national schools in the diocese, asking if some of the empty classrooms in the city might be leased was refused outright. It is very difficult for parents to remain optimistic when school year follows school year and there is no sign of a school.

The situation in North Kildare would appear to be more hopeful. There is a lot of new housing in the area with a young and growing population. Not only is there no surplus school accommodation, but there may be need for further national school places. Until recently, the North Kildare School Project had hoped that the department would sanction the temporary use of an old Methodist hall now owned by the Department of Defence. It would enable a school to get started and would provide adequate accommodation for at least three years. At the time of writing, the situation is unclear but it seems that the department would prefer to see the project putting pre-fabs on a green-field site in the short term.

A school in Dingle is likely to be a smaller school and is also likely to be all-Irish. The Dingle group was very active in 1990 and 1991 and identified possible premises, but these proved not to be available. They are currently interested in an empty school building owned by the Catholic authorities.

Terenure School Project is less than a year old. Already its pre-enrolment list has begun to build up and there could well be demand for a further multi-denominational school in the greater south city area. However, the experience of South City School Project in seeking suitable premises for a school in the area does not suggest that finding a place to start a school will be easy. On the other hand, new solutions could emerge and it makes sense for a new group to monitor the local accommodation situation closely.

Lessons learned in setting up Educate Together schools

We make no claim that Educate Together schools are 'better' than other schools in our national school system. What we seek is that the choice of multi-denominational education should be available wherever parents want it for their children. While this is a huge undertaking and is far from ideal, in our experience, it can be an exercise in local democracy with beneficial spin-offs, in spite of difficulties and frustrations. A group of parents who come together for the first time to consider setting up an Educate Together school may have little or nothing in common other than their interest in multi-denominational schooling. They are likely to come from different religious, cultural, social, ideological and political backgrounds and would probably never have met had the education question not brought them together.

Many may have little or no experience of meeting anyone outside their own religious and social circle. Issues arise that one would never consider in a more homogenous group. For example, the question of meeting in a pub or of going to the pub after a meeting has to be handled with tact and delicacy. For people of some religious backgrounds the pub is effectively out of bounds. The issue of punctuality can also arise. While punctuality is not uniquely related to religious background, we found that some traditions interpret time 'more loosely' than others, often causing tension in a group until this question was faced up to, discussed and some agreement reached.

While these are small examples, they indicate the unexpected areas where tensions can occur and which can escalate if not addressed. Deep-rooted cultural/ religious prejudice can also emerge. A confident and impressively-articulated presentation by one member of a group can be interpreted by a person from a different cultural tradition as being an arrogant and patronising speech and it may be very difficult to break down old cross-cultural suspicions.

However, in our experience, these problems are usually overcome and learning how to operate and cope with democracy is the next important milestone for new groups. The first few meetings are usually cosy and mutually supportive and parents are glad to find support in their quest for multi-denominational schooling. The next step of formalising the group can sometimes be more tricky. Usually a 'proceduralist' will emerge who is in his/her element drawing up a constitution and setting the procedures in place for future action. Many people find this stage (which is of course necessary) intensely boring and there is a danger that if it is not moved through quickly, the ultimate purpose of the group will be lost sight of and good people will drop out.

The period of consolidation between setting up the group and opening the school is very important. This is the stage when people with various strengths and skills will emerge. The challenge for the group is to harness these strengths in a constructive way and to forge ahead with the task of starting the school. Often the most valuable members of the group at this stage are those who are prepared to challenge the status quo – to question assumptions about property ownership for example, when premises are being sought, or to question various educational philosophies and methodologies. Creative and divergent thinkers can be invaluable for coming up with fund-raising ideas and a sense of self-empowerment will often become evident as the group develops. Ironically, when the school opens, those who have been most active in breaking through the various initial barriers, may find it more difficult to cope with being part of the 'status quo' and may not be particularly effective members of the school's management structure. Their tendency to question and challenge authority – which once the school is set up might well be the principal teacher and/or staff – can lead to tension and conflict which may not be at all constructive at the early stage of the school's development. It is often better for someone who has been a key person in founding the school to step aside for a while and give time and space for staff and parents to grow into the school. However, this is not an easy thing to do.

Virtually every school project provided an opportunity for women to come forward and play a key role in the setting up of the school. Many of these were women who never thought of themselves as having the kinds of skills which they proved to have. They emerged as leaders; as entrepreneurs who spearheaded successful fund-raising ventures; as public relations and marketing executives, 'selling' the new school and finding potential pupils; as excellent negotiators with officialdom at both local and central level; as counsellors and mediators who helped to resolve conflicts as they arose; and as experts in a whole range of areas which they had never previously encountered. Most of these women were working full-time in the home raising their children when they first became involved. Apart from the skills which they developed on the task, they became more confident as time went on and in many cases they subsequently took on paid employment exploiting the skills and expertise that they had developed during their time with the school project.

The chairpersons of six of the ten schools in the Educate Together sector are women. Of the 34 Patron's nominees on boards of management, 22 (64%) are women. Eight of the ten principal teachers are women and in the five schools which are large enough to have elected teachers on the board, four out of five of these teachers are women. Overall, over two-thirds of the members of the boards of management of Educate Together schools are women – which is almost certainly a higher proportion than the average in national schools throughout the country.

Religious Education

Earlier I mentioned some of the issues which cause conflict when adults from different religious and cultural backgrounds come together for the first time. While conflict is not common when the schools get underway, it would be disingenuous to suggest that there are no issues which cause conflict. Predictably the question of religious education can become a focus for difference which if not sorted out at an early stage can escalate. The religious education policy of Educate Together schools is two pronged: (a) each school offers a Religious Education Core Curriculum, which is taught by the full-time teachers; and (b) each school facilitates any group of parents that may wish to provide denominational instruction for their children. Qualified instructors may be appointed by such a group by agreement between the board of management and the parents concerned.

The development and implementation of a Religious Education Core

Curriculum has been a challenging and often exciting process in which parents and teachers participate. A number of schools have produced handbooks or guidelines on their Religious Education Core Curriculum, and Educate Together, through its in-service courses, has provided an opportunity for teachers to share expertise and experiences in this area. Educate Together has also produced guidelines for teachers which can be useful as a starting point for new schools.

Each school makes its own arrangements for facilitating denominational instruction. In some schools, denominational classes are timetabled within school hours; in others they are held on the school premises outside school hours; others have a combination of both. In schools in very cramped accommodation it may be impossible to find space for denominational instruction in school hours. On the other hand, if children depend on inflexible transport to get home, there may be no option but to timetable denominational instruction for them in school hours. Even a school with adequate accommodation may find it difficult to find space for four or five different religious groups. Consequently it might not be possible to cater for children's needs and parents' wishes in precisely the way they would like.

Almost every school has encountered tension with some parents at some stage over this question. Often the motivation of the school in taking whatever action it has taken, is misunderstood and an atmosphere of suspicion and mistrust can develop. In such cases, Educate Together recommends that the question be brought out into the open and discussed at a meeting to which all parents are invited. Such meetings have taken place in almost all our schools at some stage. Some of the meetings have initially been confrontational with emotional accusations being made. Deep-rooted resentments about 'the other side' sometimes emerge which can be disconcerting to parents and teachers who had no idea that their actions were being interpreted in this way. The aim of such meetings is to come to an agreement which will go as far as possible to meet the requests of the parents involved while at the same time ensuring that a 'majority rule' mentality does not develop.

I have attended many such meetings and find that similar issues and concerns emerge at all of them. The numerically smaller religious groups, or parents who are not affiliated to any religious group, are worried that their children might be marginalised or 'swamped' if the larger groups regularly come together within school hours for denominational instruction. They fear that their children will feel outsiders in a school where no child should be an outsider. The Catholic group, surprisingly, often feels threatened if it is asked to contribute to a compromise.

Catholic parents in the South are familiar with the tradition of Catholic schools where arrangements for religious instruction are made on the assumption that all children are Catholics. Often such parents have not fully faced the implications of sending their children to a multi-denominational school. In spite of the discomfort a general meeting produces, it has been my experience that the airing and sharing of views and attitudes has been beneficial in the long-term for the development of the school involved. In every case to date, a satisfactory compromise has been reached. However, schools must be prepared to reconsider their arrangements from time to time as the external situation or the parents' wishes change.

The Role of Educate Together
Educate Together has played an important role to date in co-ordinating the existing schools and supporting new groups which want to start a multi-denominational school. Its aims are: (a) to ensure liaison between the existing school projects; (b) to represent, where appropriate, the interests of the multi-denominational sector within the national school system; (c) to coordinate public relations activities at non-local level; and (d) to coordinate fund-raising activities at non-local level. Although its funds have been limited, it has undertaken a number of important initiatives in addition to the routine work of coordinating and supporting projects throughout the country. These have included annual Educate Together days, summer courses for teachers to share experiences in the development and implementation of the Religious Education Core Curriculum, weekend workshops for principals and training workshops for board members. A set of guidelines for teachers on the Religious Education Core Curriculum has been produced as a result of these courses and has proved very useful, particularly for new and substitute teachers. Reports have also been submitted to various education review bodies and most recently in response to the Education Green Paper. An information pack on starting an Educate Together school was prepared in 1992 and was launched by President Mary Robinson in January 1993. [27]

The only source of income available to Educate Together during its first six years, was an annual contribution of between £25 and £50 each from member projects. Subsequently full member organisations have contributed an annual amount per pupil enrolled in their school and the organisation has also received some voluntary grants. Since the setting up of the Northern Ireland Council for Integrated Education, Educate Together has maintained contact with its director and staff. We believe that this link should be strengthened, possibly through joint initiatives with teachers and parents as well as joint seminars and workshops.

Comparisons with Integrated Schools in Northern Ireland

The multi-denominational schools in the Republic and the integrated schools in Northern Ireland share many common problems and challenges. It was no co-incidence that they emerged at around the same period in the mid 1970s. The escalating violence in the north made many people think again about traditional structures in society; an initiative which might contribute to greater understanding and respect across the traditional divides was worth a try.

When the Dalkey School Project was set up in 1975, its founders kept in close contact with the founders of All Children Together and attended some of the early meetings in Belfast. From the start, it was recognised that both groups had common problems but that there were also differences in the solutions being considered. The Dalkey School Project and subsequently other Educate Together schools defined the term multi-denominational as 'all children having equal rights of access to the school and children of all social, cultural and religious backgrounds being equally respected'. Educate Together schools do not ask parents to disclose their religious affiliation (if any) and therefore no statistical breakdown of children by religion is available. Their religious education policy is based on the principle that the ethos of the schools should reflect the ethos of a society in which there are many social, cultural and religious strands co-existing in harmony and mutual respect. Consequently the RE Core Curriculum is designed to help children to understand the different traditions of life and thought that they will meet in their environment – including Catholic and Protestant, but also Jewish, Bâha'í, Muslim, Jehovah Witness, Mormon, Mennonite, humanist, atheistic, etc. Thus the RE Core Curriculum attempts to be as all-embracing as possible and to ensure that no child is an outsider whatever his/her tradition or belief.

The other main difference between the schools in the south and north is the age-level of pupils catered for. In the south, it was decided to concentrate on setting up schools at primary level. This was the level at which there was no option for parents of different religious backgrounds who wanted to have their children educated together. At post-primary level the vocational schools in the south have always been undenominational and democratically run and since the 1960s and 1970s the newer community schools were not exclusively confined to one denominational group, although their management structure gave the right to nominate a majority of board members to the local Catholic or the Church of Ireland Bishop. Although there are some areas of the country where access to un-denominational schooling at post-primary level is not easy, Educate Together has continued to concentrate on the primary level and to date all Educate Together schools are primary (national) schools.

The Main Challenges Ahead

The difficulty of getting access to suitable accommodation has been the single greatest deterrent for parents who want to send their children to multi-denominational schools in this country. All other member states of the European Community provide publicly owned buildings for basic education. Ireland is unique in requiring citizens to provide privately owned accommodation for this purpose. Of the ten national schools in our sector, only three are in permanent purpose-built accommodation and only one of these has sufficient accommodation to meet the demand for places. The other seven are in various types of temporary premises which are shared with other users. These premises are inadequate and are becoming increasingly overcrowded as demand for places grows. In addition to the existing schools, there are parent groups around the country who have demonstrated to the satisfaction of the Department of Education that there is a demand for multi-denominational education in their area but who have failed to start a school because of the impossibility of getting access to suitable accommodation.

Although classrooms and even whole school buildings have become empty because of the decline in the pupil population, they are frequently not available for Educate Together schools because though initially financed mainly from public funds, they are owned by the churches. Until this year none of the Catholic Diocesan Trusts were willing to lease or sell these buildings to Educate Together schools. Some projects were also refused access to other buildings in which the Catholic Church had an interest, e.g. sports centres, youth centres etc. However, in June 1993 an empty school building owned by the Catholic diocese of Cork was sold to the Cork School Project who plan to renovate it and move there in September. This could be an important precedent for other areas of the country.

In a number of cases the Protestant churches have provided accommodation. Classrooms have been leased from the Church of Ireland or the Presbyterian churches, or both, in Dalkey and in Cork; and the schools in Ranelagh and Dublin South City are housed in old Church of Ireland school buildings. The Vocational Education Committees in a number of areas have also been supportive.

However, because there are empty school buildings in certain areas, the Department will not provide grant aid for new buildings for multi-denominational schools. Meeting the demand for multi-denominational education and providing an effective underpinning of the constitutional rights of parents, requires a solution to the accommodation problem. In the present demographic situation it makes good sense to use existing school buildings and Educate Together would like to see some administrative changes to allow this to happen.

In its submission to the Minister on forthcoming Education White Paper, Educate Together has made a number of proposals which would help multi-denominational schools to gain access to suitable accommodation in the short term. We would also like the longer-term issue of the conditions under which grants are made available for school buildings to be addressed in the legislation. For example, parents involved in Educate Together schools have no particular interest in becoming owners and trustees of school buildings. Surely it should be possible to move towards a situation where groups like ours would have the option of being housed in public buildings which would revert to the state if the demand for multi-denominational education no longer existed in the area? The proposal in the 1993 *Programme for Government* to set up local education committees may provide solutions to this issue.

The second factor which militates against the development of multi-denominational education in the south is the practice introduced by Minister Cooney in 1986 whereby our schools are recognised in a provisional capacity only in the early years and are ineligible for capital grants during these crucial and expensive years. In the Green Paper it is stated that 'where the establishment of further multi-denominational schools represents the wishes of parents, and where such schools can be justified on the basis of demand, the Department of Education will facilitate and support the establishment of such schools on the same terms as those available for the establishment of denominational schools'.[27] Educate Together has called on the Minister to implement this commitment immediately, and to remove the discriminatory practice of provisional recognition and provide capital grants for multi-denominational schools from the start.

Conclusion

In spite of the many difficulties encountered by Educate Together schools in the past 15 years, it is probably fair to say that morale among parents, teachers and pupils is high and there is a sense of confidence that current problems will be overcome. The presence of President Mary Robinson at the launch of the Educate Together Information Pack was a great boost to the movement. The willingness of the Gulbenkian Foundation to grant aid the publication was also very important – while the grant itself was not very large, it was the first time the work of the movement was recognised outside the limited circles of Educate Together and the launch provided an opportunity to distribute accurate information about Educate Together to a wider audience. The debate on the Green Paper has also provided a platform where the difficulties and problems of Educate Together have been aired – as well its enthusiasm, commitment and success. In spite of everything, the story of Educate Together to date has been a success story. It is a story of change and development from the bottom up, of ordinary people from a variety of different backgrounds – religious, cultural and social – working together to provide an educational system where their children can be educated together.

Notes

1. Akenson, D. H., (1970) *The Irish Education Experiment: the national system of education in Ireland in the nineteenth century*, Routledge. For a more complete discussion of the historical background to the setting up of the Dalkey School Project see Áine Hyland, 'The Multi-denominational Experience in the National School System in Ireland,' *Irish Educational Studies*, Vol.8, No.1, 1989. See also A.M. Frieda McGovern, *The Revival of the Multi-denominational Concept in the Irish National School System1965 –1988*, an academic paper submitted in partial fulfilment of the requirements for the Degree of Master in Education, Trinity College, Dublin, March 1989.

2. *Annual Report of the Commissioners of National Education in Ireland*, 1850, contained in *Reports of the Commissioners of National Education in Ireland*, Vol.1 from 1834 to 1851. Dublin, 1865.

3. Commissioners of National Education in Ireland, *Rules for National Schools*, 1898.

4. Department of Education, *Rules for National Schools*, 1965, rule 68.

5. *Ibid.*, rule 69.

6. Graham Balfour, *The educational system of Great Britain and Ireland*, Clarendon, Oxford 1903

7. Preface to the *Rules for National Schools*, 1965.

8. Department of Education, *Curaclam na Bunscoile - Primary School Curriculum, Teachers' Handbook*, Dublin, 1971.

9. *Ibid.*, Introduction.

10. Fr. Colm Burke, *The Furrow*, February 1975, p.104.

11. Report of the Chairperson of the P.T.A. of St. Patrick's National School, 1974

12. Quoted in *Contact* (parish magazine of St. Patrick's Church, Dalkey), April 1974.

13. Micheal Johnston, talk entitled 'Integrated Education' given at the Methodist Centenary Church, Dublin on 7th February 1988.

14. *Irish Independent*, 12 January 1977.

15. See for example, *Irish Press,* 29 September 1975 in which Richard Burke is quoted as stating: 'There is at present a campaign for what its promoters call 'multi-denominational' education in primary schools, based on the suggestion that education in schools under the control of persons of their own religious faith and by teachers of their own religious faith promotes disharmony and dissension in the community. To my mind this is completely false. Indeed I regard it as a libel on teachers to suggest that in educating children in accordance with the particular teachings and belief of the religion of their homes, the teachers implant the seeds of intolerance and encourage attitudes of bigotry. It is also arrant nonsense.'

16. Dalkey School Project, *Survey of Attitudes and Preferences towards multi-denominational, co-educational, democratically managed National Schools,* June 1976.

17. *Demokratisierung des Erziehungswesens,* Proceedings of an international seminar hosted jointly by the Friedrich-Naumann-Stiftung and the Dalkey School Project in Dun Laoghaire from 17-19 Nov. 1978.

18. Dominic O Laoghaire, 'Some schools more equal than others?', in *Magill,* January 1988.

19. Leaflet entitled *The Dalkey School Saga: has the government surrendered to the multi-denominational pressure groups?* distributed by the Council of Social Concern, Ely Place, Jan. 1988.

20. Letter sent from the Dept. of Education to the Sligo School Project in August 1987 setting out the conditions under which recognition was given to the school.

21. Seanad Eireann (Official Report), Vol. 114, No.10 30 Oct.1986, p. 1108.

22. Extract from official lease of national schools vested in trustees (1965 edition).

23. Dept. of Education circular 1990 - *School Transport; Multi-denominational schools.*

24. Newsletter of the Ranelagh Multi-denominational School Association, 1991.

25. Newsletter of the Limerick School Project, Autumn 1989.

26. Copies of these letter were made available to Educate Together.

27. *Educate Together: Starting an Educate Together National School,* Information Pack, available from Educate Together, Áine Hyland, Chairperson, 37 Mapas Road, Dalkey, Co. Dublin.

28. Department of Education, *Education for a Changing World, A Green Paper,* Stationery Office, Dublin, June 1992 p. 142.

14
Christian Unity and Joint Church Schools
An English Perspective

Priscilla Chadwick

Jesus prayed that his disciples might be one. Disunity is contrary to the will of God. It gravely weakens the witness of Christian people and institutions before the world. There is hardly a more striking manifestation of this weakness than competition and rivalry in education and the sense of separateness which this perpetuates. Christians want their children to acquire not only mental and manual skills but a moral and spiritual formation of character. They do not want the atmosphere of the school to be at loggerheads with the values inculcated by home and parish church.

Particularly in the last three decades, there have been energetic moves to set aside the animosities of the past and to witness together to the teaching of Christ in the community of faith. These efforts have resulted in the creation of a number of joint Christian schools, notably those bringing together Anglican and Roman Catholic (the two largest Christian bodies in England).[1] These schools have developed when in Britain there is increased pressure on all schools to deliver the National Curriculum, keep abreast of modern developments (e.g. in information technology), to ensure equal opportunities, to respond to parental choice and to create a caring community, all within the context of considerable national economic stringency. What is constant in church schools, whatever may be the new situations arising, is that Christians will always seek to ensure that Christian principles are evident in the curriculum, in religious education, in admissions policy, in the ethos and atmosphere. The partnership of home, parish and school is fundamental.

A joint Christian school may be brought into existence for more than one reason. A growing mutual confidence between separated Christian communities, discovering one another to be brothers and sisters in Christ, is not only a product but in some degree a precondition of effectiveness. This prior confidence can be initially described as a vision of what is actually possible, if one looks beyond the temporary frustrations inherent in the practicalities of establishing a joint school. Where there is no will, there is unlikely to be a way. But deep convictions about the need and possibility of a united Christian school to serve the local community have already been demonstrated to be highly effective in realising the vision and have produced thriving schools. Christian groups today, though still divided by the accidents and folk memories of the past, no longer seek principally to define their own position in antithesis to one another. Differences among Christian believers have of course always existed, but today they mainly tend to run across the normal confessional frontiers. Above all, members in both groups quickly become aware of the degree of common ground in their commitment to Christ's teaching and in the upholding of Christian values. Co-operation in Christian witness creates a supportive alliance and at once marks Christianity off from the liberal secular humanism, which in practice has tended to be the principle endorsed by most county schools, in spite of the Christian context of the 1944 legislation.

Educational and Economic Issues

At this stage specifically educational arguments come into play. With current levels of funding, a small school is simply unable to offer the same range of subject choice to its pupils as a large school, especially at the secondary stage. The wide spread of ability in most comprehensive schools, while influential as a socialising factor, necessitates a reasonable number of pupils on roll to provide satisfactory group sizes. For those authorities contemplating the proposal to establish a joint school, there is a strong argument for creating an educationally viable Christian school, rather than struggling to retain two small single-denominational schools at considerable cost to the pupils in terms of educational resources. Another consideration is that staff of higher calibre are often attracted by a school that offers a wide range of teaching opportunities. In addition, the assurance of sixth form provision tends to attract both staff and parents, but is generally feasible only with a minimum intake of about 150 pupils in each year. There are, therefore, powerful educational arguments for developing successful joint church schools, rather than endeavouring to preserve less viable schools affiliated to a single communion.

Economics cannot be ignored here. In some cases, it may be that financial considerations have been excessively influential among the pressures for creating a joint school. They cannot be the top priority, but at the same time they can never be matters of complete indifference. They need the most careful scrutiny. For example, those planning a joint school have to ask the question: what is the expected ratio of Anglican and Roman Catholic pupils? If it is specified as 60:40, then the diocesan authorities need to reflect these proportions in their capital investment and contributions to maintenance.

Unlike Northern Ireland there are currently in England more joint schools in the secondary than in the primary sector; discussion continues about the feasibility of shared Christian education at different levels. Some educationists would argue strongly that joint secondary schools work more effectively if primary pupils have been 'nurtured' solely within their own tradition through their early years. Church primary schools are, in some respects, different from their secondary neighbours. They tend to be far more closely linked to a specific parish where the local priest may pay daily visits to the children and is actively involved with their catechetics or nurture. Those planning a joint primary school need full co-operation from the parish clergy in order to maintain such valuable links. Others emphasize the common elements of catechesis and religious education, suggesting that the theological content of material suitable for the younger age groups is rarely a source of division between Anglican and Roman Catholic churches; where differences are judged significant, clergy or teachers may feel the need to separate the children into denominational groups, but in general the extensive areas of common ground should in no way preclude joint Christian education from developing successfully at a variety of levels. As more joint primary schools are established, it is particularly important to support those children transferring from joint primary to single denominational secondary schools.

The Church School in England and Wales

The debate on the role of the church school continues to exercise the minds of ministers in both church and state. The essence of the debate may be briefly summarised.

The *dual system,* established by the Balfour Act of 1902 following on from legislation in 1870, recognised the value of partnership between church and state in the education of the nation's children.[2] Although there had been vocal opposition (especially from the Free Churches) towards government finance to support denominational education, producing some modifications in 1902, the 'voluntary' sector has retained its role in the partnership. Central government currently contributes 85 per cent of the capital costs of voluntary aided schools, while local authorities are responsible for their day-to-day running costs, and all the costs related to voluntary controlled schools.[3]

The Butler Act of 1944 was generally recognised as an ingenious and intricate reconciliation of, in part, conflicting interests. The fact that this major piece of legislation stood the test of time with only minor modifications suggests that, far from being one of those compromises which 'fudges' the issue, it did in fact grasp the essentials of the problem and constructed a practical solution which was made to work. Few would doubt this carefully balanced enactment would not have been possible without the skill and imagination of R.A. Butler as Minister of Education and of William Temple as Archbishop of Canterbury.[4] The Act established the framework of the present system, based on the consensus that religious education and collective worship should be an integral part of school life for both secular and religious institutions, and that the church should work in partnership with the state in educating the nation's children. This partnership preserved the religious traditions of the voluntary schools, while committing the state to considerable financial support for their maintenance, willingly given since the alternative would be far greater expenditure by the state.

The *Anglican approach* to this partnership has differed noticeably from that of the Roman Catholic Church. Some brief analysis may be needed for clarity here. The Church of England has always somehow kept before its eyes the ideal, never of course realised in practice, of holding together the idea of a 'national church' with that of the universal Church Catholic. There has been a tendency to merge its concern for the nation's general education with its involvement in Christian nurture. The role of the church of the nation has been to provide neighbourhood schools for the local children linked to the parish church.

This broad policy has meant that, especially in rural areas, the Church of England school has often been the only one available. This can present a dilemma for parents who wish their children to be educated in a secular or at least a non-Anglican environment. On the other hand, it has been an important route by which the local clergy have been given the possibility of becoming fully and profitably involved in the local community, with care for the good of all, whether their own congregation or not.

This sense of an outward-looking responsibility for education generally has been a characteristic of the Church of England for a long time; it has roots at least as far back as the sixteenth century. It was strikingly endorsed by a green paper submitted to the General Synod by the Board of Education, entitled *A Future in Partnership* (1984) and accepted by a resolution in July 1985. Strong reservations were expressed about the exclusive view that church schools ought primarily to be providing education for committed practising Anglicans. There are social disadvantages resulting from such an exclusive view, namely that in effect it would make the schools mainly middle-class, predominantly white, and limited to members of the church-going community instead of reaching out beyond these frontiers.

There is a delicate balance that is not easy to keep here. On the one hand, the Anglicans want to keep their schools Christian in spirit and ethos, not submerged in the secular liberal humanism which in county schools (though much depends on the individual teacher and the head) is likely to predominate. In the same way as Roman Catholics, Anglicans also understand their schools as bearing a responsibility to present pupils with a faith by which to live and with an experience of worship (especially important if the parents do not go to church themselves). This distinctively Christian concern cannot be overlooked. It is one of the main reasons for the existence of church schools, for many parents the main ground for choosing an Anglican school, and for many parishes the persuasive argument for parting with hard-earned funds to support their local church school. On the other hand, the tradition of Church of England schools and the public support they receive make them outward looking to society at large.

For an Anglican school, therefore, there are two parallel aims – the need to be and to stay distinctively Christian, and the need not to be exclusive or the expression of a closed society. In every Anglican school these two aims are reflected in the admissions policy, curriculum, selection of staff, and role in the local diocese. The school is there to provide the specifically Christian education which is its ultimate raison d'etre, but also to contribute to the general education in the neighbourhood, serving the community at large. The potential tension between these two aims, likely to be exacerbated by grant maintained status, shapes the continuing debate about Anglican church schools within the voluntary sector of the 'dual system'.

The *Roman Catholic school* has, until recently, never had any doubt about its aim. It was to ensure that 'the Catholic child from the Catholic home should continue his education at the hands of Catholic teachers in a Catholic school'. (Catholic Education Council, 1955) This concept has come to draw criticism from within the community, similar to that brought against the 'exclusive' Anglican approach, namely that it creates a 'ghetto' mentality and a closed society, shows disregard for the Catholic church's mission to the world, and encourages parents to rely largely, in some cases totally, upon the school for moral and spiritual formation of their children.

The new look in Catholic education has been closely related to the impact of the Second Vatican Council. That Council did not change the nature of the church or alter its doctrines, but it transformed the direction of Catholic education, dismantling the feeling of living in an embattled medieval fortress. In its final Constitution (*Gaudium et Spes,* 1965), the Second Vatican Council expressed confidence towards the world, no longer a prickly defensiveness. So rather than be set altogether apart from the world, the church can work within the institutions which shape society, and can contribute to their spiritual development. In this outward-looking mission, the Catholic school should be in the front line.

In 1981, an influential body of Catholic educationists submitted a report to the Bishops of England and Wales, *Signposts and Homecomings* .[5] They advocated a reappraisal of the model of the Church; not an institution defending a closed educational system, but a servant to the community 'involved in the general task of education for its own sake'. Not that the Catholic school ought simply to be assimilated into surrounding secular society; Catholic schools retain a prophetic role, 'making a distinctive and critical contribution'. Confidence to move outwards is based on the supportive community of faith, where initiation is into a living and growing tradition, not a static body of catechetical knowledge.

It is one thing for professional advisers to advocate such views, another for schools to adapt to the changes of attitude that such words presuppose. Recent developments in catechetical teaching aim at greater personal understanding and appropriation of Christian teaching rather than unreflecting acceptance of what is simply given by authority.[6] Syllabuses and styles of teaching, however, do not change overnight; and it is a lengthy process to bring Catholic parents to share in responsibility for their children's catechetical instruction. Nevertheless, given the essential support of the local parish, schools are becoming more confident. The atmosphere of openness seems here to stay.

Some Roman Catholic schools have recently found it difficult to fill all their places with Roman Catholic applicants. Some have had to close, but many others have encouraged the entry of children from families without a Roman Catholic affiliation. Where the latter create a very substantial minority, it is important that the school reappraise the provision of religious education and modify its ethos. There have been other instances where the cost of maintaining an exclusively Roman Catholic school has become intolerably high, and this has provided a reason for exploring the possibility of ecumenical links with other churches concerned with Christian education.

From this brief summary of the various issues facing both Anglican and

Roman Catholic schools in defining their aims, it is clear that the terms within which the debate is conducted are remarkably similar. Both bodies share the wish to balance the outward mission of the church school with the nurturing role. There is, therefore, a powerful argument for encouraging the discussion to progress in tandem, rather than in isolation. The long-term effects may prove important as increasing numbers of schools wish to see these aims realised in joint ecumenical education.

Ecumenical Education in Practice

For almost the past twenty years, the idea of 'ecumenical education' has been more than just a 'prophetic vision'. Christian schools from a variety of denominational traditions and reflecting all phases from primary and middle through to secondary and sixth forms have come together to confirm that the vision is a reality. Although some observers would acknowledge these initiatives as 'experimental', others would accept that many of these schools are now thriving examples of the true spirit of 'ecumenical cooperation' in education.

The first joint Anglican/Roman Catholic 11–16 school began in 1972 when a Roman Catholic school in Devon formally decided to admit about 30 per cent Anglicans: a common RE syllabus was accepted from the start and each denomination provided chaplaincy support. The pressure of oversubscription on the few Anglican places was subsequently considerable. In Redhill, Surrey, the amalgamation of one Anglican and one Roman Catholic secondary school into a united 12–18 comprehensive took place in 1976: here RE was taught together throughout the school, with one additional period for 12–13 year olds of denominational RE to separate groups following a common framework. The governors of this much oversubscribed school are currently considering extending the ecumenical foundation to include the Free Churches.

Meanwhile, other joint Anglican/Roman Catholic secondary schools have opened, including, Taunton (1982), Oxford (1984), Cambridge (1988) and Parkstone, Dorset (1991); and a number of primary schools, e.g. Sunderland (1972). In Harrogate, two Anglican and Roman Catholic comprehensive schools came together in 1973 to form a joint Associated Sixth Form (attracting almost 500 students in 1992). Perhaps primarily because of overall pupil numbers contracting, no opportunity has yet arisen to establish an ecumenical school from its first foundations.

These joint schools have been noticeably more successful when the parties come together from a position of strength rather than weakness, where educational managers anticipate and plan creatively rather than find themselves motivated solely by 'survival' at all costs. Each church community needs to feel confident that its interests are being best served and its children well supported; active and on-going reassurance is often needed. It is interesting to note that, while many ecumenical schools in England were established for economic as much as theological reasons, in Northern Ireland it was the parents' desire to offer their children an alternative to segregated education which created the driving force behind the integrated schools movement.

However, the hesitant response of the Anglican and Roman Catholic Churches to these developments in Northern Ireland contrasts with the encouragement generally given to ecumenical education in England. Both Anglican and Roman Catholic bishops and clergy have been regular visitors to joint church schools; diocesan authorities have been fully involved in policy and administrative matters. It will be interesting to see if such arrangements are weakened by schools opting out into grant maintained status.

The Anglican Church, with its traditionally more 'open' approach in church schools, has encouraged educational ecumenical developments: the Archbishop of Canterbury warmly welcomed the first national conference of joint ecumenical schools in June 1992 and expressed his approval. Varied levels of support among Roman Catholics have tended to reflect an individual bishop's interests: while the Archbishop of Birmingham has been critical of progressive Catholic RE and voiced reservations about his joint school in Oxford, the Bishop of Arundel and Brighton, the long-standing co-chairman of the Anglican/Roman Catholic International Commission, has always given full episcopal support to his Redhill school. Cardinal Hume has recognised that: 'Christian ecumenical schools have broken new ground...and may well be a significant indication of a way forward'.[7]

Ecumenical Religious Education

In joint schools, the issues of spiritual, moral and catechetical development are critical. First, how do we encourage young people to explore spiritual values for themselves? It is not appropriate to advocate narrow rote-learning of the Bible or catechism for today's children who demand that new ideas should relate to their understanding of the world.

Spiritual growth is more likely when children are encouraged to move beyond the superficial attractions of secular materialism and focus on the ultimate questions of God's purpose for their lives. They need to experience the mystery of God's presence through their exploration of the natural world, their appreciation of human expressions of 'the spiritual' in art, music or literature, and in their encounter with different interpretations of the divine through other world faith traditions. Religious education is central to this process. It is important also for Anglicans and Roman Catholics to work together in identifying the spiritual dimension within the secular framework of the national curriculum.

Secondly, moral values guided by Christian teaching should be an integral part of a church school community which claims to be preparing young people for adult life. Such values can be explicit in classroom discussion, for example on attitudes to Third World exploitation or sex education, but are also implicit in the quality of the relationships within the school community. Both Anglicans and Roman Catholics highlight the importance of such values. Cardinal Hume, addressing London headteachers in September 1991, argued that 'moral education is made more credible and effective if it is promoted by educators who are themselves concerned and who are seen to be living that morality in daily life'. Geoffrey Duncan of the Church of England's National Society wrote in *The Curriculum: A Christian View*: 'The ethos of the school is created by the love, care and professional concern with which staff, pupils and the community interrelate: it is a collection of positive values – including honesty, love, integrity, commitment, cooperation – to which the Christian makes a major contribution.' Joint schools need to place additional emphasis on encouraging mutual respect for individuals with differing moral views.

Thirdly, church schools are encouraged, in partnership with the home and parish community, to nurture the developing Christian faith of pupils. Such catechetical instruction in the specific tenets of Anglicanism or Roman Catholicism should be carefully distinguished, particularly in a joint school, from compulsory religious education and is often more appropriate in the context of liturgical celebrations, chaplaincy groups or retreat days where an individual's commitment of faith may be explicitly recognised. Even in this context, the professional educator has to be aware of the danger of indoctrination and the need to respect a pupil's freedom of conscience. Some would argue that specific catechetics should remain the prerogative of the home and parish to avoid such confusion; but this is not to say that the nature of Christian affirmations, the relevance of the Church to society, its sacramental and ethical teaching should be taboo subjects in ecumenical RE. These need to be tackled with a certain objectivity and even detachment, and will then be comprehended by the pupils as a matter of rational understanding that, for believers, will enrich their grasp of faith.

It seems that if religious education in a church school, and especially an ecumenical one, is to be effective, it has to succeed in the classroom by producing high standards of work and by being accepted by the pupils as a serious academic subject; at the same time, it must look at the whole person and involve itself in the pupil's spiritual development which generally takes place beyond the classroom. This wide-ranging responsibility requires a dedicated team of teachers who not only have good academic qualifications, but also relate easily to young people.

Alongside these requirements, such teachers evidently need to have a mature understanding of their own faith and a commitment to ecumenism that goes far beyond merely working alongside each other. The ecumenical task is one of great difficulty, requiring sensitivity and hard work, a resolution to remain undiscouraged by the virtually inevitable setbacks, and a vision that the ultimate aim of Christian unity is possible. For the ecumenical school is, by its very existence, a challenge to the conventional opinion that disunity has to be institutionalised to ensure its own diabolical permanence.

Notes

1. The Methodist Church has 55 primary schools, of which 27 are currently shared with Anglicans; DES figures in 1991 indicated that Anglicans had 4,685 primary and 150 secondary (aided and controlled) while Roman Catholics had 1,819 primary and 367 secondary (all aided). In 1992 there were 8 joint Anglican/Roman Catholic secondary schools, 3 joint primary and one joint sixth form college in England.

2. See Cruickshank, M. (1963) *Church and State in English Education*, Macmillan

3. There is today in Britain a mounting pressure from some religious groups, especially more fundamentalist Christians and Muslims, to establish their own religious schools with the aid of public money. Hitherto, this pressure has been resisted on, for example, the social and political ground that such a move would reinforce ethnic separation and enhance the difficulties that ethnic groups have in accepting, and being accepted by, the British society in which they live. This has been felt on balance to outweigh the force of the moral arguments, by which Anglicans, Methodists, Roman Catholics or Jews have been allowed to educate their children in schools supportive of the religious and moral values espoused by home and church. But the importance of the issue is evident in the 1985 Swann Report, *Education for All*, HMSO.

4. See R.A. Butler's autobiography, *The Art of the Possible* (1971) Hamish Hamilton.

5. *Signposts and Homecomings*, (1981) St Paul Publications.

6. For example, the Catholic R.E. programmes of the National Project on Religious Education, such as *Weaving the Web* (1988) for secondary, and *Here I Am* (1992) for primary schools, offered a flexible framework to be complemented with diocesan syllabuses and in-service training.

7. Cardinal Hume (1988) *Towards a Civilisation of Love*, Hodder and Stoughton, p. 111.

8. Duncan, G., (1990) *The Curriculum: A Christian View*, The Church of England's National Society.

15
Integrated Education and Political Identity[1]

Frank Wright

Many people in Northern Ireland want their children to be educated together with children of other traditions. There have been earlier occasions in the history of the North of Ireland when it has happened, at least in some places. Yet however much support there is for the idea of integrated education, putting it into practice seems to be exceedingly difficult. The gap between the amount of vague support there is for the idea and the actual extent of integrated education is usually wide. The purpose of this paper is to warn that there is no short cut to bridging this gap without jeopardising what is most positive about the integrated education that exists at the moment.

While I was writing about 19th century Ulster, I learned about how educational conflict had a very big part in the division between nationalism and unionism. Indeed it is hardly an exaggeration to say that at the core of each community (of Catholic and Protestant) there were fears of the threat to 'our' schools from the 'others'. The national system of education in Ireland, founded in 1831, was nominally integrated. But there was a tendency for people to support integrated education most keenly when they thought their 'side' would gain from it. For example between 1859-71, Presbyterian supporters of national education – which they described as 'mixed secular and separate religious instruction' – were less than clear about how much control they already had over the mixed schools whose role they wished to expand. No debate about the benefits of an overall integrated education policy in the North of Ireland can ever be about the abstract advantages of mixing. There is a long history of suspicion about who controls education. For good reasons, people in the North of Ireland have been very cautious indeed about who they trust with the education of their children. The future of integrated education depends on how these anxieties are coped with.

Since the 1970s the idea of integrated education has had a new burst of life. What is really new about the integrated schools of today and different from previous ideas of mixed education is that they involve parents coming together and meeting and cooperating with each other. In Dorothy Wilson and Seamus Dunn's *Integrated Schools – Information for parents*, this aspect of the school is centrally emphasised. Difficulties involved in respecting each others' tradition, whether in the syllabus, the style of teaching, the use of symbols and so on, are resolved by parents and teachers together. In a school where parents have come together freely to create a shared environment for their children, knowing the risks and that there will be difficulties to work through together, it is very possible that new relationships will grow. But if instead children are pushed together most of the old problems which led to segregated education in the first place will resurface only slightly changed.

We can say that children are being pushed together whenever integrated education is seen as a way of changing other people rather than ourselves. This matter of emphasis is very important. There have been many occasions when people said what a good idea it would be to integrate all the schools so that children would grow up together without bigotry. But such dreams about how integrated education could change everything in Northern Ireland usually leave unanswered all the real difficulties.

To explain the point further, ask yourself who you have ever heard speaking casually in favour of integrated education. Do you know either of the following? Someone with a fantasy of Catholics and Protestants standing reverently before a Union Jack fluttering from the school flagpole; or someone with the fantasy of Protestant and Catholic children dutifully absorbing a history syllabus which puts Protestants 'right about their Irishness'. These kinds of supporter of integrated schools may say how they would like to see all children being educated together and brought up without bigotry, but their desire to put something across on the 'others' is a bad omen. Of course we all may have some fantasies of this kind, but there is little integrated education can do until parents themselves are prepared to face such possible conflicts of expectation.

Parent initiative in integrated schooling has real promise for the future. If parents play some part in resolving the inevitable difficulties of integrated education, parental learning will go on and the school as a 'Meeting' of traditions will flourish. But if integrated schools multiply as a result of favourable financial incentives, they may leapfrog the growing experience that the established integrated schools have been through. This will build concealed conflicts into their foundations. At worst, people will end up rediscovering the advantages of separate education. So let us begin by trying to see what these advantages might be.

The Management of Distrust

Throughout Northern Irish history many people have sensed both that segregating children in different schools allowed bigotry to grow and also that separate education was the only secure way to ensure that schools respected the values of the children's families. Many of us know this somehow, and we cannot argue away either half of it, though we are always tempted to do so.

For example, opponents of separate schools sometimes claim that they 'cause' sectarian distrust and division. It is obvious that anything which keeps people, who might otherwise have got to know each other, apart, must be doing something to sustain an atmosphere of distrust. But the argument understandably exasperates supporters of separate schools. In a society where distrust is pervasive between adults, it can be difficult to secure trust between their children. Unless people who distrust each other have some shared trust in an authority above them both, the management of that distrust can be exceedingly difficult. Separate systems of education have often been a way of making distrust between national communities manageable.

One of the few things which northern nationalists have ever praised the Stormont Government for was its handling of education. From around 1930 onwards, it accepted an arrangement in which both communities felt their education system was secure against the encroachments of the other side. In other divided communities control over education has also been a central question. Where the communities have been more unequally placed than they are in Northern Ireland, the less powerful communities have not controlled their own education systems. Then the education systems have tended to atomise and demoralize these dominated communities, as for Muslims in secular schools in French Algeria or for the separate black (but white controlled) schools in the US Southern States.

By contrast, taking a long historical view from the 1830s, the separate school system in the North of Ireland has allowed Catholic society to build itself up to a level where it has not feared comparison with the dominant Protestant society. The Catholic middle class has built itself up around its teachers, although at the same time the boundary between Protestant and Catholic has been frozen by the parallel school systems. So even if the dual school system is a factor contributing to the present day conflict, it has also meant that the two sub-societies (roughly Catholic and Protestant) have been in a relatively more equal position in Northern Ireland than they would have been without it. There is nothing at all unusual about this: separate education has almost universally been sought by nationalist movements in Europe to build their communities and make them more cohesive.

No national group ever trusts another nation to control the education of its children – if it has any choice in the matter at all. Whenever anyone proposes integrated education in these situations, it is almost invariably suspected of being a ploy to uproot the culture of the less powerful community.

Sometimes accepting the need for separate education systems has prevented struggles which might otherwise have torn up the unity of a nation. The strength of this argument for separation of schools can be illustrated by the story of Scotland. In 1918 the state school system was placed on a firmly segregated basis. Segregated schools no doubt play a part in keeping alive Celtic v Rangers feeling today, but Scotland has by and large remained tranquil, even during the last twenty years when sectarianism might have fed back into it from Ulster. The Catholic Church has been content with a state system that contains a Catholic system within it. It is very probable that one of the reasons why the Labour party in Scotland has been able to span the gap between Catholic and Protestant has been that the truce of 1918 suited the Catholic clergy and a large enough part of the non-Catholic Labour supporters. The essential point is that existing educational arrangements are part of an unwritten treaty in Scotland, whose full implications would only become clear if an effort was made to undo it.

No one today could argue that enforcing integrated education upon Scotland would have made for a deeper peace than Scotland has actually had. There are groups in Scotland now who are aware of how far apart religious differences keep people, and they are trying to work upon their common heritage as Christians in Scotland. But no one in Scotland is arguing for a global plan for integrated education to combat dangers of sectarianism at the moment. It is easy to see that a political campaign to do this would start to politicise religion and create the very problem people suggest it might prevent. Because we have had so much sectarian conflict here in Northern Ireland it is tempting to blame it upon one of the factors which may have facilitated sectarian continuity. But the Scottish situation, which is in some respects very like Northern Ireland, helps us to underline the difference between people working together to promote integrated schools and a hypothetical policy decision to desegregate Scottish schools.

The Involvement of Parents and Teachers
The central difference between the two ways in which integrated education might come to pass have to do with how much of the dynamic is coming from the people directly involved. The hope behind most visions of integrated education in Northern Ireland is that if children mix together early enough, they will get so

used to being together that they will be relatively immunized against sectarianism in adult life. What does this mixing together mean? Upon whom does the responsibility for creating and cherishing this unusual environment fall? When few adults have experienced it themselves how do we expect that teachers will be able to do it? There is a great danger of putting onto teachers the responsibility for achieving something by magic, something they probably cannot do for our children, if we are not in earnest about wanting to do it for ourselves.

What actually happens in an integrated school will not depend on the syllabus, so much as on the human relationships within the school. Teachers are not superhuman and whether children from different national traditions can really meet as equals, sensing the acceptability of their feelings and their home experiences, depends upon how the teachers and other figures of authority in the school create the space for them. There is probably little chance of teachers developing these new ways unless the context they are working in is supportive. Here especially the input of parents may be decisive.

Any integration, if it is to avoid the pitfalls that make separate education attractive, must be a meeting on an equal basis where neither community has the upper hand over the other. Although there are many ways in which this problem could be formulated, we can see an example of it at the heart of the Anglo-Irish Agreement. In the agreement the British and Irish governments refer to two traditions in Ireland or two communities within Northern Ireland. The two traditions are defined as one wishing to have no change in the status of Northern Ireland and the other aspiring to a sovereign united Ireland. The two governments speak of diminishing the divisions in Northern Ireland and of recognizing and respecting the identities of the two communities in Northern Ireland. How do you diminish the divisions and at the same time recognize and respect the identities of the two communities or traditions, when they have such diametrically opposed opinions?

Much of this involves enabling children (and adults!) to experience differences as enriching aspects of the others that we just accept. But there are deep and antagonistic roots to the different traditions and although it will often be inappropriate to introduce children to the antagonistic aspects of their parents' different cultures, the occasions and ways for doing so will be better chosen if the parents and the teachers have themselves experienced real meeting with each other. Let us consider what is involved for parents and teachers.

'Tolerance' and Acceptance

In the beginning I distinguished abstract support for integrated education and the growing process involved in actually creating it. This is very like the difference between just claiming to be 'tolerant' and making real relationships of trust. Acceptance comes out of meeting where we both feel secure and able to trust. In such 'meetings together' we hear what it feels like to be the other and we accept each other with our differences; and we change in ways we probably cannot anticipate. We hear one another telling about each others' experiences and we are not distracted with clash of opinion. We can only have ideas about what this will mean for us politically.

We have seen that in a divided society separate school systems can make distrust manageable and allow for the growth of a polite distance between communities. This makes distrust less painful, but it also allows us to delude ourselves about how tolerant we are. Very often tolerance in the north of Ireland, as indeed in any divided society, is a kind of weapon for point scoring. 'We are tolerant, but there is no relationship between us and them, because of...xyz...which they are responsible for.'

Here are some examples of this kind of tolerance: those who say that they are tolerant of Protestants, and that most of the distrust in the north of Ireland is on the part of Protestants towards Catholics, who support the murder of (mostly Protestant) members of the security forces as part of a campaign to secure the unification of Ireland. Likewise there are those who say that there is no need for integrated schools, because the only reason the state schools are not integrated is the Catholic Church. They see no contradiction between attacking Catholic schools for creating segregation and claiming that, of course, Protestant clergy must have places on the management of state schools. These kinds of tolerance are abstract theory and have nothing to do with acceptance.

In all divided societies it can be very difficult to cope with what the others actually feel and say themselves about their own identity. When there are language differences as there are in many divided societies, they at least provide some tangible sign of difference which can be (sometimes reluctantly) accepted as a mark of national difference. But there are some societies of which this is one where people are nationally divided from each other by religion rather than language. In the Yugoslav Republics of Croatia and Bosnia, the Serbs (Orthodox), the Croats (Catholics) and the Bosnian Muslims all speak the same language, Serbo-Croatian, and they are three nations distinguished from each other by religion. Like ourselves they also have had difficulty recognizing each others' integrity. In the inter-war years in Yugoslavia the dominant Serbians used to infuriate the Croats by treating them as though they were just Catholic Serbs. During the war the Croatian fascists attempted to wipe out Serbians by forced conversion to Catholicism and extermination. Only the victory of the cross-community Communist partisans (despite their other drawbacks), brought any sanity to Yugoslavia.

Some insist that Ulster Protestants are part of the Irish nation, because it is 'only' their religion that distinguishes them from Irish Catholics. Others insist that Irish Catholics in Northern Ireland are British, because they speak English and live under British rule. But just as the Protestants' Britishness can never be reduced to a matter of denominational rights of a religious minority in the Irish nation, nor can the need for the Irish Catholic school system ever be reduced to one of mere denominational rights of a religious minority in Northern Ireland.

Like the Yugoslav nations, Catholics and Protestants in Ulster have different experiences of where threat, violence and humiliation come from. I have seen this theme unfolded many times as people tell each other about themselves. In Northern Ireland people are often attacked for who they are, not for anything they have done themselves. This is not just something about the present troubles. It has been true for much of our history. If someone is attacked, the first thing we need to know – if we want to understand it – is what religion were the attacker and the victim. We are very interested in the reasons for violence, even when we don't agree with it. Violence can spread from one incident in a chain reaction. For example a Protestant avenges an attack on his community by attacking a Catholic. Then another Catholic attacks another Protestant and so on. If people know that an attack upon some person is an attack upon a whole group of people, of whom that person is only a representative, it has a massive effect. This is quite unlike an isolated murder in a normal society. It isn't necessary for people to agree with violence. They only have to understand what is happening and to be frightened by it. Once a cycle is under way, some acts of violence are seen as self-defence, reprisal, pre-emptive strike or deterring action. 'They were provoked,' we say. 'They had good reason for their anger,' we think. An attack is on us; or it is something done by our side to them, in which case we understand it in some way. We may give reasons for it, which somehow take away from our sense of outrage. Or we may be especially ashamed of it, because we feel somehow responsible for it. This reality makes us different from each other.

Ordinary criminalization of the kind that happens in normal societies is impossible in Northern Ireland because we are so interested in the reasons why people did things, and we are not therefore united by our feelings against what they did. The law is not an anchor, but more like an axis of conflict. Some fear that the 'Law' will not protect us from 'them' and others feel the law in some way tolerates or helps 'them' against us. In Northern Ireland, no one feels entirely secure. Any tranquillity this society has known has been more like a truce than a peace. The story of the Apprentice Boys of Derry, the marching of the Orange Order (which was once explicitly about patrolling rebellious natives), and many other aspects of unionism, such as the permanent establishment of the 'B' Specials until 1969, show how tranquillity was preserved by deterrence. Peace was never taken for granted. Just as the West and the USSR spent 40 years keeping the 'peace' by using nuclear weapons to deter each other, so unionists always felt the need to deter the nationalist threat. Nationalists resented the things done to deter or control them. So even when they disagree with republican violence, they are less than enthusiastic about the British state power opposing it. Our different identities as nationalists and unionists largely depend upon the direction from which we expect violence and humiliation to come towards us and those closest to us.

It is because our experiences of threat divide us that there is such a strong aversion to talking about anything to do with politics or religion in mixed company. In fact it is an almost elementary aspect of keeping good relationships with people of the 'other' community that we do this. So we nearly always share our own trauma – the experiences which make us what we are – with those who are also traumatized as we are. Any cross-national discussion about such experiences might turn into showing how much 'we' suffered at 'your' side's hands; and an argument about whose violence is worse. Polite avoidance of these issues and feelings both ensures that we make every day life as manageable as possible and that we go on reinforcing the differences which are always there and threatening to erupt.

Seeing things in this way makes it clearer why it is rather unfair to blame the schools we have at the moment for promoting sectarianism. As a rule schools in divided societies probably only reinforce the lessons that every other situation already teaches, including homes. Distrust of the 'others' is hinted at and intuited in countless ways, even when it becomes politeness and fear of offending. Schools may for example reinforce the sense that politics, religion and history are subjects to be avoided in mixed company for fear of giving offence. We make a very great mistake to imagine that schools 'teach bigotry', if by that we imagine that they have some specially malignant influence.

If our children are to have a better future, they must experience new ways of meeting with others. Then perhaps they will become free to deal with the big things that divided their parents, who were often restricted to polite avoidance of difficult subjects. If an integrated school is a meeting place where people find that their experiences are valid and worth listening to, then it may give them this. The best integrated schools will be the ones where the parents have educated themselves together while creating and running the school. That can only strengthen the trusting environment of the 'meeting'. In the rest of this text I shall suggest a few of the things this may mean in practice.

Historical Reflections

In 1831 the British government introduced the national education system in Ireland. For the first decade the system was integrated in spirit and it involved building trusting and cooperative relationships between clergy of all denominations. In the north this meant Presbyterian and Catholic particularly. But gradually Catholics pulled away from it, and a different kind of Presbyterian also came to support it. Eventually the defence of this system turned into a crusade against the Catholic clergy without whose cooperation it could not carry on in spirit as well as in name. This is one of the reasons why the early effort to create integrated education in Ireland decayed.

The national education system was intended to become a system of mixed secular and separate religious instruction. It came into existence after Catholic Ireland had been mobilized by Daniel O'Connell to secure Catholic emancipation. The system was necessary because the existing, mainly Anglican, quality education was regarded as proselytizing. In the north the Catholics and a large minority of Presbyterians welcomed it and worked together to make it a success. They observed fairly rigorous conditions which included recognizing that each religious minister was responsible for the faith of the children of their flock.

But many Presbyterians did not accept the system until it was modified. In 1839 they were allowed to pursue their 'missionary' effort towards Catholic children in 'their' national schools, subject only to a conscience clause permitting children to leave at times of religious instruction. This modification was the beginning of a process. First, more and more Protestants who regarded Ultramontane Popery as a menace, began to support the national system on the grounds that they were only required to make minimal concessions to 'Popery'. And once the Catholic clergy opposition to national education began to harden from the late 1840s, more Protestants began to support it because the Catholic hierarchy were against it. By the 1860s many saw it essentially as a rampart against Catholic clerical control of education. These kinds of 'supporters' of national education distracted lay Catholic attention away from the sincere Protestant advocates of school integration. When in 1871 Orangemen with sashes took the platform at a meeting to defend the national education system in Cookstown, it had become very plain that many Protestants were now favouring mixed education precisely because they saw it as a way of breaking up the cohesion of the Catholic community. The liberal advocates of integrated education would have needed to do something to put a clear distance between themselves and the 'No-Popery' advocates. They would have needed to look for ways of developing trusting relationships with those Catholics, who like themselves, really valued mixed education as a way of softening prejudice.

It can be argued that because the Catholic hierarchy were completely against integrated education from around 1850 onwards, it was they who killed it. It is true that once the Catholic church had a lot of national schools under de facto Catholic management, it pressed for their denominationalisation. In fact the Catholic church sought denominational education throughout Europe at this time. But the claim that they were responsible for destroying integrated education is too simple. It fails to explore why virtually all Catholics in Ireland went along with the Hierarchy on this issue, unlike other parts of Europe. What happened in Ireland can only be understood when we see how the choices looked to Irish Catholics in the north. Where they had experience of working together with Presbyterians on a basis of equality in national schools run according to the original plan, they had something real to chose. But when they were invited to side with those who saw mixed education as a way of breaking the cohesion of the Irish nation, that was no choice at all. Even the most anti-clerical Catholic would chose the hierarchy position without a moment's hesitation when it became a power issue between the protectors of 'our' schools and the traditional enemy.

The essential point is that in this society the meaning of any proposal for integrated education depends entirely upon the terms upon which the parties to the integration meet. Given the not unfounded Catholic suspicion of anti-Irish and proselytizing intention of schools outside Catholic control, there is always a risk that schemes for integrated education might drift into de facto British-unionist-Protestant education. If it gets into deep enough rivalry with the Catholic hierarchy, its liberalism or anti-clericalism becomes a thin veneer for unionism.

This underlines the essential difference between a mixed school, where it happens that there is a large minority of one kind in the other kind's school, and an integrated school where pupils of both communities come together on equal terms. When integrated schools grow as a compact between the parents, who know and trust each other from their work together, the kinds of dangers outlined above become less threatening. Political difficulties are manageable if the relationships between the parents are close. But for integrated education initiatives to happen on any scale, it will be much easier if people from the two communities sense that they are coming together from positions of relatively equal power. If it is relatively easy for people from one community to become involved and much more difficult tor those of the other, then mixed schools will tend to be only mixed, rather than integrated. If the school systems of both communities are secure, and integrated education is not being promoted in opposition to them, then paradoxically integrated education is most likely to flower. Each national community's school system must be cherished, and seen to be cherished, if integrated education is to be able to flourish on a voluntary basis beside them.

Reconciling National Divisions

It is essential to underline the fact that integrated education will only mature if it is allowed to grow without being burdened with unrealistic expectations. There are no magical ways of overcoming national divisions through educational systems. In fact quite commonly, mixed educational systems in divided societies have been seen not as solutions to conflict but as part of the problem, a source of unacceptable power of one group over another. So what passes for peace in these societies depends on entrenching separate educational systems. This does not eradicate mistrusts, but it makes them more manageable because it leaves each group with their own space. When the problem of distrust is so real, as indeed we know it is here, it is quite unreal to think that the solution is to uproot separate education and impose an impartial syllabus in mixed schools. It is quite possible to stand in front of a class with wonderfully impartial words and to teach skin deep. The content of what is formally taught is much less important than the spirit in which it is taught. As parents or teachers, we often think that we teach with our words; yet when we reflect on our own experience as children, we recall the feelings we sensed in our parents and teachers, rather than their words.

Again Yugoslavia may have given us a warning about what can and cannot be done with a more or less impartial 'syllabus' in a mixed or integrated educational setting. Since 1945 the Serbs, Croats and Muslims seem to have lived in something like harmony in Bosnia and Croatia. The ethos of the common curriculum was provided by the Communist unifying myth, which – unlike those in other parts of Eastern Europe – had a very large core of truth. It told how all the nations of Yugoslavia had taken part in the liberation together. The story of the Partisans was like an umbrella (or transcendence) over all the Yugoslav nations. In 1988 I heard this story told often and with conviction, but it was combined with slightly over-anxious denials that the differences between the Serbo-Croat speaking nations mattered any more. For example at Jasenovac, the site of the concentration camp where the Croatian Ustashi had massacred Serbians in 1941-4, I saw school children being shown a film, which told how all the various Yugoslav nations had produced criminal elements in World War 2 who had collaborated with outside forces. Without much attention to how much, or how little support, each type of collaborator had, the harmonizing message was that all the nations of Yugoslavia could get on very well, so long as they kept clear of outside troublemakers.

But history, the history of why 'we' have cause to fear 'them', seems to have been only sleeping. Today it turns out that the divisions which so much energy went into suppressing and abolishing are again alive and well. Of course we cannot know what the unifying story of the liberation of 1945 did or did not do to bring some of the younger generations of Yugoslavs together. But it is clear that by itself integrated education has not had a great impact in mixed towns like Petrinja, where ethnic polarisation even runs through the school staff room. The communist integrated history, however well intentioned it had been, has not prepared a new generation to cope with the trauma of the past. Indeed the first outbreak of physical hostilities occurred at the Serbo-Croatian equivalent of a Celtic-Rangers match in Zagreb.

The difference between history in Northern Ireland (or any divided society, such as Yugoslavia) and histories of normal societies, is that normal societies' histories are not about relationships which are charged with any anxiety or tension today. People who live in normal societies do not realize what good fortune they have being able to see things the way they can in fact see them. Learning about how to make seriously divided societies 'normal' is like trying to teach naivety. Normal societies' histories are shared stories of how peace came. The devils cast out were the same devils for all the citizenry. And that is why the past has become the past. From that time they have lived in concord, disturbed sometimes by minor divisions, oblivious sometimes of their hypocritical unconcern with certain groups of victims, but nonetheless knowing with their being the difference between the past and the present.

For separate national communities in a divided society, for whom there is no common story of how or when peace came, the easiest way to teach about history and society is from the standpoint of 'our' community. In this history, the 'other' community appears as an obstacle or threat. The separate school system can then make the best of a bad job, by institutionalising the avoidance of real meeting. Feelings linked with 'our' history can run most smoothly when 'they' are not actually present with 'us'. This does not mean that we cannot acknowledge the pain of the 'others'. But however we acknowledge it in theory, we do not have to actually feel it as a lived reality. If any of 'them' are present as a minority in 'our' school, it is possible to ignore 'their' feelings, so that the story still runs smoothly. If this happens the result is a kind of assimilation of the minority to the community dominant in the school. Alternatively, feelings which are at the heart of the conflictual reality are avoided, while tangential bits of the story are concentrated upon and the story ends with 'what a pity' it was that the two communities ended up in confrontation. We should not understate how difficult it can be to improve on this approach, if the ethos of the school is not one of trust.

In an integrated school different feelings would be given space to be heard. In all probability it will be in historical learning that this is experienced most directly. Integrated learning of history will not just be a matter of finding an impartial approach. An integrated history would be like a vessel in which our different feelings can find expression and interact. Each of our versions of history in a divided society are related to our ways of explaining our feelings and especially our fears in the experience of our families and friends and indeed in our own everyday life. If we explore our histories together with people who have experienced the opposite side of the fear relationship, new aspects of history will become interesting and important to us. We can only find common history together when we first treat antagonistic national relationships seriously. Having recognized their coercive power over us, we are better able to see the 'other's' historic failings as mirroring our own failings. Then we begin to look at history with new eyes. Perhaps we become aware of those who stood against tides not because they thought they would succeed, but as witnesses to transcendent values, which we will need to discover as a shelter to live under together. They may provide us with role models in place of heroes of ethnic conflicts.

Note

This chapter is a shortened version of *Integrated Education and New Beginnings in Northern Ireland* first published by the Corrymeela Press.

16
Religious Identity and Integrated Education

C.E.T. Flanagan and B.K. Lambkin

The most powerful arguments both for and against integrated education are religious. In a recent television programme, religious leaders reflected the spectrum: the President of the Methodist Conference in Ireland, Derek Ritchie said that 'there is a lot to be said for integrated education'; the Church of Ireland Archbishop of Armagh, Robin Eames, said that 'integrated education has a role to play'; and the Roman Catholic Archbishop of Armagh, Cardinal Cahal Daly, said: 'If I was convinced that... integrated education were the best way to ferment good relations then I would be bound to favour it. I am not thus convinced.'[1]

It is important to understand why some church leaders are convinced and others are not. In saying that he is not convinced, the Cardinal speaks for many people in Northern Ireland, both Catholic and Protestant, who cannot see how the distinctive religious identities which they hold dear could survive and develop in the setting of an integrated school. From their point of view, the virtue of integrated education is not self-evident. There are religious difficulties with it. All the churches resisted it in the nineteenth century and again in the 1920s. The question for those promoting the policy of integration is firstly, can the sceptics be convinced? Are there religious difficulties in the way of integrated education which are insuperable? If there are not, then what evidence is needed to convince the sceptics?

The seriousness of the issue is not in doubt. Professor Norman Gibson speaks of a 'collision of absolutisms':

> At the centre of the Catholic/Protestant divide seem to be strongly opposed and apparently irreconcilable conceptions of religious truth and authority. These absolutisms are for the most part not openly and widely discussed in theological terms but manifest themselves in various ways. The most significant is perhaps education.[2]

Schools, whether day or Sunday schools, are essential to the churches. They help form religious identity. They help make Catholics and Protestants. There are, as the late Professor John Whyte has shown, two factors which do most to divide Protestants as a whole from Catholics as a whole.[3] One is separate education. The other, endogamy or separate marriage, is closely related to it. Together, separate education and separate marriage have been the two most important mechanisms for giving Protestants and Catholics their sense of distinctive religious identity and in maintaining the religious divide between them.

The two mechanisms interact. Protestants tend to marry Protestants. They tend to send their children to Protestant schools. Their children tend to marry Protestants and send their grandchildren to Protestant schools. Catholics tend likewise.[4] Religious identity is passed on most effectively from one generation to the next in this way. Church attendance is higher in Northern Ireland than anywhere else in western Europe except for the Republic of Ireland. Forty-five per cent attend at least once a week as compared with less than 10 per cent in England and Wales.[5] At the most basic level, Catholics and Protestants know that they are Catholics and Protestants because they have been sent to Catholic and Protestant schools. Protestants and Catholics can tell each other apart – as does the Fair Employment Commission – by the schools they attended. Attendance at an integrated school is problematical.

It would seem to follow necessarily from this state of affairs that it is not possible for mixed marriages or integrated education to be regarded as normal without the undermining and the eventual destruction of separate Protestant and Catholic religious identities. How, the argument goes, can Catholics know they are Catholics if they have a Protestant father or mother or if they go to school with Protestants? How can Protestants be confident that they are Protestants if they have a Catholic father or mother or if they go to school with Catholics? The inevitable consequence of mixed marriage and integrated eudcation must be confusion, indifference and loss of identity. It is this line of argument which lies at the heart of religious objections to integrated education and it is this line of argument which 'integrationists' must address if they wish to persuade the sceptics.

The sceptics who have the strongest case for resisting persuasion are those who take seriously their religious duty to pass on their faith. Segregated education works for them so why should they abandon it? Not only does it work, its success had been bought dearly. Eamon Duffy reminds us:

> Advocates of integrated education too often forget how crucial the emergence of the Catholic school system in the North was for the

preservation of the identity and self-respect of the Catholic minority, and so fail to grasp just what the surrender of the system symbolises for the Catholic community.[6]

In order to persuade the sceptics it is not enough to show that there are important problems with segregated education. Its supporters acknowledge that there are, that it needs fixing and, for the most part, they are trying to fix it. They are implementing the government's Education for Mutual Understanding (EMU) and Cultural Heritage initiative which seeks to increase contact between Protestants and Catholics and break down suspicion and mutual misunderstanding between the two sides. They are preserving separation by conceding a degree of integration.

Religious Dilemma

Here the religious believer encounters an acute dilemma which is at the heart of the Northern Ireland problem. Many of the same Protestants and Catholics who are proud of their separate religious traditions – and for that reason are suspicious of mixed marriages and integrated education – are also ashamed of the religious divide between them. They acknowledge that separation has led to regrettable ignorance, mistrust and worse. They acknowledge their shame, especially during the Week of Prayer for Christian Unity. But what should be done about it? Is it possible to break down the wall of division without surrendering one's distinctive religious identity?

This is the central question which generates the spectrum of opinion about education policy in Northern Ireland. Traditionalists stick with the old position (once held by the majority). They blame 'the other side' and actively oppose integration. Secular progressives wish a plague on both houses and advocate full integration which leaves religion behind. The rest, those who are most sensitive to the religious dilemma, seek some form of compromise, some way of breaking down the wall of division without breaking from their religious roots.

EMU and Cultural Heritage in the curriculum offer what appears to be an acceptable way out: through EMU and Cultural Heritage Catholics and Protestants become more friendly but retain their separate schools and with them their separate religious identities. They become friendly through sharing some educational experiences, but not too friendly. Those in authority can still give a clear answer to David Lodge's old question, 'How far can you go?' Polite social intercourse between schools is permitted but marriage between them – to form an integrated school – is not. In separate schools pupils retain separate identities. In an integrated school pupils gain a common identity. It is this prospect which repels sceptics. You may, they argue, have only one or the other. It stands to reason that you cannot gain a common identity without losing your separate religious identity. You cannot have separate religious identities and simultaneously share a common religious identity. If you have a common identity it must be a secular identity. Or must it?

This is the great untested hypothesis of the integrated education debate in Northern Ireland. In the absence of definitive research, the sceptics may continue reasonably to prefer their intuition to the claims of integrated schools, based on experience, that their pupils both share a common identity and retain separate religious identities. It is to be hoped that the necessary independent research will be undertaken urgently to enable the debate to move forward.

In the meantime, two observations suggest that the sceptic's intuition – that separate and common identities are incompatible opposites – is ill-founded. Firstly, Christian churches elsewhere, especially the Anglican Church and the Roman Catholic Church in England, have been running integrated schools for longer than there have been integrated schools in Northern Ireland. These integrated or joint church schools are not lay initiatives, but official church initiatives with full episcopal blessing. The principals of thirteen of these schools and three of the integrated schools in Northern Ireland now belong to an association called 'Together'.[7] No insuperable obstacles, theological or otherwise, stand in the way of setting up inter-church schools. The four largest churches in Northern Ireland are at liberty to take inspiration from the example of fellow members elsewhere and cooperate at the highest level in the running of integrated schools.

The second observation concerns the changing attitude of the churches towards mixed, or cross-community or inter-church marriage. What has traditionally been seen as a problem is increasingly seen as an opportunity. The most recent and thorough study of cross-community marriage in Northern Ireland found that most couples 'wish to maintain their links with their church'.[8] There is a shift away from the traditional notion that one partner must surrender the religious upbringing of the children to the other partner. The promise the Catholic partner must make remains a bone of contention but, as the late Cardinal O'Fiaich explained, 'the Catholic party is not giving a promise that the children will be brought up as Catholics; he is giving a promise to do his best, or what lies in his power... I would consider that any person has an obligation to try to pass on their faith to their children, and that Protestants have the same obligation'.[9] The children can belong religiously through their parents to both churches.

Clergy are increasingly being encouraged to develop joint pastoral care of mixed marriages. Archbishop Eames says that 'the concept of joint pastoral care has become a reality'.[10]   Where both partners are believers, both are being encouraged to draw on the strength of their own tradition in passing on their faith. The Roman Catholic Bishop in North London, Vincent Nichols, wrote recently to the Association of Inter-church families saying, 'Be patient, but not too patient; keep pressing and one day the walls which divide us will surely come down'.[11] The Northern Ireland Mixed Marriage Association expresses the ideal as follows:

> ...The two persons uniting remain separate and individual personalities, but nevertheless they become one within their marriage. This is surely what the ecumenical movement is trying to bring about. All churches have great riches and individual personalities, and in any 'church re-union' it is important that these are not lost. The churches need to become one, and yet retain their individuality.[12]

The message for the integrated education debate is that marriage is based on the concept that two parties share a common identity while retaining their separate identities. If separate individuals can be married successfully, may not separate schools also be married?

This is the central question which integrated schools pose for the churches. It is true that some marriages are entered into more prudently than others. Traditionally, the churches have regarded mixed marriages as imprudent and counselled against them. Now they increasingly recognise the potential of inter-church marriage as a sign of the kind of unity which the churches desire for each other.

This shift in attitude has come about through the recognition that there are in practice three main types of mixed marriage: the traditional mixed marriage where in matters religious one partner submits to the other; the secular mixed marriage where both partners lapse; and the inter-church marriage where both partners do all in their power to pass on their faith to their children. It is the inter-church marriage which the churches see particularly as the sign of unity.

These three types may also be applied to mixed education. There is the traditional type – more frequently the case of Catholics attending Protestant Grammar schools than *vice versa* – where in a school that is partially mixed the minority submits to the religious ethos of the majority. There is the secular type of mixed education where religious education is a matter for the private individual outside school. And there is the inter-church type of mixed education where the school actively co-operates with parents and their churches in the religious education of their children.

Strong and Weak Integration

Religious sceptics are understandably firm in their opposition to the secular types of mixed education in which religious traditions wither. As believers they know the importance of the school to religious identity. What is in question is the wisdom of being sceptical of all forms of mixed education. There are strong indications that the effectiveness of segregated schools in transmitting separate identitites is ebbing inexorably. Technically, the state has ceased to fund segregated schools. The terms of the education debate have been recast. No longer is it a question of choice between segregated and integrated schools. Segregation is no longer an option for state funded schools. Wittingly or not, all schools in Northern Ireland have become committed to the policy of integrated education. EMU and Cultural Heritage are now not optional but statutory requirements, and EMU and Cultural Heritage are in theory and in practice a 'weak' form of integration. They are about closer relationships between the two sides. If schools wish to remain segregated in the old way they are obliged to go independent, like the Free Presbyterian church schools.

With all state funded schools committed at the very least to a weak form of integration, the term segregation or separation ought to drop out of the debate. All schools are now integrated. It is highly significant that, in the same television programme, Cardinal Daly spoke of schools 'which work actively for reconciliation and therefore are integrated'. The debate is now about how 'weak' or 'strong' the form of integration should be. The old and new terms of the debate are represented diagramatically as follows.

Forms of Integration

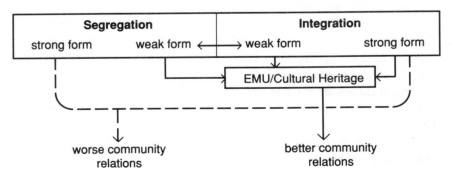

The 'strong' form of segregation meant schools were wholly Catholic or Protestant with no contact between them. The 'weak' form of segregation shades into the 'weak' form of integration, meaning separate Catholic and Protestant schools which follow the same curriculum and are in contact with each other. The 'strong' form of integration means schools in which Catholic and Protestant pupils and teachers work together daily. There are benign outcomes for community relations from both 'weak' and 'strong' forms of integration when EMU and Cultural Heritage objectives are pursued honestly.

Which form of integration, the 'weak' or the 'strong', produces the better citizen or the better Christian is therefore a sterile question. Local circumstances – the Catholic/Protestant balance in the community for one – vary from place to place and so the 'strong' form of integration (an integrated school) is not a viable option in all areas. Much more important is the possibility of malignant outcomes to both the 'weak' and 'strong' forms of integration.

The 'weak' form of integration lies between the 'strong' forms of segregation and integration. In which direction then will it tend? EMU and Cultural Heritage in practice could amount to little more than window dressing for continued, albeit better informed segregation. This is the suspicion which the strong-form integrationists have of the weak-form integrationists, namely that they are covert separatists. Conversely, the weak-form integrationists suspect the strong-form integrationists of being covert secularists. The claim of strongly integrated schools to be 'Christian' could amount, in practice, to little more than window-dressing.

Either way, cosmetic changes only will lead to deeper problems in the long run. A recent study of religious attitudes found that almost half of secondary school pupils in Northern Ireland, both Catholic and Protestant find Christianity hard to accept because of the Catholic Protestant divide.[13] However effective separate schools may have been in the past in nurturing religious identity, continued segregation is likely to alienate a growing number of young people from Christianity. They cannot understand why, if it is so good, Christianity seems to be doing nothing to heal the wounds of division. Similarly, integrated schools are also in danger of alienating young people. If Protestant and Roman Catholic traditions are not integral to the life of the school, integrated pupils will wonder why they should bother with Christianity. They may come eventually, however, to regret having been cut off from their religious inheritance.

The picture in practice is a complex one. If there is a central point to be grasped in the debate about Catholic schools, Protestant schools, and integrated schools, it is that all are now engaged in a common enterprise: integration. The argument is not about whether integration should take a strong form or a weak form. The two are not mutually exclusive. The central issue is whether or not a point is reached inevitably in the process of integration – past the stage of polite neighbourliness – at which further progress can be achieved only by the surrender of separate religious identities in the interest of a common identity and shared loyalty to the same school. Must the process of integration be held in check in case it goes too far?

The most powerful religious argument against the strong form of integration says it must. Such a point, it implies, is inevitably reached. Religious identity is most precious and may not be surrendered. Paradoxically, the most powerful counter-argument in favour of the strong form of integration is also religious. According to it, there is no inevitable point of surrender. The churches themselves use this argument in the case of inter-church marriage where both partners retain their individuality, their separate church connections and yet become one. The churches may yet decide to apply it to the case of inter-church schools.

Bishop Moriarty of Kerry said he believed that 'if the Devil got into his own controlled management the affairs of the Irish Church, he could do nothing better calculated to promote his interests than give us a separate system of education.' That was in 1860.[14] By accepting the statutory provisions for EMU and Cultural Heritage in the 1989 Education Reform Order, the sceptics have tacitly recognised that Bishop Moriarty had a point. What is needed urgently is definitive research into what is happening to the religious identities of Protestant and Catholic pupils both in schools which are weakly integrated and those which are strongly integrated. Then the sceptics may be convinced. Not convinced that integrated education is the best way forward (because they have already accepted that it is) but convinced that the strong form of integrated education – marriage between schools where the partners freely wish it – is a legitimate way forward and should be supported.

Notes

1. Television interview, *'Faith, Hope and Northern Ireland'*, BBC1(NI) 25 January 1993.
2. Gibson, N., Eonomic Growth and Political Absolutisms, in Giliomee, H., and Gagiano, J., (eds) *The Elusive Search for Peace,* Oxford, 1990, p. 136.
3. Whyte, J., *Interpreting Northern Ireland,* Oxford, 1990, p.48.
4. For a detailed discussion of the extent of educational separation in Northern Ireland, see Murray, D., *Worlds Apart: Segregated Schools in Northern Ireland,* Appletree,

1985. On the question of religion as a divisive factor in education in Scotland, the Netherlands and the USA, see McDonald, J., *Education and Community,* Occasional Paper No 9, Centre for Theology and Public Issues, Edinburgh, 1986, pp. 23-4.

5. Harding, S., Phillips D., with Fogarty, M., *Contrasting values in Western Europe,* London, 1986.

6. Duffy, E., 'The Origins of the Troubles', *Priests and People,* vii, 1, January, 1993, p. 7.

7. The inaugural General Meeting of **Together** took place in June 1992 at Fitzwilliam College, Cambridge. Present were thirty-eight delegates including special representatives of Roman Catholic and Anglican dioceses. The Chairman is Mr J Marcus, Principal of St. Bede's Anglican/Roman Catholic School, Carlton Road, Redhill, Surrey.

8. Robinson, G., *Cross-community Marriage in Northern Ireland,* Belfast, 1992, p. 51.

9. Northern Ireland Mixed Marriage Association, *Mixed Marriage in Ireland: A companion for those involved or about to be involved in a mixed marriage,* Belfast 1992, p. 9.

10. Eames, R., *Chains to be broken,* Weidenfeld and Nicholson, London 1992, p. 92.

11. Interchurch Families: *Journal of the Association of Interchurch Families,* i, 1, January 1993, p.9.

12. *Mixed marriage in Ireland,* p. 18.

13. Lambkin, B.K., 'The re-presentation of religious traditions in Northern Ireland: a study of the Opposite Religions? Project 1989-92', unpublished D. Phil. thesis, University of Ulster, Coleraine, 1993 (forthcoming).

14. Larkin, E., *The Consolidation of the Roman Catholic Church in Ireland 1860-1870* Dublin, 1987, p.122.

17
The Essential Role of the Churches in Supporting Integrated Education

Cecil Linehan, Margaret Kennedy and Sister Anna
(All Children Together)

Young parents in Northern Ireland may be unaware of two previous unsuccessful attempts at integrated education in which the churches were heavily involved in the 19th and 20th centuries. Though enabling legislation was introduced in 1978, All Children Together (ACT) failed to persuade church and state to reconsider the issue. Thus in 1981, ACT supported a group of parents in setting up the first integrated, co-educational, Christian school in Northern Ireland, Lagan College.

At first Lagan College had only 28 pupils, but expansion was rapid and 1,200 is now set as the maximum enrolment. Eighteen such groups of parents have followed suit and by September 1993, there will be 21 planned integrated schools – and still they grow. A welcome breakthrough in integrated education came with the latest Education Reform Order which included provisions for financial aid to these and other emerging integrated schools, thus extending real parental choice.

The Churches Called to Reconciliation
Integrated education is a very radical form of reconciliation. Recent research has shown the positive, durable, attitudinal change which occurs when Catholic and Protestant children are educated together, particularly at secondary level.[1] This reconciliation does not merely transform the relationships of the young but spreads out to family and friends and all associated with such schools.

ACT in 1974 envisaged the development of 'shared schools acceptable to all religious cultures, in which the churches would provide religious education and pastoral care'. The history of ACT shows that it has continued to try to bring the churches along with it through dialogue with church leaders and others. This it will continue to do.

Integration: Christian or Secular?

To allow a vaguely Christian or wholly secular integrated education system to develop in Northern Ireland would *not* be true to the letter or the spirit of the new legislation, which must, by law, 'encourage the education in school of Roman Catholic and Protestant pupils'. Nor do we believe that it would represent the wishes of most parents. Moreover, there is much recent research which shows the dominant role which the institutional churches still play in the lives of the people here, irrespective of the level of individual church attendance.[2] Hence, the positive effect on community relations of truly engaging the Christian biblical dimension in integrated schooling must be emphasised.

All Children Together has long been on record as believing that shared religious education is the linchpin of integrated education in Northern Ireland, an enriching, nourishing experience where all childrens' traditions are valued. An important milestone was reached in 1992 when the main churches co-operated in the production of an agreed religious education syllabus for use in *all* the province's schools.[3] However, in view of the widespread hostility, fear and ignorance, we feel that the proposals have to be tailored more to our crying need here, by grasping the opportunity to emphasise Christ's Gospel of reconciliation. How can religious education be justified on the curriculum of Northern Ireland's schools, unless it is being used as a reconciling rather than a divisive influence?

Threats and Fears

Integrated schools could be perceived as a threat to many in the existing schools. ACT has always worked for the development of integrated education by consent. We respect the right and the likelihood of most parents to chose state (Protestant) or maintained (Catholic) schools and the historic right of church representatives in their management. We are mindful of the financial sacrifices made by the Catholic community to ensure the continuance of Catholic education.

Yet the legislation passed in 1989 provides opportunities for church representatives and Christian parents to move into partnership in integrated schooling, and to champion this radical form of reconciliation.[4] A refusal by the churches to do so could be interpreted as placing the power and control of education above the possibilities of reconciliation through integrated education. Even worse, the churches themselves could be seen as obstacles by those who wish their children to be educated together in an atmosphere of shared Christian witness in a divided, so-called Christian, community.

To date, over 3,000 have been killed here and over 34,000 injured. Property has been destroyed along with jobs, and segregation in housing and employment has continued. Special situations require special solutions and the churches themselves are in a special position. They should be instruments of healing. Worldwide ecumenical experience demonstrates that it is possible to educate pupils of differing Christian belief together without any loss of their individual faith.[5] Indeed, the contrary is the case: the closer Christian people work together, the more they find their grasp of their own tradition deepened and strengthened. We need not be afraid of one another, as though our faith will be weakened by close contact with our fellow believers!

Could our churches here not step out in an act of faith and as an example for the good of the entire community in Northern Ireland by giving their wholehearted support to the integrated education movement? Is it not incumbent on Christian churches to show that Christian love drives out all fear?

The Churches' Own Agenda

The churches here have met regularly in the past to discuss reconciliation. They still do. They set their own agenda in the joint report of the Irish Council of Churches and the Roman Catholic Church *Violence in Ireland* in 1977.[6] It is stated in that report that members of the Working Party were not in agreement on the issue of integrated schools, but reference is made to areas where it was felt some moves could be made:

a) 'Shared sixth-form Colleges have been suggested.'
   (Are the churches jointly supporting the sixth-forms in the four existing integrated colleges?)
b) 'Common nursery schools in suitable areas could be developed. This would give mothers opportunities of meeting which it would otherwise be difficult to bring about.'
   (Some integrated primary schools have nursery wings attached. Is there joint church support for these?)
c) 'We are in agreement that the churches should promote pilot schemes and research projects to find effective ways of bringing together Catholic and Protestant young people at school level.'
   (Recently developed Education for Mutual Understanding programmes do not insist on actual *contact* between schools. Did the churches not feel that such contact was important in the first instance?)
d) 'Such schemes could include exchanges of teachers between Catholic and Protestant schools – particularly in sensitive areas of the curriculum.'

(Surely the best place for this is in the integrated schools?)

e) 'The teaching of RE in schools must have explicitly and deliberately an ecumenical dimension.'

(A start has been made here. Are teachers assured they will receive support from *all* the churches when they do introduce this ecumenical dimension?)

f) 'We recommend the establishment of Joint Committees, consisting mainly of teachers, but with representatives of diocesan and area education authorities and of parents, to consider the implementation of the above suggestions.'

(Did this take place? Has any thought been given to the fact that our colleges of education are segregated and that little provision is made for the preparation of specialist teachers with inter-denominational experience of RE?)

A final word from the same report:

'The most distinctive task confronting the churches is to promote and support reconciliation. God has committed unto us the ministry of reconciliation.'

What more tangible way of bringing about lasting reconciliation is there than by integrated education? What more practical way is there for the churches to implement their own recommendations than in integrated schools?

Possible Roles for the Churches

In our 1976 policy document entitled *ACT on Shared Schools,*[7] we envisaged a partnership between the school and supportive clergy in the enhancing of religious education, pastoral care and shared worship. We believe that the key area for the churches in integrated schools is in strengthening their whole Christian ethos. This is still our view. Clergy have invaluable expertise and while many teachers will wish to retain full responsibility for RE teaching, some may wish to invite clergy and other committed church people to be a helpful resource. This in no way diminishes the need for specialist RE teachers, a view we have constantly expressed. Rather do we see the experienced RE specialist *at all levels* from primary to secondary, encouraging a far wider and more meaningful involvement of church men and women. Places on boards of management are *not* central to such involvement. There are many other ways in which church people could support parents in integrated schools, eg:

– by appreciating that these parents care deeply for the Christian upbringing of their children in providing a sound Christian ethos for them;
– by communicating our belief that shared RE is the linchpin of integrated education in Northern Ireland;

–   by helping to correct misinterpretations about the desire for church involvement;
–   by showing the central importance of joint worship in the schools.

Church Members from the Wider Community

Church members could help greatly in the dissemination of information about integrated education by:

a) establishing an informed network in colleges for the education of teachers and clergy, and in chaplaincies of higher education;

b) seeking where possible the backing of the churches in areas where integrated schools exit, or are planned;

c) encouraging greater contacts between integrated, controlled and maintained schools;

d) making contacts with the reformed churches not traditionally involved in school management in the province and encouraging the various church bodies and organisations to discuss the new legislation;

e) inviting those in the churches who may be opposed to the principles involved to meet with members of ACT and others in the integrated movement to discuss their views, privately and in small groups;

f) reading recent research on the positive attitudinal changes in pupils attending integrated schools and discussing this with an open mind;

g) seeking, if possible, invitations to visit integrated schools, meeting staff and pupils and observing the ethos.

Hopes of All Children Together

When ACT began in the 1970s, some in the churches, and particularly within the Catholic church, may well have thought we were creeping secularists who had to be stamped out. Now, twenty years later, we and many others are still working for the development of shared Christian schools. The existing eighteen integrated schools cater for almost 4,000 pupils from nursery to sixth-form. Our longing to have the support of the churches in what has become a province-wide movement, embracing all classes and creeds remains as strong as it did all those years ago.

We are deeply grateful to all those individual clergy and other members of churches who have courageously given of their time to witness to the Christian faith in several of the schools already. As we write this on St. Patrick's Day 1993, we reflect on the fact that it was a great English Christian who brought the faith to Ireland. Will the Irish church leaders help the parents of Northern Ireland in this great task of reconciliation as the English church leaders are already doing? In a few years' time, will we be reading a statement like this from Irish Hierarchies?

> The Anglican Bishop of Southwark and the Roman Catholic Bishop of Arundel and Brighton which jointly established St. Bede's School in 1976, are convinced of its value as an opportunity, within a holistic education, for young people to be nurtured in their faith, to develop as practising Christians and to learn to grow together in response to Christ's prayer for Unity.'
> *(Pastoral letter of the Bishops of England and Wales, Catholic Media Trust, 24th January 1991)*

This is the sort of warm-hearted support from the churches that we longed for all those twenty years ago. We still do.

All Children Together

Notes

1. Irwin, C., (1991), *'Education and the Development of Social Integration in Divided Communities'*, Department of Social Anthropology, Queen's University, Belfast.

2. Stevens, D. (1991), 'A Profile of Northern Ireland Religion', *Doctrine and Life*, Dominican Publications, Dublin, July/August 1991.

3. The Churches' Religious Education Core Syllabus: Consultation Report, Northern Ireland Curriculum Council 1992 (The definitive core RE syllabus is to be published by the Department of Education in September 1993).

4. The Education Reform (N I) Order, 1989, H.M.S.O., Belfast.

5. Morrow, D. (1991), *The Churches and Inter-Community Relationships*, Centre for the Study of Conflict, University of Ulster.

6. *The Violence in Ireland Report*, (1977) A Report of the Fifth Working Party of the Irish Council of Churches/Roman Catholic Church Joint Group on Social Questions, Veritas, Dublin.

7. *ACT on Shared Schools* (1976), All Children Together, 13 University Stret, Belfast BT7 1FY.

Appendix

Northern Ireland Council for Integrated Education
Statement of Principles and Practical Guidelines

We, the representatives of the integrated schools and their supporting trusts, gathered together as members of the Northern Ireland Council for Integrated Education, define integrated education in the Northern Ireland context as:

> Education together in school of pupils drawn in approximately equal numbers from the two major traditions with the aim of providing for them an effective education that gives equal recognition to and promotes equal expression of the two major traditions. The integrated school is essentially Christian in character, democratic and open in procedures and promotes the worth and self-esteem of all individuals within the school community. The school as an institution seeks to develop mutual respect and consideration of other institutions within the educational community. Its core aim is to provide the child with a caring self-fulfilling educational experience which will enable him/her to become a fulfilled and caring adult.

We Affirm:
1. that parents have the basic rights in determining the nature of their children's education as set out in the United Nations Declaration on Human Rights, the European Convention on Human Rights and the second Vatican Council's Declaration on Christian Education;
2. that Christianity and Humanism alike demand that children be brought up to respect those who differ from them in creed, culture, race or class;
3. that children being brought up to live as adults in a plural and divided society should be educated in a context where they will come to know, understand, respect and appreciate those who differ from them and to recognise what they hold in common as well as what divides them;
4. that children brought up in a plural and divided society should be nurtured in their parents' religious and national traditions and identity, while respecting the identity and appreciating the traditions of others;
5. that children should be prepared to take responsibility for their lives as adults;

6. that children should be helped to develop self-confidence and self-respect so that they can develop confidence in and respect for others;

7. that children should learn to use and trust non-violent methods of resolving conflict;

8. that children should be encouraged and helped to be open in social relations despite difference in creed, culture, race, class, gender or ability; and

9. that children should be encouraged to identify with those less fortunate than themselves, the oppressed and victims of injustice.

In the development of integrated schools for Catholics and Protestants in Northern Ireland we are committed to the principles that we:

10. must seek to make them places where parents feel happy to send their children, where parents will feel secure knowing that the religious and cultural values and beliefs of their families will be respected in the school;

11. must ensure that they are founded with the consent of the parents, recognising that separate school systems for Catholics and Protestants are a basic right for families, parents and children who want them;

12. must ensure that there is opportunity for each child to be nurtured in his or her parents' religious and cultural traditions;

13. must seek to secure and sustain deep parental participation in the life and work of the school, and in particular in its government, in the formulation of its policy, in the creation of a working partnership with the teaching staff, and the promotion of good relations with the local community;

14. must plan the schools so that their integrated character is protected from the natural segregative tendencies of a divided society;

15. must ensure that each integrated school community welcomes, respects and cherishes the children of parents having other or no religious convictions while remaining loyal to its own essentially Christian character;

16. must ensure that the integrated school is open in its relationships with Catholic and Protestant schools and with the local community.

Practical Guidelines

In applying the above principles the governors, staff and parents of all integrated schools in Northern Ireland must make every effort to implement the following guide-lines.

Equality

There shall be equality of status within the schools for the two main ethno-religious communities of Northern Ireland. There shall be equality of respect and treatment for all children, regardless of creed, culture, race, class, gender or ability.

These commitments to equality shall be fostered both structurally within the Board of Governors, the staff and the pupils and culturally within the overt and hidden curriculum of the school. To achieve these ends all reasonable steps shall be taken to ensure that:

(a)   at least 40% of the first year intake in any year are pupils of the Catholic tradition and at least 40% of pupils are of the Protestant tradition;

(b)   at least 40% of the teaching staff are of the Catholic tradition and at least 40% of the Protestant tradition;

(c)   at least 40% of the governors are of the Catholic tradition and at least 40% of the Protestant tradition;

(d)   the Catholic and Protestant communities within the schools are accorded equal respect and standing;

and furthermore to:

(e)   promote the learning of shared culture, beliefs and traditions;

(f)   promote the learning of what is specific to the other tradition;

(g)   nurture within each pupil what is specific to his or her own tradition;

(h)   promote an atmosphere in which pupils will neither conceal nor flaunt their own cultural identities;

(i)   ensure that no symbol likely to be seen as offensive or divisive shall be displayed in the school premises or worn by pupils;

(j)   ensure that when inviting well-known visitors to the school they are selected even-handedly, having regard to the perceptions of the two major communities within Northern Ireland;

(k)   be democratic in all relationships between staff, parents and governors and, where possible, make decisions affecting school life on a consensual basis.

Religion

The school shall provide a Christian rather than a secular approach and context.

(a)   The children shall learn together all that we can reasonably expect them to learn together.

(b)   Where the school population includes significant numbers of children of a particular religious community, separate provision should be made to prepare such children for sacramental and liturgical participation in that specific religious community if their parents so wish. In addition the school shall encourage ministers of such religious communities to visit the school, take a pastoral interest in the children and get to know the parents and teachers.

(c)   In a manner appropriate to their age and ability, pupils shall be introduced to the ideas, beliefs and practices of the major world religions and humanist philosophies.

(d)   All parents should be encouraged to allow their children to follow the common elements in the religious curriculum.

(e)   Where parents do not wish their children to be given any specific sacramental or liturgical preparation their wishes shall be respected and proper alternative provision shall be made for their children.

(f)   In the selection of prayers (e.g. the Lord's Prayer), texts, readings and music for school assemblies and gatherings, care shall be taken to ensure equal prominence for the two major traditions and fair representation of other groups of significant size within the school community.

(g)   Where there are significant differences in liturgical practice between the two major communities (e.g. in the making of the sign of the cross) children should be encouraged to continue with their normal practice.

Parental Involvement

The school shall promote and encourage parental involvement at all levels of school life.

(a)   There shall be a Parents' Council to mobilise and organise parental support and participation and to advise the Board of Governors of matters of concern to the parents.

(b)   The Governors shall consult the Parents' Council when drafting or redrafting their statements of curriculum policy and discipline policy.

(c)   The Governors shall ensure that the parents are briefed when major changes in the curriculum take place.

(d)   The Governors shall consult the Parents' Council before determining the school calendar, start and end times of the school day, school uniform, homework policy and other such matters of evident import to parents.

(c)   The Governors shall establish appropriate arrangements and procedures for individual and collective communication between parents and
    (i)   the principal,
    (ii)   other members of the teaching staff,
    (iii)   the Governors themselves.

(f)   The Governors shall take steps to ensure that parents understand their
      obligations to play a full part in school life, for example by:
      (i)   regular attendance at school functions, meetings and events;
      (ii)   helping during the school day;
      (iii) helping on school outings and at school events;
      (iv)   taking an active interest in their children's school work and homework;
      (v)   encouraging their children to show respect for parents, teachers and
             other pupils by their manner and in their care for their appearance;
      (vi)   seeing that their children attend school regularly and punctually;
      (vii) taking part in fund-raising activities for the school.

Educational Philosophy

(a)   The school shall wherever possible be co-educational and all-ability in
      character and shall seek to educate each child according to his or her
      educational needs.

(b)   Resources and teaching strategies shall be organised to accommodate the
      all-ability nature of the school. In particular the school shall provide special
      help:
      (i)   for children with particular learning difficulties; and
      (ii)   for children at the top of the ability range.

(c)   The school curriculum shall reflect not only the external demands of the
      Northern Ireland Curriculum, the inspectorate and the economy but also the
      all-ability character and integrative purpose of the school itself. In particular
      the school shall make provision for:
      (i)   a history syllabus which reflects the historical roots of the two major
             communities within Northern Ireland so as to illuminate both their
             separate and shared history;
      (ii)   music and dancing which reflect the culture of both major traditions;

      and, on an optional basis, for

      (iii) Irish language;
      (iv)   Irish games.

(d)   In selecting texts for English language, literature and drama, care shall be
      taken to illustrate the contributions both of writers born in Britain and those
      born in Ireland, North and South.

(e)   The school curriculum and the manner in which it is delivered shall encourage
      the development of autonomous individuals with the capacity to think,
      question and research.

Selected Bibliography

ACT on Shared Schools (1976) All Children Together, 13 University Street, Belfast BT7.

Akenson, D. H., (1970) *The Irish Education Experiment: the National System of Education in Ireland in the Nineteenth Century*, Routledge.

Akenson, D. H., (1973) *Education and Emnity: The Control of Schooling In Northern Ireland*, David and Charles.

Boal, F., and Douglas, J., (Eds.) (1982) *Integration and Division: Geographical Perspectives on the Northern Ireland Problem*, Academic Press, London.

Cairns, E., (1987) *Caught in Crossfire: Children and the Northern Ireland Conflict*, Syracuse University Press.

Caul, L., (1990) *Schools Under Scrutiny The Case of Northern Ireland*, Macmillan.

Civil Liberties in Northern Ireland: The CAJ Handbook, (1993) Committee on the Administration of Justice, Northern Ireland.

Clarke, D. M., (1986) 'Freedom of Thought in Schools: A Comparative Study', *International and Comparative Law Quarterly*, Vol. 35, April 1986.

Community and Curriculum, (1990) Conference Proceedings; Co-operation North and Education Studies Association of Ireland.

Darby, J., P., Murray, D., Dunn, S., Farran, S., and Harris, J., (1977) *Schools Apart?: Education and Community in Northern Ireland*, New University of Ulster.

Department of Economic Development; *Fair Employment Code of Practice*, HMSO 1989.

Department of Education (N.I.) *The Way Forward: Educational Reform in Northern Ireland*, H.M.S.O. Belfast 1988.

Department of Education (N.I.) *Cross-community Contact Scheme 1992-93*.

Department of Education (N.I.) *The Parents' Charter for Northern Ireland*, 1992.

Department of Education (R.o.I.), *Curaclam na Bunscoile - Primary School Curriculum, Teachers' Handbook*, Dublin, 1971.

Department of Education (R.o.I.),, *Education for a Changing World, A Green Paper*, Stationery Office, Dublin, June 1992.

Dunn, S., Darby, J., Mullan, K., *Schools Together?* (1984) Centre for the Study of Conflict, University of Ulster.

Dunn, S., (1986) 'The Role of Education in the Northern Ireland Conflict', *Oxford Review of Education*, Vol 12, No 3 pp 233-242.

Dunn, S., (1989) 'Integrated Schools in Northern Ireland', *Oxford Review of Education*, Vol 15, No. 2.

Dunn, S. (1990), 'A Short History of Education in Northern Ireland', 1920-1990, Annex B to *Fifteenth Report of the Standing Advisory Commission on Human Rights*, London, HMSO.

Eames, R., (1992) *Chains to be broken*, Weidenfeld and Nicholson, London.

Education and Libraries (Northern Ireland) Order, HMSO, 1986.

Education Reform (Northern Ireland) Order, HMSO, 1989.

Educate Together, *Starting an Educate Together National School*, 37 Mapas Road, Dalkey, Co Dublin.

Gallagher, A., (1989) *Education and Religion in Northern Ireland*, The Majority-Minority Review No 1, Centre for the Study of Conflict, University of Ulster .

Greer, J. E., and McIlhenney, E. P., (1985) *Irish Christianity: A Guide for Teachers*, Gill and Macmillan.

Harbison J., and Harbison J., (eds) (1980) *Children and Young People in Northern Ireland: A Society Under Stress*, Somerset Open Books.

Harbinson, J., (ed) *Growing Up in Northern Ireland.*

Hulmes, E., (1989) *Education and Cultural Diversity*, Longman.

Hume, B., Cardinal, (1988) *Towards a Civilisation of Love*, Hodder and Stoughton.

Hyland, Á.,'The Multi-denominational Experience in the National School System in Ireland,' *Irish Educational Studies,* Vol.8, No.1, 1989.

In Re: Application by Lagan College for Judicial Review, Judgements Office, Belfast, 10 April 1992.

Irwin, C. J., 'Integrated Education: From Theory to Practice in Divided Societies', Prospects, *UNESCO Quarterly Review of Education.* Vol. XXII, No.1.

Irwin, C. J., (1991) *Education and the Development of Social Integration in Divided Societies,* Northern Ireland Council For Integrated Education, Belfast.

Irwin, C. J., (1992) *Integrated Education: A Moral Issue, First Call for Children,* UNICEF, New York.

McDonald, J., (1986) *Education and Community,* Occasional Paper No 9, Centre for Theology and Public Issues, Edinburgh.

McEwen, A. and Salters, J., *Integrated Education: The Views of Parents,* School of Education, Queen's University of Belfast, 1992.

Morgan, V., Dunn, S., Cairns, E. and Fraser, G., (1992) *Breaking the Mould: The Roles of Parents and Teachers in the Integrated Schools in Northern Ireland,* Centre for the Study of Conflict, University of Ulster.

Mulvenna, J., 'Integrated Education; A Definition', *Bulletin of the Belfast Charitable Trust for Integrated Education*, 1/3, 1986.

Murray, D., (1985) *Worlds Apart: Segregated Schools in Northern Ireland,* Appletree.

Mulcahy, D. G., and O'Sullivan, D., (1989) *Irish Education Policy: Process and Substance*; Institute of Public Administration.

Northern Ireland Council for Integrated Education, *As Easy as abc - Anti-bias curriculum*, NICIE, Belfast.

Northern Ireland Council for Integrated Education (1992), *The Growth of Integrated Education: an Outline*, pamphlet produced by NICIE, Belfast.

Proposals for a Core Syllabus in Religious Education, The Churches Religious Education Drafting Group, 1991.

Richardson, N., (1990) *Religious Education as if EMU really mattered,* Christian Education Movement.

Robinson, A., (1987) *Education for Mutual Understanding: Roles and Responsibilities,* Report and proceedings of a Conference held at theUniversity of Ulster, Coleraine.

Robinson, G., *Cross-community Marriage in Northern Ireland,* Belfast, 1992.

Rockeach, M., (1960) *The Open and Closed Mind,* New York Basic Books.

Salters, J., McEwan, A., *Something Different: Integrated Parents in Northern Ireland;* Research in Education No. 49, May 1993.

Smith, A., and Robinson, A., *Education for Mutual Understanding: Perceptions and Policy*, Centre for the Study of Conflict, University of Ulster, Coleraine.

Spencer, A. E. C. W., 'Integration and Segregation in the Northern Ireland Educational System: Lagan College and its Context', *Queen's News*, November 1982, Queen's University of Belfast, 1982.

Spencer, A.E.C.W., (1987) 'Arguments for an Integrated School System, in Education and Policy in Northern Ireland', in Osborne., R., Cormack., R., and Miller R., (Eds) *Education and Policy in Northern Ireland*, Policy Research Institute, 1987.

Standing Advisory Commission on Human Rights (1990), *Religious and Political Discrimination and Equality of Opportunity in Northern Ireland*, Second Report, HMSO.

Standing Advisory Commission on Human Rights (1990), *Seventeenth Report 1991-92*, HMSO.

The Violence in Ireland Report, (1977) Irish Council of Churches /Roman Catholic Church Joint Group on social questions, Veritas, Dublin

United Nations Convention on the Rights of the Child, adopted by the General Assembly of the United Nations on the 20th of November 1989.

United Nations Education, Scientific and Cultural Organisation, *Convention against Discrimination in Education*, adopted by the General Conference, Paris, 14 December 1960.

Whyte, J., (1990) *Interpreting Northern Ireland*, Oxford.

Wilson, D., and Dunn, S., (1989) *Integrated Schools Information for Parents*, Centre for the Study of Conflict, University of Ulster.

Wright, F., *Integrated Education and New Beginnings in Northern Ireland*, Corrymeela Press, Belfast, 1991.

Index

joint sixth forms, 15, 206
Joseph Rowntree Charitable Trust, 28,
    38

Lagan College, 34, 70, 126, 204
liberal *view of integrated education*,
    191
local control of integrated education
    development, 149

maintained schools, 62, 97, 98, 134
management of change, 103-5, 123,
    133
Mawhinney, Dr Brian (former N.I.
    Secretary of State), 39
Methodists, 64, 107, 145, 195
minority community, 71-2, 194, 199
'mixed' marriages, 38, 96, 143, 196,
    198
    Northern Ireland Mixed Marriage
    Association, 199
'mixed' schools, 66, 114, 122, 124, 154
    in 19th century Ireland, 183-4, 190-
    2, 199
    secular, 199-200
moral values,
    in integrated schools, 38, 58, 65-7,
    80, 83
    in joint church schools, 180
monitoring intakes, 143; *see also*
    integrated education – admissions
    and enrolments
Mormons, 167
multi-cultural education, 50-1, 125, 146
multi-denominational education, 146,
    180
multi-denominational schools in R.o.I.,
    153-71
Muslims, 126, 147, 167

National Curriculum (G.B.), 94, 172
national schools, 34, 69
    in R.o.I., 153-171
    rules for, 154
nationalists, 62, 188, 189
'national' (Anglican) Church in Great

Britain, 175
North Armagh Group for Integrated
    Education, 112-5
nomination procedure, 119, 135, 139;
    see also integrated schools –
    governors
non-denominational education, 69, 146
North Dublin National School, 158
Northern Ireland Council for
    Integrated Education (NICIE), 27,
    37-8, 107, 136, 149, 166
    Statement of Principles, 27, 41, 43,
    46, 113, 117, 119, 136
Northern Ireland Curriculum, 44, 121,
    129
Nuffield Foundation, 25, 29
nursery provision, 29-30, 206

Oakgrove Primary School and College,
    L'Derry, 31-40
open enrolment, 144-5
'opting out' (Conservative
    Government policy), 14, 26, 148
O'Fiaich, Cardinal, 198
Orange Order, 124
    in 19th century Ireland, 189-91
O'Rourke, Mary T.D. (Education
    Minister, R.o.I.), 157-8, 159

parent(s),
    action, 114, 127
    background, 96, 110
    commitment, 26, 85, 97, 41-2
    contact, 33-4, 74, 185
    founder, 89-91, 96, 110
    and management, 31-2, 97, 162-4
    power, 31
    representatives, 97; *see also* boards
    of governors
    responsibility for faith nurture, 64-
    7, 198
    and teachers in integrated schools,
    101, 128, 147
parental involvement, 43, 90-1, 98-
    100, 106-7, 117, 119, 132, 138,
    147, 167, 185